CONFEDERATE CORSAIR

CONFEDERATE CORSAIR

THE LIFE OF
LT. CHARLES W. "SAVEZ" READ

Robert A. Jones

STACKPOLE
BOOKS

Published by
STACKPOLE BOOKS
5067 Ritter Road
Mechanicsburg, PA 17055
www.stackpolebooks.com

Printed in the United States of America

10 9 8 7 6 5 4 3 2 1

FIRST EDITION

Library of Congress Cataloging-in-Publication Data
Jones, Robert A. (Robert Allen)
    Confederate corsair : the life of Lt. Charles W. "Savez" Read / Robert A. Jones.
—1st ed.
        p. cm.
    Includes bibliographical references (p.) and index.
    ISBN: 0-8117-1532-9
        1. Read, Charles W. (Charles William), 1840–1890.   2. Ship captains—
    Confederate States of America—Biography.   3. Confederate States of America.
    Navy—Biography.   4. Confederate States of America. Navy—History.
    5. Privateering—United States—History—19th century.   6. United States—
    History—Civil War, 1861–1865—Naval operations.   I. Title.
    E467.1.R27 J66 2000
    973.7'57'092—dc21
    [B]
                                                                            99-089006

TO ELAINE

who encouraged me to finish this book
and had the love and patience
to put up with me as I did.

CONTENTS

Acknowledgments   ix

Preface   xi

ONE   A Wolf in Fisherman's Clothing   1

TWO   A Young Mississippian   15

THREE   CSS *McRae*   29

FOUR   Götterdämmerung   47

FIVE   Iron Warrior   63

SIX   Aboard the CSS *Florida*   85

SEVEN   Raising Cain and the Price of Fish   107

EIGHT   In Old Abe's Domain   125

NINE   On the James River   139

TEN   CSS *Webb*   157

ELEVEN   An Old Pirate   169

         Epilogue   173

         Appendix 1: Ships Captured by Read   *175*

         Appendix 2: Sail Plan   *177*

         Appendix 3: Naval Glossary   *179*

         Notes   *185*

         Bibliography   *209*

         Index   *221*

ACKNOWLEDGMENTS

During the many years I have taken preparing this book, I have been helped by more people than I can possibly acknowledge. Even so, I wish to thank the following people. For those I have forgotten to mention, please accept my apologies.

I have relied on several friends and relatives for editorial help. Harry Learch has spent countless hours reviewing my rough drafts and always gave helpful comments. His wife Sharon enthusiastically supported his editing. Thanks to Walt Kropp and Jerry Snyder who generously provided editorial advice. Peter Gingras provided a nautical scrub of the work. Judy Trull showed me how to put a manuscript together plus commented on the proposals to editors. I need to thank my daughters, Jeri Benner and Robin Klein, and their husbands, Mike and David, plus my stepchildren, Gordon and Martine Hartogensis and Grace Chao. Thea Hall graciously analyzed Read's handwriting. Mark Henry patiently listened to my history lessons in our car pool and provided suggestions. Other good folks who have patiently endured my "What do you think of this?" include: Steve Arnston, Ron Smith, Fran Humberd, Jim Griffin, Steve Magdits, Andy Anderson, Fred Jones, Tom Lloyd, Rick Holliday, Kim Horn, Jean Schloo, Mike Royle, Don Neuman, Jim Claffey, and Keith McAllister.

Librarians and historians are invaluable to anyone writing a biography. These include the staffs of the Naval Academy Library, Navy History Library, Naval Historical Center, National Archives, Department of Archives and History of the State of Mississippi, Maine Historical Society Library, Boothbay Harbor Library, Wilson Library of the University of North Carolina at Chapel Hill, and especially Pat Prentice and John Reilly.

I have been fortunate to have interviewed and corresponded with some of Read's descendants including the late Mallory Read and Roxie Read. Mr. and Mrs. John Read Maynard and Mr. and Mrs. B. Maynard have been most helpful.

I owe a special thanks to all of those authors listed in the bibliography. Historical writing builds on the work of those who have gone before. Mention must be made of the untold numbers of civil servants who labored and compiled the *Official Records of the Union and Confederate Navies in the War of the Rebellion* and the *War of the Rebellion: A Compilation of the Official Records of the Union and Confederate Armies*.

I would be remiss if I did not thank our cat, Muffin J. Wellington Mouse Ripper, who by walking across my computer keyboard provided imaginative text.

I certainly need to thank our old English sheepdog, Anne Boleyn (Annie), and our Australian shepherd, Brumby, for their many "pet the dog" breaks. Finally, I want to give special thanks to my wife Elaine who read and commented on my many drafts and never failed to encourage and support me.

Although many have helped me, if there are any mistakes in this book, the fault is mine.

PREFACE

I have always loved sea stories. During the '50s, I watched *Victory at Sea* with my father. He had served aboard the USS *Cabot* during World War II. My evenings were spent eagerly reading the books of Forester, Melville, Monsarrat, and Nordhoff and Hall. Part of me is not a land animal.

More years ago than I wish to recall, I read a book about the CSS *Florida*. Charles W. Read's adventures sounded like a good sea story. After discovering the Library of Congress did not have a complete biography of Read, I started researching his life. What I found was that Read's career encompassed almost all facets of the naval side of the war. At the battle of New Orleans, his mortally wounded captain gave him command of the CSS *McRae*. He directed the stern guns on the ironclad CSS *Arkansas*. As captain of the CSS *Tacony*, he sank Yankee ships off the East coast. While in a northern prison, he made three escape attempts. His reconnaissance work set the stage for the last action of the James River Squadron. He ended the war by trying to sneak the CSS *Webb* past Union-held New Orleans.

Read was brave and cool under fire. His ever-active imagination was always full of ideas about attacking the enemy. He was not shy about voicing his strong opinions. Read had a great deal of common sense and a sense of humor. In my writing I show Read's character, personality, and the way he thinks. My deductions are based on the writings of those who knew him and are corroborated by a graphological analysis.

The telling of Read's tale is more, however, than a *veni, vidi, vinci* war story. The breadth of his experiences shows the impact of sea power. Alfred Mahan defined sea power as "the military strength afloat, that rules the sea or any part of it by force of arms . . . also the peaceful commerce and shipping." With sea power, a country can project its forces anywhere it wants and can deny the same to its enemy. The North had it and the South struggled to get it.

But enough of this, for as Ishmael said, it is "high time to get to sea. . . ."

CHAPTER ONE

A WOLF IN
FISHERMAN'S CLOTHING

Secretary of the Navy Gideon Welles, at his desk in Washington, D.C., pondered the telegram before him. Adm. Andrew Hull Foote, his boyhood friend and champion of the Union cause, was dead. Although hardly unexpected, the news hit hard. Welles had followed Foote's declining health for the last several days. The country had lost the fighter whose drive brought needed victories at Forts Henry and Donelson. Welles needed a dozen more men like Foote who would seek out the enemy and sink him.[1]

But Foote's victories were last year's memories. This year—1863—the war effort stalled. The early hopes for a quick trouncing of the South had vanished. That June evening, Washington again panicked; the Army of Northern Virginia once again marched northward.

Lee's invasion engaged the Army, but not the Navy, little comfort to Welles. His Confederate counterpart, Stephen Mallory, kept sending out armed raiders to prey on the North's merchant ships. Welles denounced them as pirates. The Southern buccaneers would make their captures on the high seas, then remove the crews and torch the Union ships. The shipowners bombarded Welles with telegrams demanding protection.

Politicians complained that the Navy lagged in doing its duty; at the same time they objected to the expense of sending warships to protect the merchant fleet. That very evening, the CSS *Alabama, Florida,* and *Georgia* were at large in the Atlantic. Closer to home, another raider sank ships just off the East coast. The headline of the June 26 edition of the *New York Daily Tribune* boasted "THE PRIVATEERS TO BE HUNTED DOWN, A POWERFUL STEAM FLEET READY FOR PURSUIT!"[2]

Stevedores slowly loaded cargo from the Boston wharf on board the side paddle steamer *Forest City* as baggagemaster Reuben Chandler dutifully checked his manifest.[3] It would take all night to get from Boston to Portland, Maine. Once there, 1st Lt. James H. Merryman would take command of the United States Revenue Cutter *Caleb Cushing*. The previous skipper, Capt. George Clarke, had died of a heart attack. The executive officer, 1st Lt. Dudley Davenport, was temporarily in charge. Since Davenport had earlier failed his examination, the Revenue Service did not feel him qualified to be captain.[4] Merryman, who had been a first lieutenant for five years, hoped to earn the rank of captain by capturing a Confederate pirate.

First, though, he had to get to Portland.

The citizens of Maine believed in the preservation of the Union and eventually almost one-eighth of the state's population would wear suits of blue. Portlanders read the *Portland Argus* for accounts of the 20th Maine. Pine Tree State boys saw combat at Antietam, Maryland, and Fredericksburg, Virginia. In a few days, some of them would lose their lives on Little Round Top at Gettysburg.

Earlier in the day the Portlanders watched their Poppenburg concert band go off to war, as it marched down the Franklin wharf playing "The Flag of Columbia." In another part of Portland, quite a different procession took place. A train pulled into the station; in a boxcar lay the body of Lt. George S. Kimball Gardner; a dead cavalryman had returned home.[5]

The war had made the Portlanders suspicious. Although born in Maine, Ruggles Sylvester Morse had made his fortune in New Orleans. There he married a southerner with whom he spent his summers in Portland to escape the heat. At the start of the war, the people of New Orleans did not trust him because of his northern birth. Taking his wife to Portland, he encountered the Portlanders' distrust because of his long stay in the South.[6]

Morse was not the only one under suspicion. Born in Georgia, Davenport, the temporary commander of the *Caleb Cushing*, had joined the Revenue Service in 1847. Despite being on board the cutter since the start of the war, he had been accused by a fellow officer of being a southern sympathizer.[7]

To the Portlanders, however, the war remained a distant conflict. The nearest known Confederates were five hundred miles away. The Portlanders knew the Confederates were somewhere off the eastern seaboard, but the *Caleb Cushing* had just returned from an unsuccessful search for raiders. The townspeople were confident in their harbor, sheltered behind barrier

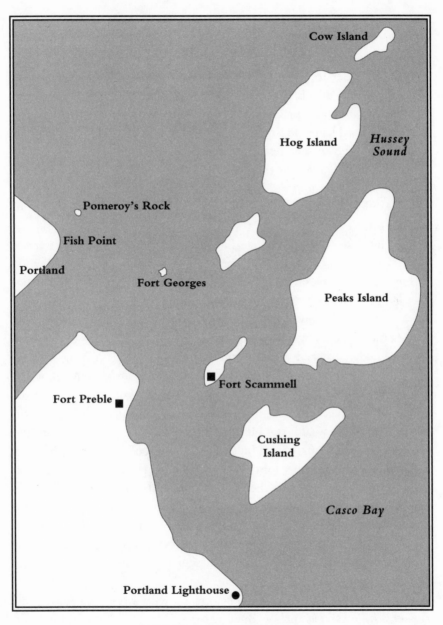

Cow Island

Hog Island

Hussey Sound

Pomeroy's Rock

Fish Point

Portland

Fort Georges

Peaks Island

Fort Scammell

Fort Preble

Cushing Island

Casco Bay

Portland Lighthouse

PORTLAND HARBOR

islands, and protected by three forts. No enemy ships had attacked Portland since the British burned the city in 1775.

That night the Portlanders were unaware that 2nd. Lt. Charles William Read, Confederate States Navy, had anchored the captured mackerel schooner *Archer* off Fish Point near Pomeroy's Rock. The twenty-three-year-old Mississippian, nicknamed "Savez" (savvy), was about five and one-half feet tall and had sandy-colored hair and brown eyes. His mustache and goatee partially concealed his fair complexion and narrow face. A blue frock coat hung loosely over his thin, gangly frame. Savez's high-pitched voice sounded almost feminine.[8] Three years before, he had graduated from the Naval Academy. When his state left the Union, he resigned his commission to fight for the South.

By June 26, 1863, a change in what the Prussian military strategist Clausewitz called "Conduct of War" had occurred.[9] The Civil War was turning into a war on civilians. Warriors like Grant and Sherman understood the change. Savez's character, forged by fighting Yankees on the Mississippi River and at sea, showed he was of similar mettle. Yet in appearance, he looked more like an overgrown boy than the intrepid captain of the Confederate raider that had spread panic from the Virginia Capes northward.

The eighty-two-foot high Portland Observatory stood on Munjoy Hill across from where the *Archer* had anchored. Signals from the masts on top of the red-shingled tower denoted the approach of ships coming into the harbor. Portland's wealth was built on trade with Canada, Europe, and the West Indies. Brick warehouses bulged with barrels of flour, grain, fish, and corn, plus cords of lumber for export or to supply the Federal armies. Cotton bales were also piled on the docks. Apparently some "patriotic" Yankees had profited from trading for southern cotton. Two new gunboats, the *Agawam* and the *Pontoosuc*, were moored at the Franklin wharf for work on their side-wheel machinery. Secretary of the Navy Welles planned to send the gunboats south to fight the Confederacy. Nearby, the New York steamer *Chesapeake* lay berthed for the night.[10]

In the harbor the *Caleb Cushing*, graced with a rounded stern and a clipper bow, rocked at anchor. Built in 1853 at the Hood shipyard in Somerset, Massachusetts, the cutter was slightly over one hundred feet in length with a twenty-three-foot beam. Her raked mainmast and foremast with topsail showed she could sail fast. On her deck was visible a pivot-mounted, large black 32-pounder cannon.[11]

The only cannon aboard the *Archer* was a small bronze 12-pounder boat howitzer.[12] In the two months since leaving the CSS *Florida* in the South Atlantic, Savez, with his four officers and twenty men, had captured twenty-one ships from the Virginia Capes northwards. The orders he had received from the *Florida's* captain John Maffitt allowed him wide discretion. In his fishing boat he was a wolf in fisherman's clothing. Newspapers taken from captured ships told him that Welles had dispatched more than thirty ships to catch him. He had dodged them all.

Albert Bibber and Elbridge Titcomb, two fishermen Savez had picked up that morning out in the Gulf of Maine, provided the information he needed to take the schooner into the harbor. The brandy, cigars, and twenty-dollar gold pieces he had given them convinced them he was a smuggler, because smuggling had been commonplace in New England since before the Revolutionary War. The *Archer* had come in on the flood tide on a moderate breeze, boldly sailing past Forts Preble, Scammell, and Georges without arousing suspicion. Had he been challenged, Savez's cover would have been that he had run out of bait. No flags on the observatory signaled his arrival. No one noticed that the *Archer* did not tie up to the wharf to off-load its catch or send a boat ashore. Even Bibber and Titcomb did not catch on until the Confederates broke out pistols and cutlasses as they neared the harbor entrance.[13]

Below deck Savez had already put his crew to work making firebombs of oakum soaked with turpentine.[14] Although the wind needed to whip the fire into conflagration was dying, fire on the wharf would spread panic and confusion, allowing him to make off with the *Chesapeake* or maybe take the *Forest City* when she arrived from Boston.

All of Savez's officers concurred with his plan except Eugene H. Brown, the ship's engineer, who explained that the steam was not up on the *Chesapeake* and even if he had steam on the *Forest City,* he could not run the engines alone.

Brown, who had served as third assistant engineer on the *Florida,* lacked experience. But the summer nights were short, and if Savez and his crew did not clear the forts before being discovered, everyone would spend the rest of the war in a Federal prison.[15] The attack plan was off; Portland would be spared the torch.

Savez formulated a new plan—a cutting out expedition. If the soldiers in the forts noticed the *Caleb Cushing* slipping anchor, they would think it was going out to hunt for Confederates. The *Caleb Cushing* swinging on a single anchor chain, its bulwarks low to the water, could easily be climbed by a boarding party. Only one sailor appeared to be on watch and he did not come out from under the ship's awning to challenge the passing boats. The cutter's 32-pounder would be an improvement over the little boat howitzer Savez had on the *Archer*.

As the evening hours passed, Savez watched a small steamer leave the wharf at Portland and head across the anchorage toward a party at the Ottawa house on Cushing Island.[16]

About nine o'clock Savez had one of the crew take Bibber and Titcomb below and handcuff them. He told the sailor to caution the fishermen that if they did not attempt to come back on deck or make noise or resistance, it would be all the better for them.[17]

After midnight, when the party was over, Savez made his move. He assembled his crew, then slowly and deliberately whispered instructions. To take the *Caleb Cushing* would require quick work to avoid sounding the alarm. Three men remained on board the *Archer* to sail it out after daybreak.

Half the crew climbed in the *Archer*'s dory and the other half into Bibber and Titcomb's boat. The tholepin oarlocks were muffled with marlin and rags to prevent the noise of rowing. Savez took command of one boat and John E. Billups the other.[18] Silently the Confederates started for the *Caleb Cushing*.

The Confederates were just about at the stern of the cutter when the watch hailed them. When Savez did not reply, the watch hailed again then turned and disappeared. Read ordered his men to pull on the oars. The rowers beat the water to foam as the boats vaulted the last few yards. The Confederates pulled in the oars as they came alongside the cutter. Read stood and leaped for the bulwark. Grasping it, he swung up on to the deck. Savez's crew hurridly boarded and dropped down the main hatch to capture the Federals.

A figure in a nightshirt appeared at the aft hatch. The watch had not rung its ship's bell to sound the alarm, but had instead gone to get the executive officer. Pointing his revolver at Lieutenant Davenport's head, Savez claimed him as a prisoner of the Confederate States of America.[19] Two of Savez's sailors clapped Davenport in irons, then took him below.

Below deck the Union crew were handcuffed and gagged. Chance had aided Savez. Davenport had given most of the cutter's crew shore leave to arrange for Clarke's funeral. It was 1:30 A.M. The boarding, unreported by the one Portlander who saw it but did not know what to make of it, had taken about five minutes.[20]

Savez then went below to check on his prisoners in the forward end of the berth deck. He explained that he wanted the *Cushing,* not the Yanks. If they behaved themselves, they'd be put off on an island; if they made trouble, they'd be shot and thrown overboard. Davenport pleaded not to be locked up, saying that he was an officer and a Georgian. Savez agreed on hearing Davenport's word that he would not attempt to escape.[21] Leaving two of his crew as guards, Savez returned to the deck.

Trying to get the *Caleb Cushing* under way, the crew discovered that the anchor chain could not be slipped because it did not have a shackle to release it. Since the links were impossible to cut, the Confederates manned the windlass for nearly thirty minutes to noisily house the anchor.[22]

Savez immediately had the sails set, but the cool of the night had killed the sea breeze. To make matters worse, the cutter drifted aground as the anchor came up. Portland harbor had gone through ebb tide around midnight, which meant there was eight feet less water under the *Caleb Cushing* than when the Confederates came in. There was only one choice—"white ash breeze"—tow the *Caleb Cushing* out of the harbor. Savez ordered the towline broken out and *Caleb Cushing*'s boat launched. Across from the cutter an unattended bark lay anchored. The Rebs rowed the line over to the bark and secured it to the ship's mizzen chains. Heaving the line in with the windlass, the Confederates pulled the *Caleb Cushing* off the mud bar. The line was next freed from the bark and tied to two boats. The Southerners finally started towing the *Caleb Cushing* out of the harbor.[23]

Savez realized that inconspicuously taking the cutter out the main channel past the forts was now impossible. Before sunset, he had noticed that there appeared to be a passage to the north around the harbor islands. Savez sent a boat back to the *Archer* for the imprisoned fishermen. When the boat returned, Savez ordered Bibber aboard and sent Titcomb back to pilot the *Archer* out of the harbor after sunrise.

Waiting for the moon to set so that the darkness would lessen their chance of being spotted,[24] Savez encountered the tide, which had started to come in again, making the rowing difficult. The land breeze was late in coming.

Questioning Bibber, Savez learned that the passage beyond the islands ahead, Hussey's Sound, was very shallow at low tide. Savez urged Bibber not to ground the vessel.[25] Savez also called for a sailor to sound with the lead line.

Meanwhile the *Forest City*, returning from Boston, rounded the Portland lighthouse and headed up the channel. Baggagemaster Reuben Chandler noticed the *Caleb Cushing* being towed out and waved. Lieutenant Merryman, its new skipper, demanded that the captain make for the cutter so he could board her. Capt. John Liscomb, intent on making his railroad connections, would not stop.[26] At 4 A.M. the *Forest City* finally approached the Franklin wharf. Merryman discovered part of the *Caleb Cushing*'s crew wondering why their ship had left without them.

Just as the *Caleb Cushing* was towed past Hog Island, the breeze freshened. Savez recalled the towing boats. Ahead lay Cow Island, the last island to pass. On the other side of Cow Island lay Hussey Sound and the Atlantic Ocean. Between the two islands lay a narrow passage.

Informed by the fisherman that it was a very bad passage, Savez considered going around Cow Island, a course that was at least a mile and a half long. Sailing it would take the better part of an hour. Aware that the *Forest City* had observed him, Savez did not have an hour to spare. He judged the passage to be about one hundred and fifty yards wide, but only three hundred yards long: a distance of nine boat lengths. The rocky shores could barely be seen in the dim light. The *Caleb Cushing*, he figured, probably had about a nine-foot draft. Hitting one of those jagged boulders would rip the hull open and sink the cutter. But the tide was coming in and that meant more water over the rocks. Savez ordered the helmsmen to bring the cutter before the wind.[27]

The *Caleb Cushing* slowly turned and started down the passage. Pointing to the rocks, Read cautioned the helmsman to keep the cutter off. The water gurgled past the hull as they crept on. The granite boulders passed abeam, then fell astern. The *Caleb Cushing* was clear.

The cutter headed down Hussey Sound and out into the Atlantic as the sun came up.

Bibber now repeatedly approached Savez and asked to be let go.[28] Savez responded that he first wanted to wait for the *Archer* to catch up with them so that he could get Titcomb off the schooner.

To prepare for the fight ahead, Savez urged his officers to search for powder and shot for the ship's 32-pounder. He realized that breakfast would be a good opportunity to interrogate Davenport about munitions. Since the cutter's cook was back in Portland arranging the funeral, the Confederates had to make do with the cook's fifteen-year-old assistant.[29] Savez appealed to their common Southern heritage. Davenport responded that Savez had acted humanely and if they were taken, Davenport would represent him favorably to the United States authorities.[30]

When asked where the shot was, Davenport denied that it had been taken aboard. He had noted that the door to the shot locker, concealed by a mirror in the aft part of the captain's cabin, had not been opened. The *Caleb Cushing* had been modified at the Boston Navy Yard to add the 32-pounder, so the shot locker was not obvious.[31] Taking advantage of his freedom, Davenport had briefed his crew to tell the Confederates that they were supposed to load shot that day. The four hundred pounds of powder onboard would be easy to find. With the exception of the locker behind the mirror, the remaining shot had been loaded first and stowed behind the powder in the magazine.

The crew backed up Davenport's story. Not trusting the answer, the Confederates pulled open the hatches in the berth deck, but only found five shots, one in a potato locker. More than ninety solid shots were onboard.[32]

Back in Portland, the church bells rang out the alarm. Capt. John Moody in his post atop the observatory spotted the *Caleb Cushing* moving out to sea and sent word into town. The Portlanders grabbed guns and cutlasses. Harrison B. Brown, a local artist, grabbed his sketchbook. A good illustration could sell.[33]

Since the *Caleb Cushing* belonged to the Treasury Department and since Jedediah Jewett, the port collector, was the highest ranking official of that department, he assumed command of the chase. Davenport, Jewett quickly concluded, had turned traitor and made off with the ship. After he took his shave from the town barber,[34] Jewett telegraphed Federal agents in Boston and New York from the Custom House. Next, he sent for the United States Army, dispatching messengers to Fort Preble for men and guns from the 17th U.S. Infantry. He then sent word to Camp Lincoln for more men and guns from the 7th Maine Volunteers. Jewett wrote out charters for the tug *Tiger* and the small steamer *Casco,* which were needed to bring the soldiers into Portland. Knowing that he would need a "man-of-war" to haul his "army," he wrote another charter for use of the *Forest City* and then headed to the Franklin wharf.

At the waterfront, chaos reigned. Some residents took practice shots at boxes and debris floating in the water. Reuben Chandler, watching from the *Forest City,* thought the Portlanders were as mad as hornets. Two black signal balls flew from a mast on the observatory. The cutter was still in sight, taking a south-southeasterly course. Seeing the signals, the mob wanted to take the *Forest City* and start out after the *Caleb Cushing.* Captain Liscomb directed his crew to turn the fire hose on the rabble to prevent them from capsizing his ship.

When Jewett arrived, he found Mayor Jacob McLellan readying the *Chesapeake* for the chase. McLellan had had to offer his home as security before the owners of the *Chesapeake* would let him take their steamer.[35] Portlanders toted cotton bales on board to serve as makeshift armor. The mayor provided guns for those lacking them. Ample provisions were unloaded. Aboard the steamer, the enginemen worked to get steam up in the boilers.

The *Casco* arrived from Fort Preble carrying Capt. Nathaniel Prime and thirty-five of his men together with two cannons: a 6-pounder fieldpiece and a rifled 12-pounder. In good military order, the infantry filed aboard the *Forest City.* Assuming that the presence of the army would calm the locals, Liscomb let the volunteers on his steamer. Merryman, having rounded up the crew of the *Caleb Cushing* on shore leave, hustled them aboard the *Forest City.* At eleven o'clock, the *Forest City* was ready for the pursuit. The Boston steamer, followed by the *Casco,* started out after the *Caleb Cushing.*

By then, the *Tiger* docked with Col. Edward Mason, the troops from the 7th Maine, and their band. The colonel had obtained two brass 6-pounder cannons from the state arsenal. They boarded the *Chesapeake* along with more Portlanders, including Harrison Brown. McLellan pronounced the local naval inspector, William F. Leighton, commander of the vessel. Leighton asked the mayor for orders. "Catch the damned scoundrels and hang everyone of them," bellowed McLellan.[36] With the band playing and the crowd cheering, the *Chesapeake* left the pier and followed after the *Forest City.*

In all the excitement, no one noted the *Archer* as she raised anchor and set out to sea.

Back on the *Caleb Cushing,* Savez, having finished breakfast, ordered all hands below to rest. When the watch called out a steamer was in sight, Read bounded up the ladder and onto the deck. Taking the spyglass from the watch, he looked over the steamer that had just passed the Portland lighthouse. Savez noted the side paddle wheels and guessed it was the *Forest City* bound out to Boston. A second steamer appeared with soldiers on the upper deck. Savez ordered his crew to clear for action.[37]

The Confederates released the lashings that had held the 32-pounder amidships. Dropping the in-tackle, the sailors swung the cannon around on its races to point it aft toward the approaching Portlanders. The cannon halted on the stops at the end of the races. The main mast prevented the cannon from pointing directly astern.

After Savez ordered the helmsman to bring the cutter around so the cannon could get off a good shot,[38] Bibber again pleaded to leave. This time Savez replied that he could take either of the boats alongside.[39] As Bibber rowed away from the *Caleb Cushing,* a Confederate yelled to row quickly as they were about to open fire.

Read surveyed his ammunition: five cannon balls—a fact unknown to the Portlanders. Pryde, Savez's gunner, pushed a priming wire down the tiny vent on the back of the cannon and punched a hole in the powder bag inside the barrel. With the vent clear, he slid the primer in the opening and flattened the explosive wafer over the primer. Pryde then wound the firing lanyard onto the gunlock. Pulling the lanyard taut he stepped back and looked across the breech sight at the approaching *Forest City.* The elevating screw was quickly turned to give the cannon barrel five degrees elevation for a 1,930-yard shot.[40] Savez watched the ball splash directly in front of the steamer.[41] He had the bearing, but not quite the range. He called for more elevation. A second shot skipped across the calm water only to fall short.

Meanwhile, on board the *Chesapeake,* the Portlanders had decided to sail up to the *Caleb Cushing* and ask what the crew planned on doing with the ship. Savez's first shot at the *Forest City* ended all doubts about the intentions of the crew of the cutter. On deck, a private from the 7th Maine cheered. Naval Inspector Leighton told the pilot to "run her down or go to the bottom!"[42]

The 32-pounder fired again, and again the shot fell short. The citizen army aboard the *Forest City* became concerned about the steamer's vulnerability. Liscomb decided to wait for the *Chesapeake* to catch up. She had cotton bales to absorb the hits and her screw propeller made it less likely that she would be disabled by cannon fire. Aboard the *Forest City,* Prime wanted to press on and seize the cutter.[43]

As the *Chesapeake* came alongside the *Forest City,* the cutter fired a fourth shot. This time the *Chesapeake* was the target. The attackers held an impromptu council of war as the fifth shot fell within thirty feet of the two steamers. Both the *Forest City* and the *Chesapeake* could be put out of action before they got close enough for their guns to bear.

While the talking proceeded, some of the volunteers on the *Chesapeake* fired their brass 6-pounder even though the range was too great to hit the cutter. After one shot an old tar from the Navy hugged the barrel and patted it as if it was his child.[44]

It was decided that the *Chesapeake* would steer straight for the cutter, followed by the *Forest City*. When Mason turned to the 7th Maine and announced that they would take the cutter, his men broke out with three loud and spontaneous cheers. The cheering was returned by the *Forest City*. One man on the *Chesapeake* cried out, "Stand by your flag!" Everyone cheered.[45]

The bright midday sunlight danced across the calm water. As the *Chesapeake,* black smoke pouring out of her smokestack, charged toward the *Caleb Cushing,* Savez realized the raid was over. He had fired his last cannonball. Gone was the chance to link up with Maffitt's *Florida* in attacking other seacoast towns in Maine.

Savez ordered the cutter set afire, then sent a sailor below to release the prisoners. Savez also told the gunner to keep firing the cannon with scrap metal, nails, anything. The range was too great for the scrap to be effective, but the sound of the cannon might rattle the attacking Portlanders. He needed time to abandon ship and for the fire to catch hold. A Dutch cheese from the officers' mess was loaded and fired. The Portlanders would later claim that the Rebels were firing "stink pots."[46]

Below deck, the Confederates broke up furniture and tore apart bedding. A match was thrown in. The cabin immediately burst into flames. To make sure the cutter would be destroyed, a sailor strung out a long fuse from the powder magazine and lit it. When Savez's crew returned to the deck they had scorched eyebrows and mustaches from working close to the fire. The Confederates launched boats, then helped the prisoners climb into them and tossed them the keys to their handcuffs.

Savez gathered up some money, and since his coat was threadbare, grabbed Captain Clarke's coat. By that time, the flames were leaping up the open hatches toward the rigging. Savez ordered his crew to abandon ship and they boarded two boats. He then told the crew to throw their arms overboard for their safety. Pulling out a bag of coins, he passed out money that would be helpful in Yankeedom. The Confederates finally tied a white handkerchief to a boat hook and waved it.[47]

The *Forest City* approached. It looked as though every citizen had his musket trained on the boat. The Confederates made Masonic signs. An officer with a drawn sword stepped in front of the threatening Portlanders and ordered them not to fire.

A line was tossed to the boat and the Confederates were ordered up one at a time. Savez climbed onto the deck and stated he was a prisoner of war, then surrendered his side arm to an angry Merryman. The lieutenant briefly questioned Savez, then ordered him tied up and turned over to Captain Prime. The rest of Savez's crew were then brought on board.[48]

The *Chesapeake* picked up the original crew of the *Caleb Cushing*. A few of the Portlanders on the *Chesapeake* rowed over to the *Caleb Cushing* hoping to put out the blaze, but the fire was too far along. Roaring flames licked their way up the rigging. Cinders and burning bits of sails shot upwards. Smoke bellowed, darkening the sky. The ship was ablaze from stem to stern. Giving up, they towed back a half-swamped boat.

At 1:48 P.M. the flames racing through the dying ship reached the four hundred pounds of black powder. In an instant, the magazine exploded with a thundering roar. The deck buckled, then split apart as fire erupted, sending black smoke rolling skyward in a huge column. Fragments of deck, masts, booms, and charred timbers catapulted hundreds of feet in the air only to fall back onto the spectator fleet. The sound was heard in Portland, over twenty miles away. Pivoting backwards, the cutter's stern dipped below the water. The now silent 32-pounder fell off the deck and plunged into the sea. The *Caleb Cushing* slid below Casco Bay sinking in thirty-three fathoms of water, ten to twelve miles from shore. As the cutter vanished, the water swirled in a whirlpool and a spar rose from below, then sank again.[49] Aboard the *Forest City,* Harrison Brown recorded the event in his sketchbook.

In the captain's cabin, a pleased Savez heard the explosion. He still was wearing the coat of the late captain of the *Caleb Cushing.* Clarke had weighed 260 pounds.[50]

After the *Forest City* picked up Bidder, the Portlanders learned of the *Archer.* They steamed over to the schooner and captured it. Everyone started back to Portland.

As the *Forest City* passed the Portland lighthouse and steamed up the channel, the soldiers at the forts fired their cannons in celebration. The church bells of Portland rang out. The townspeople lined the shore and cheered.

The mood of the citizen army suddenly turned ugly; they wanted to lynch the captives. Prime decided that the walls of the fort would be safer than the jail in Portland. Prime assembled his soldiers and took charge of the prisoners.

When the *Forest City* docked, Prime marched the Confederates over to the fort under the guard. The Portlanders jeered the Confederates along the way with taunts of, "How does your neck, Johnny Reb?" and "Hang the pirates!"[51] The soldiers kept the townspeople at bay.

The only fatality happened after Savez was captured. A curious Portlander slipped past a guard on the *Archer*. He picked up a rifle and cocked it without realizing it was loaded. The rifle fired and mortally wounded a bystander.[52]

The crew of the *Archer* took their schooner and resumed fishing. In 1868, a ship from Gloucester hit the *Archer*, sinking her almost immediately. The crew barely had time to escape.[53]

The *Chesapeake* was destined to play another part in the Civil War. In December 1863 a band of Confederates seized the steamer while she was in route to Portland. The Southerners wanted to take the steamer to Bermuda, but needed coal to make the trip. They went to Canada for fuel, but were captured by the Union Navy before they could take on coal. The *Chesapeake* was returned to her owners.

The *Florida* did come northward. With the capture of the packet ship *Sunrise,* Maffitt learned of Savez's exploits from the New York newspapers on board the ship.[54] In July, Maffitt docked in Brest, France, where he suffered a heart attack. The *Florida* sailed on under a new captain, only to be captured in Bahia, Brazil, and taken back to the United States. The Brazilian government protested the seizure and while negotiations were under way, the Federal Government sank the *Florida* under the guise of an accident.

Jedediah Jewett would, in a report to the secretary of the treasury, state that he regretted suspecting Davenport. Later in the war, Jewett would again send out a ship looking for more Confederates. At the end of the war, Jacob McLellan left office, only to again become mayor three years later. Merryman became captain in 1864, but Davenport still failed to pass his exams and had his rank revoked in 1865. Artist Harrison Brown made photographic copies of his sketch. They sold well. Reuben Chandler continued on as a baggagemaster, retiring in 1907 after forty-seven years of service. Titcomb and Bibber denied helping the Confederates. The Revenue Cutter *James C. Dobbin* was assigned to replace the *Caleb Cushing*. Jewett took two Confederate flags and a red burgee found on the *Archer* and hung them in the Custom House. Savez's firebombs ended up on display in the reading room at the Merchant's Exchange. The boat that the *Chesapeake's* crew rescued from the *Caleb Cushing* was named *Trio* and displayed in the North Star Boat Club.[55]

CHAPTER TWO

A YOUNG MISSISSIPPIAN

Savez, born Charles William Read, was born May 12, 1840, in Yazoo County, Mississippi, the first child of William Francis and Maria Louise Read. His farmer parents, who traced back their ancestry to the Jamestown settlement, married in 1837. After Savez's birth, the family expanded with the births of John, Jeremiah, Joseph, and Elizabeth.[1]

In 1844 twenty-eight-year-old William took a mortgage from his father for six hundred acres at Brownsville near Edwards Station in Hinds County. Four years later William and Maria decided to try farming without his father. They signed a one-year lease for everything they needed. By the end of the year, the Reads were to have grown and turned over to the lessor's agent in Vicksburg, eighty-two bales of cotton weighing 400 pounds each.

The farm was not prosperous and in 1849, the Reads were in debt. About this time William was asked by his father to take his uncle, thought to be sick with tuberculosis, to California in the hopes of improving his health. William was reluctant to leave the pregnant Maria, but finding gold would help the family finances.

He and his uncle joined a large party of Mississippians leaving for the goldfields. On July 6, 1850, William died in Nevada City, California, while taking care of his uncle, who later returned to Mississippi.[2]

Growing up without a father forced Savez to be independent and sure of himself, but also impulsive.

The homestead that Maria inherited, worth eight hundred dollars by 1850, was hardly successful. Most farms in the county were valued for at least twice that amount.[3] Maria knew she could not continue to run the farm with only children as help. She had relatives in Jackson, Mississippi, so she moved her family to the state capital to start anew.[4]

The capital of the "Magnolia State" had a hustle and bustle that contrasted it with the quiet dull farm life. School, however, was not exciting for young Savez. He daydreamed of a sailor's life on the high seas.

In search of excitement, the teenager aspired to work with his uncle, who had a job with a Jackson newspaper, the *Mississippian*. With his uncle's influence, he got an after-school job.[5] The newspaper office provided the activity of running the press and getting out the paper. Being a printer's devil was better than doing schoolwork.

The youth, wanting to do more, organized the boys in the office and started a newspaper of his own. He called the broadsheet *Scraps of Little America*. One of his frank articles ired the editor of the *Vicksburg Sun*.

When the editor, who had a tradition of settling his differences with his fists, came to town, Savez had a bit part as a sailor boy in a nautical melodrama from Boston entitled *Black Eyed Susan*. The editor's friend, who had told him that his antagonist was in the play, offered to go with him to the performance to identify Read. The boy, fifteen years old and small for his age, looked even younger in his sailor costume. As the sailor boys came out onto the stage, the hero of the drama began a dialogue with another actor:[6]

"What service?" inquired the hero.

"I'm the law."

"Umph!" the hero snorted. "Belongs to the rocket boats. May my pockets be acuttled if I didn't think so! Tis Beelzebub's ship, the law neither privateer, bombship nor letter-o-mark. . . ."[7]

The editor's companion pointed Savez out to him. The chagrined editor arose, proclaiming he had come to Jackson looking for a man to fight not a boy.[8] As he stomped out, the hero, as if to mock the editor, concluded his soliloquy with, "She always sails best in a storm and flounders in fair weather. . . ."

After the newspaper and the theater became boring, Savez decided to make his daydreams come true. Without telling his mother, he left Jackson for New Orleans and signed on aboard a sailing ship. Maria, after much difficulty, obtained her son's release with help from friends.[9]

She then sought help from her congressman, W. A. Lake. Realizing the boy's desire to go to sea, Lake wrote the required letter to James C. Dobbin, President Franklin Pierce's secretary of the navy. Dobbin placed Charles William Read's name on the list of applicants to the United States Naval Academy.[10]

Savez fired off a letter of acceptance to Dobbin. Next, he wrote one to the superintendent of the Academy, asking if he could get the jacket, vest, and pantaloons after he reached Annapolis and if the regulations permitted examination of more than one person from the same congressional district.[11] The answer was yes to the former and no to the latter.

By 1856 eleven years had passed since Secretary of the Navy George Bancroft established the Naval School, later renamed the Naval Academy. The War Department gave the Navy an old army post on the Severn River, which consisted of seven buildings and a small fort. The Academy quickly outgrew the old post.[12]

Academy regulations stated that the candidates could present themselves to the superintendent only during the last ten days of September. Upon arrival, Read passed both the medical and academic examinations and on September 20, 1856, the Academy Board pronounced him duly qualified to become an acting midshipman in the United States Navy.[13]

Of the fifty-two young men who made up the class of 1860, half would graduate. Several graduates of the Academy between 1856 and 1860 achieved fame. Winfield Scott Schley led the fleet in the Spanish–American War's battle of Santiago and made admiral for it. Alfred Thayer Mahan wrote *The Influence of Sea Power upon History*, a work that inspired Presidents Theodore Roosevelt and William Howard Taft, British statesmen, and Kaiser Wilhelm II. George Dewey emerged the hero of the battle of Manila Bay.[14]

Article 10 of the *Regulations of the U.S. Naval Academy* required an entering midshipman to immediately furnish himself with everything from uniforms to a pair of hair combs. Savez's uniform consisted of a navy blue, double-breasted jacket with nine small buttons per side and a gold fouled anchor on each collar. Under the jacket he wore a white shirt, a black silk handkerchief for a necktie, and a vest.[15]

Fifty-one-year-old Comdr. Louis M. Goldsborough, the fourth superintendent, had the responsibility for the discipline and good management of the Academy. A giant, Goldsborough weighed almost three hundred pounds and stood six feet, four inches tall. He had a deep voice, penetrating stare, and brisk, salty manner. Although he would lecture the Academic Board on the enforcement of discipline, he maintained a "boys will be boys" attitude, probably because he had first gone to sea at the age of eleven.[16] He could, however, be pushed too far. The previous March,

Goldsborough wrote the secretary of the navy: "Midshipman Simon Mish exhibited himself in the chapel . . . in a state of excessive intoxication. . . . Subsequently, on the conclusion of the service he had to be conveyed out of the church and thence to the police office and his quarters."[17]

Goldsborough continued that although he knew he was not a severe man in his official conclusions, he wanted Mish dismissed and not allowed to resign. Goldsborough later relented and did allow Mish to resign, but swore he would never enter the Navy again.[18]

The acting midshipmen of the Academy were organized into four classes, with the neophytes in the fourth class. Savez was assigned to a gun crew for drill and mess, a practice used by a ship's company on a man-of-war. Each crew had about fifteen to twenty members and was under the tutelage of two first-class men, designated first and second captain.

The school day began at 6:15 A.M. with the morning gun and beating of a drum for reveille. Then came policing of quarters, inspection, and roll call. The students next marched to chapel in close order and perfect silence.[19]

To the drumbeat "Peas upon a Trencher," the gun crew marched to the mess hall for breakfast. They then marched to the recitation hall. The Navy stressed training in two broad areas: those things necessary to command a fighting ship, and everything else. Grades were computed by a complicated system resulting in a class ranking for every subject.

At one o'clock, with the drummer beating "Roast Beef," the midshipmen returned to the mess hall for dinner. After forty minutes, they marched back to the recitation hall. At four o'clock, they either marched to Fort Severn for gunnery drill and fencing practice or to the parade grounds for infantry and light artillery drill. At sunset came evening roll call and parade.

The drummer beat "Canteen Call" as the young men marched to supper. Study followed. Tattoo was at 9:30 P.M. and at ten o'clock lights were extinguished.

The regulations permitted bathing once a week. The gun captains marched their charges to the bathing rooms. Anyone bathing more than once a week had to pay six cents to the barber.[20]

Just as he did in Jackson, Savez lacked the discipline to study. He daydreamed and his grades suffered accordingly. By the time of the semiannual examination in February 1857, he ranked forty-sixth in his class in mathematics, thirty-sixth in grammar, and thirtieth in geography.[21]

The young Mississippian discovered that while good marks were hard to earn, demerits were not. He collected demerits for everything from not sweeping his room to throwing a snowball at a friend. A classmate reported Read for using profane language; ten demerits resulted. Ten days later he got into a fight with his accuser. The regulations called for ten more demerits.[22]

When the year ended with examinations in June, Savez retained the same class academic ranking.[23] The ten months had passed without hazing. Very little hazing occurred before the Civil War. Read's class then became the third-year class.

That September Capt. George S. Blake replaced Goldsborough. The fifty-four-year-old Blake came to Annapolis with over forty-three years of service. The acting midshipmen would find their new superintendent a likable, but firm disciplinarian.

For the third-year class mathematics continued, but history replaced geography and French replaced grammar. For Savez, French was incomprehensible. His entire knowledge of French consisted of one word: *"savez"*—you know. He repeated the word hundreds of times, even ending sentences with it. For the rest of his life, he would answer to "Savez" Read.[24]

Savez's drillmaster, Henry H. Lockwood, had graduated from West Point. Even though Lockwood had left the Army, he had been dubbed "The Shore Warrior." Some of Savez's "shipmates" hanged Lockwood in effigy. When court-marshaled, the accused said that they were not guilty because Lockwood was not an officer and the regulations did not mention respect toward civilians. The scheme did not work; new charges were brought and the accused convicted. To prevent future usage of that argument, Lockwood received an equivalent rank resulting in an increase in pay of about $400 a year. The acting midshipmen quipped that for that amount of money, Lockwood should be hanged annually.

Since Lockwood stuttered, he needed a bugler to sound the calls. One day, however, the bugler got sick. That day's drill required the acting midshipmen to move the 6-pounder cannons forward, firing blanks as they progressed. Savez's classmates headed their cannons toward the superintendent's house. As Lockwood struggled to yell "Halt," the gun crews blasted the board fence that surrounded the garden.[25]

The roar of cannon was not the only noise at the Academy. One evening the back wall of one of the dormitories collapsed. The builders had failed to attach the wall to the floors.[26]

Life at the Academy, as George Dewey would later write in his autobiography, meant "no system of athletics except our regular drill . . . no adequate gymnastic apparatus . . . one endless grind of acquiring knowledge."[27] Some acting midshipmen "frenched out" by scaling the wall and going into Annapolis to drink. The Academy soon banned drinking clubs such as the Owls, the Crickets, and the Corn Hill Riot.[28] In December when two of his classmates were caught, Savez and thirty-one others signed a pledge stating that they would abstain from alcohol if the Academy would look favorably upon the cases of Stanton and Doolittle, their accused classmates.[29] The pledge did not work. Stanton and Doolittle were dismissed, because Blake knew the students would not keep their pledge.

Savez's concern for others impressed his classmates. Years later, Winfield Scott Schley wrote that Savez was "active in movement, generous and loyal in character, firm in his friendships, and decided in opinions. The place he took in his class was in no sense the measure of his intellectual worth, but arose from his lack of application to study. He possessed in high degree common sense, or ought I to say an uncommon sense, as everyone does not possess it. He had sublime courage . . . conspicuous dash . . . great originality . . . and was aggressive in all that he did."[30]

By June Savez ranked twenty-sixth in a class that then numbered thirty-three. His standing was better in one area, demerits. About half the class had more than his eighty-three.[31]

In 1858 the Academy received a ceremonial bell that Commodore Matthew C. Perry had brought back from his expedition to Japan. It joined the collection of flags in the Lyceum, such as Oliver Hazard Perry's dark blue flag with the white letters "Don't Give Up the Ship," which served to instill in Savez the Navy's tradition of duty and valor.[32]

The Lyceum had been placed under the care of George Jones, the Academy's first chaplain. "Old Slicky" delivered numerous "hell's fire and damnation" sermons. One December Sunday, a small dog wandered into the chapel and started barking a response. The young parishioners scarcely contained their laughter.[33]

By the end of the year Savez's classmates were divided over the Hackett Affair. The Academy had a tradition that one first-year classman would not put another first-year classman on report. Alfred Thayer Mahan put Samuel Hackett on report for talking in the ranks during gun drill. Most disagreed with Mahan and placed him "in Coventry," refusing to talk to him.[34] Savez could not side with Mahan.

When the June 1859 examinations were completed, Savez's class standing had fallen to twenty-fifth out of twenty-five. This time he had 157 demerits. Two hundred demerits would have brought dismissal. Only one man received more demerits and he was held back a year.

Class rank not withstanding, Savez boarded the USS *Plymouth* for a summer cruise with one hundred and six other acting midshipmen.[35]

Built in the Boston Navy Yard in 1844, the *Plymouth* was a 147-foot-long sloop rigged with a full spar deck. In appearance, she looked like a merchant packet ship designed to sail between America and Great Britain. Considered by many officers to be the finest ship of her class, she had the reputation of being a stiff ship and dry in heavy weather, but very fast in both light and strong wind.[36] The *Plymouth* had gone with Commodore Perry in his 1853 expedition to Japan. She carried a battery of four 8-inch-shellguns and eighteen 32-pounders.

At 11 o'clock on June 22, Comdr. Thomas T. Craven came aboard and ordered the first lieutenant to get the ship underway.[37] The acting midshipmen were bound for England, France, Spain, and Madeira. After twice running aground, the *Plymouth* started to sail down the bay. After three days the *Plymouth* anchored fifty-five miles down the bay off New Point Comfort near Mobjack Bay, Virginia.

At 6 A.M. on June 26, a pilot came aboard to take the ship out of Chesapeake Bay. On a port tack and under clear sky, the *Plymouth* sailed past Capes Henry and Charles. After the capes were cleared, the pilot left in his boat.

Once out into the Atlantic, the ship's motion changed. The long ocean swells passed under the hull, rolling the ship back and forth. Several acting midshipmen felt dizzy and nauseous. As the *Plymouth* continued eastward, they grew accustomed to the ship's motion and all recovered from their seasickness.

The ocean suddenly seemed to change color from dull green to deep indigo blue. The waves changed from long rolling swells to shorter, choppier seas, with little ripples marking the division. Seaweed drifted by and overhead meandered a few white, cumulous clouds.[38] Turning northeastward the *Plymouth* entered the Gulf Stream.

A typical day at sea began with a roll of the ship's drums. The bugler then sounded reveille. Inspection and scrubbing the decks with holystones came before breakfast. Two bells (9:00 A.M.) brought the changing of flags, lowering the night pendant, and raising the ensign.

The first lessons of the day were held aloft, working with the sails. Mizzen, topmast, mainstays, fore topsail, and a hundred other terms became easily recognizable to the young sailors. The boatswain showed the acting midshipmen marlinespike seamanship: knotting, worming, splicing, serving, parceling, and doing fancywork with rope. The sailmaker taught them to patch worn sails and sew grommets into canvas. At noon the decks were swept and grog issued before the acting midshipmen were piped below for their meal.

In the afternoon, lessons were conducted on deck. The acting midshipmen learned the art of helmsmanship, steering the *Plymouth* on course. Whenever weather conditions permitted, the acting midshipmen also drilled with the gun batteries, firing at barrels they had set adrift as targets.

After the evening meal came time for relaxing, singing, and telling sea stories. Sunset brought the lowering of the ensign and the raising of the night pendant. All hands stood by their hammocks. A long drumroll followed by a bugling of the night call ended the day.[39]

The ship continued sailing northward in the Gulf Stream, past the New England coast and south of Nova Scotia. On July 5, as the *Plymouth* approached the Grand Banks, a frosty wall of fog rose from the ocean. Above the fog the sky remained clear. The warm Gulf Stream was colliding with the cold waters of the Labrador Current coming down from the Arctic Ocean.[40] The boatswain sounded the foghorn, the ship sailed on, and the fog cleared almost as quickly as it had formed.

The next afternoon a school of porpoises swam by, hunting the bountiful fish of the Grand Banks. Porpoises were not the only ones that fished there. Commander Craven ordered the *Plymouth* to hove to in an area called the Tail of the Bank and sent a boat over to a French fishing brig to buy six hundred pounds of codfish.

The eighth ring of the ship's bell had just sounded when the first lieutenant passed the captain's command to reef the topsails to lower the pressure on the masts. What had been a strong breeze from north-northeast that morning now blew at near gale strength. On the sea white foam shredded into streaks.[41]

The acting midshipmen ran to their places. Some went aloft to shorten sail. Some stayed on deck to man the rigging. The days of drill would now pay off. At the ship's railing, young men grabbed the lower shrouds and pulled themselves up and around onto the rope ladders. At fifty-five feet above the deck, the lower shrouds converged on the tops that extended beyond the shrouds. To get around them, they grabbed the futtock shrouds, leaned backwards, and with a chin-up pulled themselves up and over. Then began the final ascent up the topmast shrouds. Even though the *Plymouth* was a stiff ship, she did roll.

Reaching the topsail yardarms, the acting midshipmen lunged for the horizontal spruce timbers, draped their arms over them, and swung their feet onto the footrope four feet below the yardarms. They shuffled sideways down the footrope pressing their chests firmly against the fourteen-inch-wide yardarms. With the deck eighty-six feet below, falling meant death. Even if they landed in the ocean, they would drown before a boat could be launched to rescue them. All remembered the sailor's maxim "one hand for yourself, one hand for the ship."

On deck, others slacked off the halyards and hauled in the clew lines. The windlass was manned to pull the weather braces and turn the yardarms. Wind spilled from the sails, making it easier to pull them in.

Those aloft grabbed the canvas sails and pulled them up. When the reef points appeared, they tied the ropes around the yards. The danger of blown-out sails was over; the acting midshipmen beamed.[42]

The storm lasted for three days. By the time it had stopped, the *Plymouth* was approaching Ireland. Several ships were sighted.

On July 21 the lookout spotted the Scilly Islands off the port beam. The next evening the Eddystone Light appeared in the distance. To avoid the rocks, Craven had the *Plymouth* sail a course thirteen miles to the east of the lighthouse.

The following day, the *Plymouth* beat to windward past the ruined St. Michael's chapel on Rame Head and sailed into the harbor at Plymouth, England. Plymouth, the acting midshipmen's first port of call, was home to the British Naval Docks. The *Plymouth's* port watch of acting midshipmen visited the docks first. When they returned, the starboard watch went ashore. One shipmate, Morgan Ogden, went instead to a pub and returned so drunk he had to be lifted aboard. Upon sobering up, Ogden wrote a pledge to Craven pleading to be allowed to remain at the Academy by promising "never to touch another drop of liquor of any kind."[43] He was, nevertheless, dismissed when the *Plymouth* returned to Annapolis.

At 8:15 P.M. on July 25, the *Plymouth* left England. Three days later the ship passed Ushant Island and rounded Pointe de Saint-Mathieu. Heading up the steeply banked channel, Craven and his crew brought the ship to anchor in the harbor of Brest, France, a sixty-square-mile, deep-water anchorage. The harbor was also a French naval base, the reason for the visit.

On July 30, as the *Plymouth* started out of the harbor, both of the bowsprit's inner bobstays broke. Craven ordered the ship back to Brest for repairs. That this was wise became apparent as the *Plymouth* headed southward toward Spain across the Bay of Biscay. The ship's course, together with a fresh breeze and heavy swell, caused her to pitch heavily. If the repair had not been made, the bowsprit would have let go, causing the loss of the foremast.

The *Plymouth* sailed under an overcast sky, which prevented taking a sextant reading to determine the ship's latitude. Suspecting the storm had blown the ship into the Atlantic, Craven turned the *Plymouth* eastward until they sighted the rocks of Cape Finisterre, Spain.

With the ship's position verified, Craven resumed a southerly course. For two more days the *Plymouth* sailed through rain and cloudy weather. On August 9, the lookout spotted the cliffs of Cape St. Vincent on the southwest corner of Portugal.

The following day, the *Plymouth* sailed into the harbor of Cadiz, Spain. Spanish officials, perhaps seeking a bribe, placed the ship under quarantine. Craven sent a complaint ashore to the American consul, but the Spanish objected to the landing of the boat. To the disappointment of the young sailors Craven signaled for a pilot.

The *Plymouth* set course for the island of Madeira. During the early morning hours of August 17, she entered Funchal harbor. In anchorage lay the USS *Constellation,* flagship of the African Squadron. The *Constellation* was bound for the east African coast to suppress the slave trade. Four of the Academy's previous graduating class were serving on board the *Constellation.*

On August 20 Craven ordered the *Plymouth* to get underway. The acting midshipmen saluted the flagship with three cheers and a manning of the rigging, standing aloft on the yards. The entry in the ship's log read, "and then we turned the ship's head to the westward and were—*Homeward Bound.*"[44]

Craven followed the Canary Current until it divided north of the Cape Verde Islands. He then took the westward, North Equatorial Branch, toward North America.[45] Besides learning to use ocean currents, the acting midshipmen studied navigation and every aspect of seamanship as they sailed home. Each gun crew got to use the sextant to determine the *Plymouth*'s position. The honor of plotting the position went to the acting midshipmen whose observation came closest to the class average.[46] Savez's observations never equaled the average, but to him that mattered little.[47]

The tranquillity of that summer would not last for long. The approaching war would affect both the ship and those on board. The *Plymouth* would make one more summer cruise and eventually die in a funeral pyre at the Gosport Navy Yard at Portsmouth, Virginia. Eight of the twenty-five members of the third class would resign and go south.[48] By the end of the war, Craven would be court-martialed and found guilty of failing to engage the CSS *Stonewall*.

On September 15, the *Plymouth* dropped anchor off Old Point Comfort, Virginia, twenty-six days after leaving Funchal, Madeira. Craven said in his report to Blake that he had never known a more perfect landfall at Cape Henry.[49] When the *Plymouth* arrived back at Annapolis, the acting midshipmen enjoyed their biggest meal of the summer.[50]

That fall, Savez's grades dropped lower and lower, with his highest marks in the theory of gunnery, and in that, he only placed fourth from the bottom of his class.[51] As a member of the first class, a bored Savez stood watch as officer of the day in the guardhouse and recorded in the log the weather, the number of laborers employed for the day, and the coming and going of his classmates.[52]

In the fall of 1859, the country was drifting toward war. The slavery issue destroyed the spirit of compromise. At Annapolis, the acting midshipmen debated current events on Saturday nights, in what they called "reformed banquets." Tempers flared over such things as John Brown's raid on Harpers Ferry and South Carolina congressman Preston Brooks's 1856 caning of Massachusetts senator Charles Sumner. Sumner had been sharply critical of Brooks's uncle on the floor of the United States Senate.[53]

On June 10, 1860, Charles William Read graduated as anchorman of his class. His scholastic rating had fallen until he finished twenty-fifth in a class of twenty-five.[54] One of his classmates later said, "After a magnificent struggle extending over four years, Savez triumphantly graduated, at the foot of his class."[55]

As a midshipman in the United States Navy, Savez was assigned to the newly commissioned sloop USS *Pawnee* at the Philadelphia Navy Yard. Before the *Pawnee* could sail, he was detached and ordered to report to Capt. Samuel Mercer aboard the USS *Powhatan*.[56] The pride of the service, the 253-foot-long side-wheeled steamship *Powhatan* represented the transition of the Navy from sail to steam. The ship had served as Perry's flagship when he sailed into Tokyo Bay.[57]

Among the young officers already on board, Savez found former class-mate George Dewey. At the end of August, the ship set sail for Veracruz, Mexico. A storm off Jamaica, during which lightning hit the main mast, provided the only excitement of the voyage. On September 17, the *Powhatan* dropped anchor at Veracruz.[58]

The ship served as the flagship for the squadron, hosting visiting digni-taries. Monotonous months followed. Back home the mood worsened. After the November election of Abraham Lincoln, the South acted.

On December 20, South Carolina withdrew from the United States and declared herself to be an independent and sovereign people. Mississippi, on January 9, 1861, became the second state to secede. Nine days later when the mail steamer *Tennessee* arrived in Veracruz from New Orleans, she brought Savez word of his home state's secession.

The next day, Savez wrote a letter to the secretary of the navy, Isaac Toucey, resigning his commission. Despite the friendships he had made at Annapolis, and his loyalty toward the Navy, his family and neighbors were in Mississippi. Honor and duty demanded that he must abide by their decision.[59]

Savez's letter of resignation troubled Captain Mercer. Resignations by Southerners would leave the ship shorthanded. The captain agreed to for-ward Savez's resignation on the mail steamer if Savez would stay until the ship arrived in New York, assuring him that a relief ship would arrive any day. Savez agreed as a favor to the captain.[60]

At the end of February, the *Tennessee* brought word that the Navy Department had accepted Savez's resignation.[61] Finally, the new flagship USS *Macedonian* arrived. Five days later the *Powhatan* left Veracruz. Mercer did not hold gunnery drills, seeing no need to practice a skill that depart-ing crew and officers might someday use against him.

Upon reaching New York, Savez left the *Powhatan* on March 14 to board a southbound train. Three days later Mercer had Savez listed in the ship's log as absent without leave because he had not returned by sunset on the fourteenth.[62]

At Annapolis, Superintendent Blake urged the Southerners to stand by the Navy and to hold to their oath of allegiance to the Constitution and the United States. Tears in their eyes, the Southerners left with a handshake and a pledge of friendship to their Northern classmates.[63]

Savez stopped briefly in Washington at the Navy Department to con-firm that his resignation had been received.[64] The Navy had it, although the new secretary of the navy, Gideon Welles, was then listing all resigning officers as "dismissed," thereby denying them future rights to pensions. His predecessor Toucey had been censured for having been too lenient.[65]

Savez luckily left Washington when he did. In a little more than a month, the city would be under martial law with the army guarding its exits. The pass to the south would prescribe death for the user if thereafter he bore arms against the government of the United States.

As Savez moved southward, the temperament of the people changed. Bands played "Dixie" and "The Bonnie Blue Flag," while people waved the new flag of the Confederacy. Savez finally reached Montgomery, Alabama, the capital of the new Confederacy.[66] The Exchange Hotel, considered to be the more refined of the city's hotels, served as the temporary offices of Pres. Jefferson Davis and his cabinet. The accommodations, however, were hardly luxurious. Davis had his desk moved into a hotel parlor, a room he shared with his secretary. Davis ate his meals in the dining room with the other guests. Until a private residence could be secured, Davis remained content to live that way.

On his arrival, Savez made his way through the Exchange lobby, swarming with cotton merchants, officers, adventurers, office seekers, faro dealers, ladies of the night, and politicians.[67] Savez managed to talk with Jefferson Davis and also with Confederate secretary of the navy Stephen Mallory. From them he received assurance of a commission if hostilities started.

Leaving Montgomery Savez traveled to Raymond, Mississippi, to spend some time with his mother, who had moved there from Jackson. During his stay at home Savez fell in love with Miss Rosa Hall, the seventeen-year-old daughter of a wealthy hotel owner.[68] It would be six years, however, before he could marry her.[69]

On April 12, the commander of Federal Fort Sumter in Charleston Harbor refused to surrender and was notified that the Confederates would fire on to the fort. At 4:30 A.M. that morning, the Confederates fired a signal mortar. The shell exploded directly over the fort. The Civil War had begun. The next day, Savez was appointed acting midshipman in the Confederate navy.[70] On May 8, Read received orders to report to Capt. Lawrence Rousseau in New Orleans for duty aboard the CSS *McRae*.[71]

The war would not only bring Savez to the fighting, but also his brothers. William Read, too young to join the army, would serve as a courier for Brig. Gen. Francis M. Cockrell. John Read would serve as a regimental adjutant. Joseph Read would serve in the infantry where he would lose a leg to gangrene while being held prisoner. Even Elizabeth stood up to the Yankees who were imprisoning two Confederates in her uncle's house.[72]

Not all the Reads supported the war. Savez's grandfather threatened to disown him for resigning his commission from the United States Navy. John Read considered himself an Old Line Whig and a Union man.[73]

Savez arrived in the Crescent City on May 21, prepared for the glory of war. New Orleans' own Pierre Gustave Toutant Beauregard had commanded the Confederates at Charleston, and the townspeople were wild with excitement. Even the riverboat gamblers joined up, organizing themselves into companies like Wilson's Rangers and the Perrit Guards. It was rumored that the Perrit Guards had to cut, shuffle, and deal on the point of a bayonet.[74]

CHAPTER THREE

CSS M<u>c</u>R<u>ae</u>

In the naval war of which Savez was so eager to be part, the North would have a huge nautical advantage: sea power. Savez's Annapolis classmate, Alfred J. Mahan, influenced by the Civil War, would later define sea power as "the military strength afloat, that rules the sea or any part of it by force of arms . . . also the peaceful commerce and shipping. . . ."[1] By 1861 the Federal navy had 7,600 officers and men and ninety ships, although only forty-two were in commission and half of those were in the Pacific Ocean. The American merchant marine dominated world trade. Although Southern officers were allowed to resign their commissions, Southern enlisted men, who had enlisted for a period of time, could not resign.[2] The Confederate navy started with 321 men and ten ships, one in need of so much repair that she never put to sea.[3] The South, with a few exceptions, would wage a defensive fight. Savez would be one of the exceptions.

When Savez reported for duty Captain Rousseau told him to go across the river to Algiers to report to Lt. Thomas B. Huger aboard the CSS *McRae*. Huger, a bearded South Carolinian, had gotten captaincy of the *McRae* after he commanded the south-end batteries on Morris Island below Fort Sumter. Huger gave Savez the job of sailing master.[4]

Huger explained that he was in a hurry to get his ship to sea. Seven days after the firing on Fort Sumter, Lincoln had issued a proclamation calling for a blockade to close southern ports to foreign commerce. In the previous year New Orleans had exported nearly two million bales of cotton, which was more than all other United States ports combined.[5] The Federals would act quickly to blockade the Mississippi River and thus the Crescent City. Savez admired Huger's zeal to get out before the Union navy arrived and took a liking to him.[6]

As sailing master Savez would be responsible for trimming the sails to get the maximum speed once the *McRae* got to sea. The *McRae* was about forty feet longer than the *Plymouth*. Although classified like the *Plymouth* as a sloop, the *McRae* was a bark-rigged steamer. Her three masts had an aft rake, with the main mast farther abaft of amidships than the Academy training ship. The *McRae*, by comparison, had bigger fore, main, and mizzen sails; smaller topsails; bigger topgallants; and no royals.[7]

Starting with almost no navy, Secretary Mallory was forced to purchase steamers until he could get them built. One of the first obtained was the *Marques de la Habana*. The ship had been captured the previous year from a band of Mexican revolutionaries by the USS *Saratoga*. The Navy took the *Marques de la Habana* to New Orleans and turned the ship over to the civilian authorities. When the Confederates bought her, they renamed her the *McRae* after Rep. Colin J. McRae, a member of the Committee on Naval Affairs.[8]

The Confederates planned to offset their deficit in ships by using a strategy that the United States had used during the War of 1812 when they were outnumbered by the British navy. Mallory would commission, arm, and provision ships such as the *McRae* to hunt Northern merchant ships. The crews of captured ships would be removed, and the ships would either be sent back to Southern ports with a prize crew or burned. The commerce raiders—commissioned—were not pirates (Northern claims notwithstanding). From 1812 to 1815 American privateers had taken about 2,500 British ships and badly injured Great Britain's merchant marine fleet.[9] The potential was there to hurt the North, which had about five million tons of merchant shipping. The destruction would also increase insurance rates. Stopping shipping might force the North to end the war. If not, the search for Confederate raiders would at least draw part of the Union navy from the blockade of Southern ports.

The Federal navy hurried to sea. The task of blockading was enormous. The South's more than 3500-mile shoreline was longer than the distance from Norfolk to Plymouth, England. By the war's end, the Navy would build more than 200 ships and purchase more than 400.[10]

Converting the *McRae* to a raider required major changes. Savez and the other officers had to direct the laborers. The *McRae* needed more firepower. A 9-inch Dahlgren was being mounted on a pivot amidships. This big gun would be the main battery; the existing six 32-pounder smoothbore cannons would supplement it. Gun ports were being cut in the bulwarks and training tackle rigged. The deck was reinforced with timbers to carry the Dahlgren's four-and-one-half-ton weight. Extra storerooms and coal bunkers were built because Federal cruisers would try to prevent the Confederates from making port calls to resupply. The ship's accommodations were increased to provide room for the crews from captured ships. Timbers and one-inch flat bar iron were added to protect the engines and boilers in case of attack by Union warships.

Working on the *McRae* was not like outfitting the *Pawnee* back at the Philadelphia Navy Yard. Although Algiers had eight shipyards, Huger could not get skilled carpenters, materials, and workshops to outfit his ship. The officers and crew had to do most of the work.[11]

The war had stopped river traffic. Tied-up riverboats meant the waterfront had a surplus of out-of-work rivermen.[12] Here were men to fill the places of the Southern sailors who could not resign from the Federal navy.

Not everything was delayed. Savez got his travel allowance for the trip from Raymond to New Orleans on May 23, just three days after he submitted the voucher. He signed at the paymaster's office for eighteen dollars and ten cents: 181 miles at ten cents a mile.[13]

The *McRae* was not the only ship hurriedly being prepared to hunt Northern ships. Nearby Raphael Semmes was working his crew to get the CSS *Sumter* ready. Later in the war, Semmes would earn fame aboard the CSS *Alabama*.

Despite all their hurrying and hard work, the Confederates lost the race. On May 26 the USS *Brooklyn* arrived off Pass a l'Outre at the mouth of the Mississippi River. The Federals sent word ashore announcing the beginning of the blockade of the river. Later the *Powhatan* and *Massachusetts* joined the *Brooklyn*.[14]

As Savez and his shipmates prepared the *McRae* to go to sea, a battle raged ashore. The army generals, the Louisiana governor, and the politicians bickered over who had the authority and cannon to fortify Ship Island. The small sandy strip of land, nine miles long by less than one-half mile wide, lay about twelve miles southwest of Biloxi, Mississippi, in the Gulf of Mexico. On the island was a partially completed horseshoe-shaped fort, a lighthouse with its keeper, and a few other buildings. Because of its position, the island guarded the water route between New Orleans and Mobile. In the War of 1812, the British had come through the sound for their attack on New Orleans.

In late June Union raiding parties from Navy ships started capturing Confederate schooners in the sound behind the island. The raids were a threat that could not be ignored.

The Confederate Navy was asking to mount an expedition to catch the marauders. Savez eagerly answered Huger's call for volunteers.[15] Rousseau provided the cannons: an 8-inch columbiad, a 32-pounder, and two 12-pounder boat howitzers. Savez and the other volunteers quickly loaded the cannons on two lake steamers, the *Oregon* and the *Swain*. The expedition spent July 8 searching the sound without any luck.

By late afternoon, the Confederates decided to land their cannons on Ship Island. The steamers docked at the wharf near the fort. Lt. Alexander Warley, executive officer of the *McRae*, took charge of the landing party. The steamers returned to New Orleans for reinforcements.[16]

Warley ordered the cannons moved to the highest point on the eastern end of the island. Savez was placed in charge of the columbiad. Weighing over four and a half tons, the cannon required backbreaking effort to move up from the beach through the soft sand. When the Confederates reached the ridge they found some pine trees and solid ground. They built wooden gun platforms, dug protecting parapets, and finally set the cannons in place. Tents were pitched and a flagstaff raised. By the time they completed the fortifications, darkness had fallen.[17]

The Confederates had just finished their work when the *Massachusetts* steamed up. As the ship approached, she fired a gun to signal the lighthouse keeper to light the light. Despite the start of the war, the keeper kept the light going. The *Massachusetts* anchored in ten fathoms of water, a mile offshore from the Confederates.[18]

The Confederates heard the sound of "beat to quarters."[19] They had been spotted. The lieutenant announced they would open fire in the morning when they could better see the target.

At dawn, the *Massachusetts* still rode at anchor. Warley gave the order to commence firing. After an engagement of about an hour, the *Massachusetts* steamed off to the cheers of the Southerners.

That afternoon a steamer returned from New Orleans with the 4th Louisiana Regiment. Savez and the rest of the sailors returned to the city.[20] The Confederates did not retain this pugnacious spirit; two months later, they withdrew from Ship Island without a fight.[21]

Shortly after Savez returned to the *McRae*, the refitting was done. All that remained was to go upriver to the Confederate Arsenal at Baton Rouge and load ammunition. Just before the *McRae* reached Baton Rouge, part of the ship's machinery broke down.[22] Repairs would have to wait until the ship returned to New Orleans. Baton Rouge lacked the parts and machinists.

Faulty steam engines were destined to plague the Confederates through-out the war. The South's industrial capability to fabricate engines was min-imal. Spare parts were also difficult to obtain. Because of the blockade, the old sources in Great Britain and New England could not be used. Aged, worn-out engines, the Confederates found out, would have to suffice.

When the *McRae* reached Baton Rouge a sailor hoisted a red flag on the foremast to show that the ship was loading ammunition. Before joining his fellow officers, Savez carefully emptied his pockets. No metal objects were allowed. The black powder handlers wore worsted shirts, without metal buttons, that came down to their knees. A spark would mean disas-ter. Watched by the officers, the crew loaded powder tanks into the maga-zine. Other handlers also stowed solid shot, shell, shrapnel, grapeshot, canister, and fuses in the shell room.[23] When they finished, the *McRae* stood ready for battle.

At Baton Rouge, Acting Midshipman Jimmy Morgan joined the ship. Morgan had gone to Annapolis the year Savez graduated. Like Savez, Mor-gan was small and frail. Savez took a liking to him and started a friendship that lasted long after the war.[24]

The *McRae* returned to New Orleans. Huger had the coal bunkers topped off and steamed down the Mississippi. The *Sumter* had recently run the blockade. If the *Sumter* could make it out, perhaps the *McRae* could also. Seventy-five miles below New Orleans were Forts Jackson and St. Philip; Huger anchored the *McRae* and waited.[25] Twenty-some miles downriver lay the wide delta and offshore, waiting, were the blockaders.

At the Head of the Passes, the Mississippi fanned out into three major branches: Pass a l'Outre, South Pass, and Southwest Pass. The fifteen-mile-long Pass a l'Outre was the deepest, at seventeen feet. The thirteen-mile-long South Pass was the shortest but the shallowest, with a depth of only six feet. The Southwest was twenty miles long and had started to fill with silt, leaving a depth of thirteen feet.[26]

Breaking out through the blockaders presented Huger a problem. Since the *McRae* had a thirteen-foot draft, the South Pass was out. If he took the *McRae* to the Head of the Passes, to try either of the other two passes, the Union ships would spot him across the low marshy delta. Once the *McRae* started down a pass, the blockade would move to intercept the Confeder-ates after they entered the Gulf of Mexico.

Sometimes the blockaders left their stations. The Federals often went out into the Gulf of Mexico to check on approaching ships that might be trying to run in. If there was only one blockader left and the Federal was off the Southwest Pass, the Yankee would have to steam almost forty miles to get to Pass a l'Outre; time enough for the *McRae,* aided by a four-knot current, to go the fifteen miles. Semmes took the *Sumter* out Pass a l'Outre when the *Brooklyn* was off chasing a ship.[27] Huger relied on the small steamer CSS *Ivy* to check when the coast was clear. If the timing was right and they were lucky, the *McRae* could get to sea.

Huger had moved the *McRae* down to within ten miles of the Head of the Passes; the *Ivy* had reported that the blockaders had gone. Suddenly a steamer approached with the *Ivy* in the lead. The French flag flew from her masthead. The stranger had gotten past the blockade the night before, only to go aground trying to get across the bar at the Southwest Pass. The French man-of-war reported that the gunboat USS *Water Witch* had arrived that morning. Huger ordered the *McRae* back to the forts.[28]

Despite his fondness for Huger, Savez found the false starts exasperating. Although the *McRae* drew thirteen feet of water, Savez was certain she could run out South Pass where there were no blockaders. He refused to believe the pilot's opinion that South Pass was too shallow. Full of youthful inexperience, he declared to Morgan and the other midshipman that the *McRae* could plow through the soft mud bottom.[29]

Knowing Savez wanted action, the second lieutenant approached him with an idea. They would write a letter to the Mississippi state government requesting that they be given permission to organize an artillery company. They would take field pieces from Jackson and serve in either Virginia or Missouri. Savez quickly agreed. Although they sent the letter, they never received a reply.[30]

Even though the *McRae* did not get to sea, she did serve a useful purpose. The Union Navy could not come upriver with the *McRae* there to fire on them. Huger, unfortunately, failed to realize this and took the *McRae* back to New Orleans.

At New Orleans some changes had been made. Secretary Mallory had replaced the ailing Rousseau with Capt. George N. Hollins as commodore. Hollins had already received fame when he and a few companions had seized the steamer *St. Nicholas* during a cruise from Baltimore, Maryland, to Washington, D.C. With the *St. Nicholas,* he went on to capture three more ships: the *Monticello, Mary Pierce,* and *Margaret.* Hollins then turned everything over to the Confederate authorities at Fredericksburg, Virginia.[31]

With the river undefended, the Federal navy moved up to the Head of the Passes. The USS *Richmond* grounded while trying to cross the bar. The Union sailors labored for three days removing powder and shot to lighten their ships, then reloading them after they moved upriver. The *Preble, Vincennes,* and *Water Witch* accompanied *Richmond.* These ships carried a combined battery of twenty-six cannons of at least 8-inch caliber plus many smaller ones.[32]

Hollins commanded a makeshift collection of ships and riverboats dubbed the "mosquito fleet": the *McRae, Ivy, Tuscarora, Calhoun,* and *Jackson,* plus tugboats. Besides *McRae's* pivot, the only guns of any caliber were 8-inch on the *Ivy* and *Tuscarora.*[33] Despite the uneven odds, Hollins wanted to fight.

For reinforcements, Hollins sought the *Manassas.* The namesake of the Confederate victory was a 143-foot-long steam-driven ram. Resembling a turtle in the water, the ship had a humped back of 1½-inch thick iron plating over oak. Enemy cannonballs were supposed to bounce off her curved back. A tall smokestack protruded from her top. For armament she carried a single 64-pounder Dahlgren.[34] The *Manassas* could ram her opponents with her cast-iron prow. For protection against boarders, pipes could carry scalding water from the boilers onto the turtle back.

The ram had been converted from the twin-screw Boston-built ice-breaking tug *Enoch Train.* New Orleans' businessmen had financed the conversion to drive the Union navy from the river and get prize money. They, consequently, set the price too high for Hollins to buy.

Hollins was determined to have the *Manassas.* Using *McRae* as his flagship, the flag officer had Huger bring the ship alongside *Manassas* where she lay anchored in the river. The crew of *Manassas* threatened death to anyone who stepped on the ram. Ignoring the protests, Lieutenant Warley quickly took *Manassas* as her crew jumped overboard and swam to shore.[35]

In the early evening hours of October 12, 1861, the Union ships lay anchored out of view of *McRae.* Only *Ivy* had been allowed to move in close enough to check on them. Hollins hoped to lull the enemy into complacency.

The moon had set and a fog hung low over the water. Although the river was only three-quarters of a mile wide, the hulls of the fleet disappeared in the mist. Only the masts and spars gave away the locations of the ships.[36]

Warley, in command of the ram, had been given orders to seek out a suitable target, ram it, then withdraw and launch a signal rocket. Four fire rafts loaded with burning cotton were chained together in pairs to snag the bows of the Federal ships.[37] The mosquito fleet would follow at dawn. Clouds made the night seem darker. Warley's signal rocket ascended, and flames leaped from the burning rafts as the tugs pushed them out into the current. A few colored lights appeared downriver then vanished. Everything became quiet.[38]

Luck alone had saved the *Richmond* from being holed by the *Manassas*. Despite intelligence that a vessel capable of boring holes in wooden ships was being built in New Orleans, Capt. "Honest John" Pope, the squadron commander, had not set out the picketboats. The *Manassas* was able to approach unnoticed but plowed into a coal schooner lashed alongside before crashing into the *Richmond*. Still, the impact left the *Richmond* with three broken planks and a five-inch hole in her hull two feet below the waterline. When he saw the fire rafts coming, Pope signaled for the squadron to retreat down Southwest Pass.[38]

Warley meanwhile struggled to escape upriver with the *Manassas*. The shock of impact had knocked the ship's boilers and engine loose. The coal schooner's anchor cable had fouled the smokestack. The stack broke off at the deck, causing the crippled ship to fill with smoke.

In their haste to retreat, the Union squadron ran into more trouble. The *Vincennes* grounded with her stern upriver. The *Richmond* plowed into a sandbar and swung broadside in the river. Only the shallower drafted *Preble* and the *Water Witch* with her captured prize, *Frolic,* escaped. The fire rafts beached on the riverbank and burned harmlessly.[40]

At first light, Hollins got the "mosquito fleet" underway. Steaming downriver, they passed the damaged *Manassas* and the abandoned coal schooner. Soon the *Vincennes* and *Richmond* came into view and the Confederates opened fire.

The *McRae's* shells were falling short of their targets.[41] Savez declared to his friend Morgan that the *McRae* should move alongside *Vincennes* and destroy her. Morgan flinched as a Union shell from the *Richmond* burst overhead. Savez, not letting his fear show, let Morgan think he considered the shells as no more annoying than the mosquitoes.[42] The *Water Witch* then returned to help the stranded Federals, and Hollins ordered a retreat.

The captain of the *Vincennes* had misread a signal from the *Richmond* and, wrapped in his ship's flag, reported to Pope that he had ordered

Vincennes destroyed. One of the *Richmond*'s officers later wrote that although Pope was not a profane man, he was sure that Pope's language forced the Recording Angel in Heaven to shed a tear. Fortunately, the sailor who had been told to light the slow match in the magazine of the *Vincennes* remained calm. He followed orders and lit the fuse, but then cut the burning end off and threw it overboard. The action became known as "Pope's Run."[43]

In New Orleans the townspeople held a bell ringing. Bands serenaded Hollins, and the Crescent City named a new company of soldiers for him.[44]

An embarrassed Savez thought the attack should have been continued the next night. The Federals should have been destroyed, but they were only driven into the Gulf. The blockade remained unbroken.[45]

Huger again attempted to go to sea, but the *McRae*'s engines failed. After repairs, the ship set out only to have most of the officers and crew come down with swamp fever. Returning to New Orleans, Huger finally received orders not to run the blockade.

If the *McRae* had put to sea, her career as a raider would have been short-lived. With her limited coal supply and faulty steam engine, she could not long have avoided the Federal cruisers. Savez and the others would almost certainly have ended up in a Union prison.

The *McRae* rode at anchor across from Jackson Square at New Orleans. With Huger and the other senior officers ashore recovering from illness, Savez had become the executive officer. The only other officers on board were Morgan and another midshipman.

As Savez stood on the quarterdeck, the sailors stowed the ship's boat after a day spent drinking ashore. The mood turned ugly and some of the more intoxicated crew started talking about taking the boat ashore to get more liquor.

Now, Savez decided, was the time to act. He quietly told a midshipman to get on his side arms. When he returned with his pistol, Savez ordered: "Shoot down the first man who touches a boat fall without my orders!"[46]

Astonished, the crew moved back from the boat. An apparently unworried Savez strolled over to the ship's rail and looked out over the city. If the crew mutinied, he had only two other midshipmen to stand against them. The bluff worked. The crew went below.

Just after seven bells, a loud pounding on the cabin door awakened Savez. Morgan announced that the crew had gotten into the ship's whiskey. Cutting a hole in the spirits locker, they had drained out liquor with a piece of lead pipe. When Morgan found them they were drinking and playing cards by candlelight. Later Morgan would confess that one of them had told him to "go tell your mammy she wants you."

Savez leaped from his bunk, tucked his pistol in his belt, and then grabbed his sword. Reaching the forward hatch he dropped down to the berth deck. The mutinous crew jumped up from the table, scattering cards, money, and whiskey. Savez lunged his sword toward the head of the nearest sailor. At the last instant, he turned his wrist and cracked the sailor with the flat of the blade. The mutineer screamed in pain and ran for the open hatchway. The others followed amid oaths and screams as Savez continued to flail them with the flat of his blade. Reaching the deck Savez ordered them aloft. Seeing some hesitate, he reached for his pistol. Their mild-mannered sailing master had vanished. Grabbing the shrouds the crew scampered up the ratlines. When they reached the upper yardarms, they pleaded that there was no room. Savez ordered them to lie on the yards. Sobered with the excitement, the crew walked out on the footrope while holding on to the yardarm.

When they were all perched, Savez lowered his voice and said, "I will shoot the foot off the first man who steps down a rattling [ratline]."[47]

The *McRae*'s crew spent the night like birds on a telegraph wire. With the first light of morning, Savez ordered them down and started the normal morning's work by washing the deck. Savez had turned into an officer that his crew could idolize.

The Federal warlords, meanwhile, were developing the Anaconda Plan, which required encircling the South to squeeze the life out of the Confederacy. The Union knew that more than a blockade would be required to assure a Federal victory. They needed to control the Mississippi River to split the South in two—keeping Texan beef and Mexican supplies from the rest of the Confederacy.

Opening the Father of Waters would require a joint army-navy thrust. The Navy would provide the transportation and heavy firepower to dislodge the Confederates while the Army would seize the river cities. In preparation, the Union had started building ironclad gunboats near St. Louis and at Mound City, Illinois.

The Confederate government in Richmond—they had moved there from Montgomery after Virginia seceded—grew alarmed.[48] Mallory ordered the *McRae* upriver to help stop the Federals. The ship's 9-inch Dahlgren could throw a 70-pound shell almost a mile. Being mounted on a ship, the big gun was mobile enough to be used against either troops or gunboats. The Confederate high command felt Forts Jackson and St. Philip could hold the Federal fleet back from New Orleans.

Huger, recovered from his illness, departed by train with Hollins for Columbus, Kentucky. This left Savez with the job of bringing the *McRae* upriver.[49] Savez learned that, in war, the battle you plan to fight is not always the one you end up fighting. After taking on a load of coal, the *McRae* departed. With the *McRae* was a small squadron consisting of the *Tuscarora, Livingston,* and *Ivy.*[50]

As the squadron moved along, people flocked to the riverbanks to watch the *McRae* and her consorts. Some of them had never seen a seagoing ship. When the ship stopped they were asked where the paddle wheel was kept.[51]

The *Livingston,* hampered by faulty engines, made slow progress. The crew joked they were used to going slow. They claimed that, in the past, when the *Livingston* went full speed downstream they could not sleep because of the noise that drifting logs made as they caught up with the ship and bumped into the stern.[52]

On November 23, the *Tuscarora* caught fire. A strong wind quickly spread the flames. The engineer barely had time to flood the magazine before jumping overboard. The captain and crew escaped unharmed although the ship was a total loss.[53]

The slowness of the *McRae*'s companions was not the only problem navigating upriver. The Mississippi was rising toward spring high water. Like the steamboats, the *McRae* hugged the inside of the many bends in the river because the current was slower there than in the middle or outer bend. The slow current, however, deposited mud and sand into submerged bars, indicated by circles and lines on the water's surface. Drifting trees grounded on the bars producing snags that would foul the ship's propeller. Night obscured the shallows and made the curving shoreline into straight lines. The *McRae*'s thirteen-foot draft meant hitting the bars became inevitable.

Once while moving through a heavy fog, the *McRae* grounded on the levee in front of Brierfield, the plantation of Jefferson Davis. A tug pulled the ship off the bank.[54] Savez learned that what he thought to be "soft Mississippi mud bottom" could glue a ship in place.

The squadron finally reached Columbus, Kentucky, at the foot of high bluffs above the river, and joined the CSS *General Polk* and *Jackson.*[55] North of Columbus the Confederates had constructed formidable batteries. During the battle of Belmont, the Southerners had plunged cannon fire down on the Union gunboats *Tyler* and *Lexington*. The Federals were unable to elevate their guns high enough to return fire and so retreated upriver.

With support from the New Orleans naval squadron, the Mississippi River downstream from Cairo, Illinois seemed secure. A land attack, however, coming from the Union base at Paducah could outflank and bypass Columbus. The Confederates believed that Fort Henry on the Tennessee River, and Fort Donelson on the Cumberland River, would deter the Yankees, because a Union attack on Columbus would expose the Federal rear to sorties from these forts.

After arriving at Columbus, Savez and a few other officers urged that the squadron be allowed to steam the scant thirty miles upriver on a raid. Only one fort stood between the Confederates and Cairo, which was being turned into a supply depot for outfitting the Western Flotilla under the command of Flag Officer Andrew Hull Foote. Savez argued that they should destroy the supplies before the Yankees could use them against the South.[56] The raid was never approved.

At the time Read's suggestions were rejected, he was promoted to second lieutenant.[57] In peacetime rising from midshipman to lieutenant could take a lifetime. To Savez the rank did not matter; he wanted to fight.

As the Confederates waited, Forts Henry and Donelson in February 1862 fell to the combined Federal army-navy attacks employing ironclad and timberclad gunboats outfitted at Cairo. Excessive caution had cost the Confederacy its northwest cornerstone. Columbus had to be abandoned and the cannons sent thirty miles downriver to Island No. 10.

The riverboat pilots numbered the islands coming down the Mississippi from Cairo. The two-and-one-half-mile-long island that lay in the first bend in a great "S" turn in the river was Island No. 10. There, on the Tennessee, Kentucky, and Missouri borders, the river snaked through the marshy lowland. New Madrid had been built on the Missouri side of the second bend. Tiptonville, Tennessee, was farther downriver. Reelfoot Lake extended from behind Tiptonville almost up to Island No. 10. Since there were few roads through the swamps, almost all supplies had to be moved on the river.

These swamps also prevented the Federals from advancing overland through Kentucky. Confederate fortifications at New Madrid would stop the Federals in Missouri. The keystone in the Confederate defense was Island No. 10. The Confederates supplemented forts with a floating battery. The river channel flowed by the island, and as the Western Flotilla

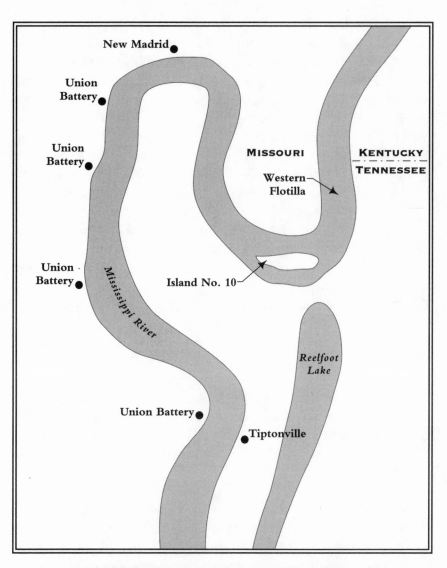

MISSISSIPPI RIVER—ISLAND NO. 10

approached and went through the turn, Confederate firepower would prevent Foote from steaming downriver.

The Confederates hurriedly moved troops to New Madrid. Forts at each end of the town were connected with a line of earthworks. Savez thought that New Madrid was poorly fortified.[58] The cannons of the forts defended the ends of the line, but more firepower was needed in the center.

Now the high water worked to the Confederates' advantage. The *McRae* floated high enough to bring her cannons just above the top of the levee.[59] The open city streets gave the ship's gunners a clear shot at any Union soldier approaching the line. No sooner had the Confederates finished digging their cannons into position than the Union Army, under Brig. Gen. John Pope, appeared.

The *McRae* positioned at the head of Main Street. A lone rider suddenly galloped toward the boat from behind the buildings at the far end of the street. The horseman shouted that he wanted to see Flag Officer Hollins. Hollins moved to the rail and asked the rider what he wanted.

Identifying himself as Gen. Jeff Thompson, the Swamp Fox of Missouri, he informed Hollins that there were 100,000 Yankees after him, who were prepared to board the *McRae* in less than fifteen minutes.

By that time, another man appeared atop a small brass cannon mounted on buggy wheels pulled by a worn-out mule. Pointing toward the artillery, Thompson announced that he had invented it and the Yanks had its mate. He then galloped off.

"I can't keep up with Jeff," complained Thompson's companion as he cracked the whip on the mule's bony back.[60]

The next day, March 2, was cold, windy, and cloudy. An early morning rain had washed the decks of the *McRae*. In the distance, the Confederates could hear the muffled thunder of the Federal cannons shelling abandoned Columbus. By evening Pope had brought 20,000 troops to the outskirts of New Madrid. The Confederate defenders numbered less than 5,000.[61]

The following morning the Federals attacked. Union troops drove the Confederate skirmishers back to their lines.[62] As executive officer of the *McRae*, Savez directed the gun captains. Since the Dahlgren had the greatest range, Savez ordered spherical shrapnel shell and selected a fifteen-second fuse.[63] The 9-inch ball flew over the heads of the Confederates. With a roar, the exploding powder ripped apart the thin shell, sending 350 .85-inch-diameter iron balls into the attacking troops.[64] The forts joined in on the barrage. The rest of the Confederate fleet provided little support, since the high levee prevented them from bringing their guns to bear. The Confederate fire repulsed the Northern assault.

The unoccupied buildings of New Madrid limited the *McRae*'s field of fire. Hollins ordered them burned. Savez's friend Morgan led the Confederate torch men ashore. A minié ball nicked Morgan's left arm. Later Savez listened as Morgan told him that his great-grandfather had built the town he had just burned.[65]

Pope resorted to siege war and set his troops to digging trenches. Needing more firepower, he sent word back to Cairo for his heavy guns. Later Pope wrote in his battle report that although he could have taken the Confederate entrenchment, he would not have been able to hold it because of the *McRae*'s fire.[66]

The Union sharpshooters did manage to get close enough to hit the *McRae*'s crew. The enemy fire did not bother Savez who told Morgan they "could hold the place until the day of judgment."[67]

Morgan was being used as a courier to carry messages between Hollins and the army generals. One day an infuriated Morgan returned from his mission to ask Savez to send a challenge to an army major. An aide to General Bankhead, noting Morgan's small stature, had remarked, "What a damned shame to send a child into a place like this."

Savez soothed his friend's feelings by saying that "the commodore would not approve of such action, and anyhow don't mind what the major said, as he is nothing but a damned soldier, and a volunteer at that, and of course, did not know any better."[68]

The Union Army continued its attacks on New Madrid. The Confederates fell back under the cover of the fortifications near the river, leaving the town to the Federals. Savez kept the guns of the *McRae* busy, so the blue-coated soldiers could not reach the river.

Always probing, a company of Federals unlimbered a light battery of cannons at the end of Main Street. Savez ordered a shell with a five-second fuse fired from the Dahlgren.[69] The ensuing explosion sent horses, men, and guns flying into the air. A second shell was loaded. This time its defective fuse burned through before the shell had left the Dahlgren's barrel. The explosion tore the big gun apart. The Confederates replaced the damaged gun with one from the floating battery at Island No. 10.[70]

Held off by the *McRae* and the Confederate forts, Pope decided to outflank New Madrid.[71] The Federals moved their artillery down the Missouri side of the river to try to cut off supplies sent by ship to Island No. 10. The Union horse-drawn cannons could be quickly set up and quickly moved. The *McRae* would steam up and drive them off only to have them return the next day.[72]

As dawn broke on March 13, a fog lay over the battlefield. Suddenly the roar of cannon smashed the silence. The balance of power had shifted;

Pope's siege guns had arrived. Their fire covered not only the town, but also the river.[73] Hollins did not have enough ships to fight siege guns. His only reinforcements had been two small steamers: CSS *Maurepas* and *Pontchartrain*.[74]

The Confederate leaders, knowing they could no longer hold New Madrid, met that afternoon on the *McRae*.[75] They decided to evacuate the town rather than risk losing all the defenders. The Confederates' plan was to fall back downriver to Tiptonville and attempt to hold off the Yankees there. The withdrawal would be made at night under the cover of an impending storm. Hollins's fleet was to transport the demoralized soldiers.

At midnight, the ships drew up alongside the riverbank. A thunderstorm had started an hour earlier.[76] The *Ivy's* sailors became concerned as soldiers stampeded on board. The small steamer almost capsized as the passengers rushed to the outboard rail to get as far away from the enemy as possible.

Next it was the *McRae's* turn to load. When the sentry at the *McRae's* gangplank ordered the soldiers to halt, the throng surged forward. Savez announced that they could come on board if they behaved like soldiers rather than a mob. The crowd started to threaten Savez. When he asked who their headman was, a big soldier stepped forward declaring that he "has as much to say as any other man."

Savez instantly drew his sword from his scabbard. The flat of the sword cracked across the soldier's head. The startled crowd backed up. The technique Savez used in New Orleans worked again.

The mob meekly marched on board.[77] The *McRae* left for Tiptonville; the next day Union troops marched into New Madrid.

With the town in Federal hands, the holding of Island No. 10 became essential. The Confederate batteries on the island kept the Federals from bringing their ironclads to New Madrid. Pope needed ironclads to fight the Confederate Navy, since the guns of the *McRae* and her cohorts would keep him from advancing downriver to attack Fort Pillow, which was vital in the defense of Memphis.

Foote brought the Union fleet down the Mississippi. With the gunboats came the mortar boats with their squatty cauldronlike cannons. The Federals hastily moored the boats in position just beyond the range of the Southern guns. On March 16 the mortars opened up long-range bombardment of the island.[78]

The island's beleaguered defenders needed Hollins's fleet to bring them supplies. The shallowness of the channel and the Union gunfire made the job hazardous. The *Maurepas*, with a draft of only seven feet, made the run at night to avoid the cannonading.

One morning while the *McRae* rode at anchor off Tiptonville, the lookout spotted men tearing down a woodpile across the river that had been used by the Confederates to fuel the boilers in their ships. Just as Hollins prepared to investigate, the men fired a cannon. As the ball hit the bank near the *McRae*, Hollins called for the flags to be set that would order the fleet to engage at close quarters.[79] The Federals had dug earthworks to protect their battery of cannons. The *Maurepas* lost a ship's boat. The *General Polk* got hit so badly that the Confederates beached her to keep her from sinking. The *Livingston* received a shot in the ship's pantry that smashed all the crockery.[80]

During the action Savez asked Huger why the *McRae* did not beach itself in front of the battery and drive out the Federals with canister. Savez knew a canister round would act like a giant shotgun shell. Huger replied that the Federals also had canister.

Savez reponded that in the canister game one side always grew tired and wanted to quit. The soldiers in the battery could leave whenever they wanted to, but the *McRae* would have to stay until a tugboat pulled her out of the mud.[81] Huger simply refused.

The Confederates finally drove the Federals from their guns. Only one Union gun remained in action, and it fired slowly and wildly. Hollins ordered the signal raised to withdraw from action.[82]

Later another gun battery appeared. Savez asked Huger for permission to lead a boarding party ashore, claiming that the crew would follow him anywhere. Huger again refused.[83]

Impatient with their stalled advance, Foote decided to take a chance. He ordered the ironclad USS *Carondelet* to run the gauntlet past the guns of Island No. 10 to New Madrid. Relying on a torrential downpour to mask her movements, the *Carondelet* safely passed the island on the night of April 4, 1862. Two nights later, another ironclad, the USS *Pittsburg*, made the same trip.[84] The supply line to Island No. 10 was cut. The Union also had the fire support to move across the river to Tiptonville.

The Union ironclads at New Madrid tipped the scales against the Confederates. Although Savez and a few of his fellow officers still wanted to fight, Hollins refused to pit his wooden boats against ironclads. The flag officer instead decided to retreat eighty miles to Fort Pillow.[85] There he hoped the 32-pounders of the fort would stop the Federal advance. Island No. 10 was left to its fate.

While the *McRae* had been busy upriver, Union flag officer David Glasgow Farragut had been assigned the task of taking New Orleans by Secretary Welles. Farragut had spent fifty-one of his sixty years in the service, serving in both the War of 1812 and the Mexican War. As enthusiastic as a midshipman, Farragut would not consider himself old until he could not turn a handspring on his birthday.[86]

The Union Navy used Ship Island as a base for its supplies. On March 12 the Federals returned to the Head of the Passes, unchallenged by the Confederates. Farragut had undone the Confederate effort of the previous October. The Union was ready to squeeze the southern pincer to connect with the northern one at New Madrid.

Hollins, shocked to learn that the Union fleet was back in the river, telegraphed the secretary of the navy for permission to go downriver. Mallory replied that Hollins should remain at Tiptonville to harass the enemy. Hollins wired back that upriver he faced the ironclad fleet, downriver he could challenge wooden ships. Hollins accordingly ordered the *McRae* to go downriver after his replacement, Comdr. Robert F. Pinkney, arrived from Memphis. Hollins then left with Morgan on the *Ivy*.[87]

Richmond was furious and relieved the flag officer of his command, ordering him back to the capital. He died shortly after the war while serving as a crier in a minor court in Baltimore.[88]

Huger, temporarily in command of the fleet until Pinkney arrived, decided to steam upriver for reconnaissance. That night a man waving a torch hailed the *McRae* and warned them that the Yankee fleet lay anchored just ahead around the bend. The next morning Huger sent the *Pontchartrain* upriver to confirm the enemy's presence. Union gunboats, seven abreast, chased the *Pontchartrain* back. The fleeing Confederate fleet finally stopped after it passed Fort Pillow, and the Federals turned their attention to shore and started shelling the fort.[89]

A few of the gunboats of what was known as the Montgomery Fleet, commanded by Louisiana riverboat pilots with no love for the regular Navy, arrived at Fort Pillow. Savez knew the pilots had ridiculed the Navy in every waterfront tavern from Fort Pillow to New Orleans, and wanted to show them what the Navy could do.[90] Pinkney finally arrived and the fleet headed south to New Orleans.

CHAPTER FOUR

GÖTTERDÄMMERUNG

The *McRae* stopped at New Orleans. Huger wanted to replenish his coal bunkers; there was no guarantee it would be available at the forts. While loading coal, he dispatched Savez ashore for the latest news.[1]

The confident air of the previous fall had vanished from the Crescent City. Many of the city's youth had marched off to fight at Shiloh. The lists of casualties—"the butcher's bill"—had sobered the city. New Orleans had accorded Gen. Albert Sidney Johnston—slain at Shiloh—a hero's funeral. His bier had proceeded up St. Charles Street to the beat of muffled drums.

Food was scarce, Savez learned. Gold and silver were no longer exchanged, and the value of Confederate money was dropping. Spies were believed to be everywhere; lists were drawn up of suspected Union sympathizers. The mayor had even banned masquerading during Mardi Gras.[2]

With Farragut's fleet below the forts, a near panic gripped the city. Every man was supposed to rush out at the sound of twelve taps of the fire alarm bell to defend his home.[3] People tried to convince themselves the forts would hold the dreaded Yankees at bay. Fort St. Philip had prevented the British from coming upriver during the War of 1812. Since then Fort Jackson had been built. One hundred and fifteen cannon could be brought to bear on the river.[4]

No one seemed to notice that since then navies had gone from sail to steam. The narrowness of the river that made navigation difficult for sailing ships was not a problem for steam-powered ships. The steam engine allowed the Union Navy to go wherever it wanted.

To augment the forts' firepower, the Confederates were constructing two of the biggest ironclads to be built during the Civil War: the CSS *Mississippi* and *Louisiana*. Only the CSS *Virginia* was larger.[5] Their batteries of smoothbore and rifled cannons were to sweep the river clean of the invader's wooden ships. Laborers worked round the clock trying desperately to finish them.

Read returned from his reconnaissance. Coaling completed, Huger ordered the *McRae* to continue down the Mississippi. On April 16, 1862, the *McRae* anchored close to the riverbank, above Fort St. Philip. The enemy lay beyond the next bend in the river, a mile and a half below Fort Jackson.[6]

Farragut commanded seventeen steam warships, of which eight were larger than the *McRae*. For armament, the fleet carried 245 smoothbore Dahlgrens, rifled Parrott guns, howitzers, and mortars. An experienced Dahlgren gun crew could fire the 90-pound shells at the rate of one every minute and forty-five seconds.[7] Eleven of the ships had the big Dahlgrens. To bombard the forts, Farragut's foster brother Comdr. David D. Porter had brought twenty mortar-carrying schooners. Numerous other smaller ships provided logistical support. Farragut had assembled the fleet for one purpose, to slug his way to New Orleans.

The main line of defense of the Confederate preparations was the forts. Their casements and parapets bristled with cannons. Fort Jackson was a bastioned brick pentagon with fronts about 100 yards long. A 127-pound shot from Fort Jackson's 10-inch columbiad could smash its way through the wooden Union hulls.[8] At the river's edge next to Fort Jackson, a battery of more cannons augmented the fort's firepower. The battery's low-fired shots would perforate Union ships at their waterlines. Seven hundred yards upriver on the opposite side was the quadrilateral Fort St. Philip. The forts' interlocking fields of fire meant that Northern ships would be under Southern guns for three miles.

Just downriver from Fort Jackson the Confederates had constructed a chain barricade. Supported by mastless schooners the chain stretched across the 700-yard wide river. A narrow passage around each end was left open. The water appeared to be moving at three to four knots.[9] The current would slow the Federal ships, and the chain would snare them, making them easy targets for Southern guns.

Across the river from the *McRae*, the Confederates built fire rafts like those used at "Pope's Run." They would be lit at night and sent through the openings in the barricade to drift into Federal ships. Not all the rafts would be sent, though. When the battle came, unarmed tugs would push burning rafts against the Federal ships. The flames would illuminate the targets for Confederate gunners at the forts while blinding and confusing their Union counterparts.

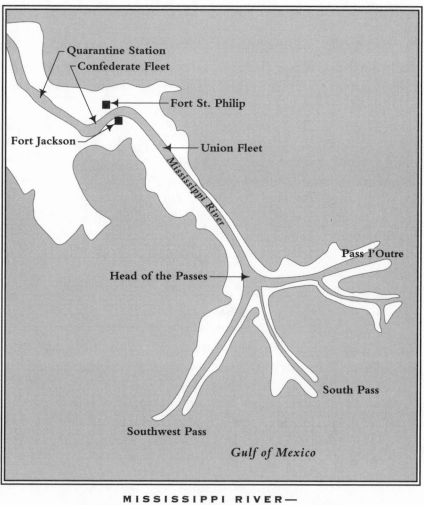

**MISSISSIPPI RIVER—
QUARANTINE STATION TO THE DELTA**

Any Union ships getting past the killing field would be prey for Confederate forces afloat. The Confederate navy, other than the *McRae*, was composed of the *Jackson* and *Manassas* plus a couple of launches. The state of Louisiana supplied its own navy: the *Governor Moore* and *General Quitman*. The River Defense Fleet consisted of the *Warrior*, *Stonewall Jackson*, *Defiance*, *Resolute*, *General Lovell*, and *R. J. Breckinridge*. A few unarmed tugs and tenders made up the rest of the fleet.

Between the forts and the ships, the Confederates manned 166 cannons.[10] This was more than the cannons General Lee would fire at Gettysburg before "Pickett's Charge." In size, Lee's cannons were dwarfs in comparison.

The barricade, the water battery, the forts, the fire rafts, and the forces afloat would form a ring of fire. Stopping the Yankees should be simple enough. If, however, Farragut could get his fleet through the ring, nothing would stand between him and New Orleans.[11]

As Carl von Clausewitz, the author of *On War* observed, everything in war is simple, but the simplest thing is difficult. Working together gave the Confederates their biggest challenge. The Southerners, rebelling against an authoritarian government, could not even agree on a single commander to lead their ships. Comdr. John K. Mitchell had been given command of the naval forces on the lower Mississippi River. His command, nevertheless, did not extend to the Louisiana State Navy, which Lt. Beverly Kennon controlled, and Capt. John Stevenson commanded the River Defense Fleet.

Stevenson sent a note to Mitchell saying:

Every officer and man on the river defense expedition joined it with the condition that it was to be independent of the Navy, and that it would not be governed by the regulations of the Navy, or be commanded by naval officers. In the face of the enemy I will not say more. I will cooperate with you and do nothing without your approbation, and will endeavor to carry out your wishes to the best of my ability, but in my own way as to details and handling of my boats. But I expect the vessels under my charge to remain as a separate command. All orders for their movements addressed to me will be executed, if practical, and I undertake to be responsible for their efficiency when required.[12]

Stevenson, who had been instrumental in the conversion of the *Enoch Train* into the *Manassas,* still fumed over the way the Navy had taken the ship from him.

At nine o'clock in the morning of April 18, Good Friday, Savez heard a low boom.[13] Porter's mortars had opened fire. The Federal gunners quickly found the range. Fort St. Philip and the *McRae,* beyond their range, were spared.

The Union gunners increased their tempo until each mortar got a shell off every five minutes. Often, several 218-pound shells could be seen in flight at once. The star-shaped Fort Jackson was not the only target. The water battery also got hit. The shots that missed burst in midair or fell into the Mississippi. The river surface boiled with the explosions and dead fish floated downstream.[14]

The gunners in Fort Jackson and Fort St. Philip returned fire as best they could. The schooners were at the maximum range of the forts' guns. The gunners did manage to hit and sink a single one.

Toward evening, flames rose from Fort Jackson. The bombardment had ignited several wooden buildings in the fort. Too many shells burst on the parade ground to risk sending fire fighting parties. One shell struck the parapet over one of the magazines, but luckily did not explode.

At 7:00 P.M. the Union gunners stopped firing for the day, having shot almost 3,000 shells. The following day the mortars resumed. This time they continued firing thoughout the night.[15]

On April 20 tugs arrived from New Orleans towing the ironclad *Louisiana*. It had rained earlier in the morning and with the rain had come wind. The tugs struggled to move the boxlike structure against wind and current. If a line broke, the *Louisiana* would be swept into the *McRae*; but the lines held and the tugs got the *Louisiana* anchored just downriver of the *McRae* by Fort St. Philip.[16]

The *Louisiana*'s sea trials at New Orleans had been disappointing. The bulky ironclad was underpowered and could not move against the current. The Confederates were forced to use the ironclad as a gun battery. The *Mississippi* had been left at the city; she needed even more work.

Once in position, the *Louisiana*'s sailors made an alarming discovery. In their haste, the builders had cut the gunports too low for the guns to fire through. The captain of the ironclad borrowed part of the *McRae*'s crew to correct the mistake.[17]

As Confederates readied the *Louisiana,* Farragut, under cover of an even heavier mortar cannonade, sent two gunboats up to the chain barricade. With difficulty, the Federals cut the chain and it was breached.[18] The Confederate defenders had earlier gone to Pensacola and Savannah for the chain.[19] Chain was in short supply; there was no replacement.

Savez waited with the other officers and crew of the *McRae.* They waited the way sailors have waited since the Greeks waited for the Persian fleet before the Battle of Salamis. They waited and wondered. If the Yankees broke through, the battle would not be like shooting at soldiers across a riverbank; Union sailors were well trained. The heavy shells from their ships could crush the *McRae.* All thoughts of glory vanished. They disciplined themselves to carry on as though they were unafraid, yet only fools are truly not afraid.

On April 23 the strong north wind of the previous day had subsided.[20] Huger sent Savez over to Fort Jackson to try to figure out when Farragut would attack. The bombardment was still going on. Savez left the boat at the landing and crossed the bridge over the moat that surrounded the fort. Entering the fort through the sallyport, he asked the sentry for Lt. Col. Edward Higgins, commanding officer of both forts. Everyone other than the sentry was still under shelter.[21] Savez accompanied Higgins to the parapets. There both men observed that the Union ships were forming three battle lines. Savez quickly returned to the McRae to report that the attack would come that night.

Huger reacted quickly, ordering Savez to prepare the McRae for battle. Savez went about the ship making sure everything was ready, then put one-half the crew on watch and sent the rest below deck to get some sleep.[22] When the battle came, Savez would command the guns. The 9-inch Dahlgren would be critical to the ship's survival. Pivot-mounted, the big cannon could be turned and fired at the Federals without turning the McRae.

Savez stayed on deck until after midnight; the moon had not yet risen.[23] Before going below Savez ordered the officer of the deck to call the moment any ship came in sight.[24]

Two hours later, a blue-jacketed sailor on the USS Hartford hoisted a pair of red lanterns up a halyard. This was Farragut's signal to attack.

Farragut had ordered his ships grouped into three columns. The USS Cayuga led the first column, followed by Pensacola, Mississippi, Oneida, Varuna, Katahdin, Kineo, and Wissahickon. The first column were to steam up the right side of the river through the opened barricade and past Fort St. Philip. The Federals hoped that the fort's gunners, their guns trained on the middle of the river, would overshoot their targets. As the first column moved, the second column would move up the opposite side of the river. These ships, the Hartford, Brooklyn, and Richmond, carried the heaviest guns. Farragut had to knock out Fort Jackson with his broadsides to make safe the passage for the third column. The Sciota, Iroquois, Kennebec, Pinola, Itasca, and Winona were the lightest and least able to withstand damage.[25]

As the Union ships started quietly moving upriver, Acting Master Charles B. Fairbanks saw them. He had picket duty in launch number six. Instead of sounding the alarm by firing the boat howitzer to launch signal rockets, he panicked, beached his launch, ran into the swamps, and disappeared. It was later reported that Fairbanks was tracked down by Confederates and killed. Others said he survived.[26]

At the water battery a sergeant saw the lead column of Union ships. He quickly passed the word and a bugler at Fort Jackson sounded the alarm.[27] As the Confederate guns thundered, the battle began.

Savez dashed up the ladder onto the deck of the *McRae* upon hearing the call from the watch.[28] The drummer sounded "beat to quarters." Sailors scrambled to their battle stations. Gun captains yelled orders as powder monkeys quickly brought up gunpowder. Black smoke bellowed from the stack as stokers spread out the burning coal across the fire gate and threw on pine knots to rapidly bring up the fire.

Downriver was a Götterdämmerung. The Federal fleet grappled with the forts. By then the moon had risen.[29]

As the *McRae* readied, so did the *Governor Moore, Stonewall Jackson,* and *Manassas.* The tug *Mosher* chugged by, shoving a blazing raft.

Not all the Confederates answered the call. Most of the officers and men of the River Defense Fleet panicked at the sound of the first gun. Fleeing into the swamps, they burned their ships behind them.[30]

Suddenly, at 4:00 A.M. the USS *Cayuga* appeared out of the cloud of battle smoke. The Confederate ships pounced, eager for their first kill. Huger, aware that the *McRae*'s steam pressure had not come up enough to join the assault, told Savez to hold his fire until the *Cayuga* came up abeam of them. The *McRae*'s signal lights, the same as the Federals', might confuse the Northerners.

The *Cayuga* fought alone. The determined Federal gunners managed to drive off their attackers. One Confederate ship was left in flames and adrift.[31]

Huger called for the anchor to be slipped, then rang up the engine room to get underway. Seconds later a sailor swung a sledgehammer to knock loose the hook holding the anchor chain. With fifteen pounds showing on the steam pressure gage, the *McRae* gradually swung out into the Mississippi with her bow pointed upriver. The current helped the ship to hold position.

The *Cayuga* approached fast. On the opposite bank, the deserted ships of the River Defense Fleet burned like beacons. Their smoke drifted over the *McRae,* partially hiding the ship.[32] The enemy might confuse the running lights.

When the *Cayuga* drew up alongside, the Union gunners did not fire. Savez shouted the command. The *McRae's* guns blasted a broadside into the unaware Federal. The surprised *Cayuga* did not fire a shot, but rather moved upriver to get out of range.[33]

Two federal ships, the *Varuna* and *Oneida,* were now coming out of the smoke. Behind them more Federal ships worked their way past the forts. Where were the other Confederate ships?[34] Savez resolved to fight with his ship, even if alone.

As the two Federals drew up, the *McRae's* guns thundered. These Union ships returned fire as they passed. Their shot tore through the bulwarks, rigging, and smokestack. The USS *Brooklyn* appeared out of the smoke. The crew of the Dahlgren's gun frantically worked to reload. The Federal passed within ten feet, but did not fire. Later Comdr. John R. Bartlett would write that he held the lock string on the Union cannon taut, ready to fire, when he heard the order not to fire because it was the *Iroquois.* Bartlett yelled back that it could not be the *Iroquois* because her smokestack was abaft of her mainmast.[35] Capt. Thomas T. Craven, former captain of the Naval Academy training ship *Plymouth,* repeated the order and unknowingly prevented the sinking of the *McRae.*

More ships steamed out of the darkness. At the tenth round the *McRae's* Dahlgren overstressed and burst, wounding a gunner.[36] This time Savez could not get a replacement. The Confederates would have to rely on their 32-pounders.

Savez spread the Dahlgren's gun crew amongst the remaining guns. Huger now noticed that the *McRae* had drifted near the riverbank and ordered the helmsman to steer back into the middle of the river.

As the *McRae* turned, Savez could see the *Iroquois* approaching. The Union ship's bulwarks seemed low enough to board. Huger agreed. Savez called to load grapeshot and copper slugs. Huger would bring the *McRae* into the *Iroquois,* beam to beam. At the last minute, Savez would order the guns fired. The cannons would act like huge shotguns and drive the Federals back from their guns long enough for the Confederates to climb aboard.

Unfortunately for the Southerners, the *Iroquois* steamed past before the *McRae* could ram. Disappointed, Savez ordered the broadside fired anyway. The surprised *Iroquois* returned fire with canister. Although torn up by the blast, the *McRae* kept up the chase.[37] The steam engines, however, were overheating; Huger had no choice but to order the ship to stop.

As the engine's temperature dropped, the *McRae* floated back toward the forts. By the time the engine cooled enough to restart, the *McRae* had again drifted over to the riverbank. Huger ordered the helm put over to port. Savez stood by to fire at a passing Union ship. The battle-damaged *McRae* moved sluggishly. The Federal, with greater speed, moved quickly ahead of the *McRae* before the Confederate guns could line up on the target.

The *Hartford* and *Mississippi* were now closing in on the *McRae,* one on each quarter. The *McRae,* responding to her helm, was turning onto a collision course. Huger yelled to reverse helm. Instantly, the helmsman spun the wheel in the other direction. The *McRae* slowly turned upriver. Since she was in a position to be boarded, Savez called for the crew to stand by to repel boarders. The Federals mistook the *McRae,* headed upriver, for one of theirs and passed without firing a shot. Huger resumed turning the *McRae* to port and then to starboard as Savez ordered each battery fired.[38]

As the *McRae* fired, the Union ships discovered their mistake. One Federal shot crashed through the *McRae's* bow. The shell exploded in the sail locker, setting the ship on fire. The flames signaled the approaching Union ships that a crippled Confederate lay ready for the kill.

The *McRae's* fire bell sounded as Huger ordered Savez to take a party forward to extinguish the blaze. The captain's parting words to Savez were to let him know when the flames reached the bulkhead. On the other side of the sail locker was the powder magazine.

Huger then grounded the ship near the riverbank to persuade the passing Yankees that the *McRae* had already been destroyed. Also, if the fire could not be extinguished, the crew might have a chance to escape ashore.

In the sail locker, flames were rapidly consuming the dry canvas and licking toward the two-inch-thick pine bulkhead.[39] Sailors manned the pumps and ran the hose to the fire, as others cleared away the wreckage with axes. The rest of the party flailed the flames with wet blankets. After Savez sent the news to the captain that the blaze was extinguished, the ship was backed off the bank.

On the river, the *Katahdin, Kineo,* and *Pinola* were hammering away at the *McRae.* Farther out in the river two other ships had joined in. Just then, the Federals fired a broadside of grapeshot. In the flashes of cannon fire, Savez noticed a large white number "6" on the stack of a nearby steamer. In the next flash, he looked back at the quarterdeck and saw Huger fall.[40]

The captain had been hit in the groin. A sailor helped the captain up,

but Huger refused to leave. The Union guns roared again as they fired canister. One piece struck Huger in the temple and also took off part of the
head of the sailor that helped him. Savez called for help to carry Huger
below.

As the sailors lifted the mortally wounded Huger, he pleaded with
Savez saying, "I always promised myself I would fight her until she was
underwater." Savez swore to his captain that he would fight as long as the
McRae floated.[41]

Savez took command of the *McRae*. The broadsides had wrecked the
ship. The signal halyards were cut, the wheel ropes were carried away, and
her flag hung over the side. The Federals continued their fire. Under Savez's
direction, one Confederate recovered and raised the flag, while others
cleared away the wreckage and rigged tiller ropes to steer the ship. The battered *McRae* suddenly got help as *Manassas* appeared out of the darkness.
The attackers spotted the ram and quickly moved upriver.

Savez ordered the *McRae* to steam upriver after Farragut's fleet. The
starboard 32-pounders fired at the Federals. The damaged *McRae* moved
slowly and the Union ships easily outran her. When the Confederates
rounded the first bend above the forts, they were startled by the sight at the
Quarantine Station of every Federal ship that had made it past the forts.
Savez ordered the helmsman to bring the *McRae* about.

As the *McRae* turned, the Federals opened fire, hitting her in the stern.
Moving downriver the ship got caught in an eddy current in the river and
started to swing around. Savez called for the helmsman to turn the helm. As
the sailor obeyed, the tiller ropes broke, damaged by the last hits. The
engines were reversed, but it was too late. The *McRae* plowed into the river
bank, sticking hard aground across from Bolivar Point.[42]

The morning sunlight revealed that Farragut's fleet had successfully run
the gauntlet. Of the seventeen ships that started, fourteen made it past the
forts, the barricade, the fire rafts, and the Confederate ships. Only the *Kennebec, Itasca,* and *Winona* had failed to get past the forts.

In later years some Confederates claimed that the *Louisiana* should have
been moved downriver into a better position to fight. Savez disagreed, saying that the top of the ironclad, the weakest part, would have been sub-
jected to plunging fire from the mortar schooners. Others complained that
not enough fire rafts were used. Savez, however, stated that their value was
exaggerated because their smoke was so dense.[43] Porter countered that the

three 100–foot–long fire rafts "were very formidable and troublesome." He counted fifteen that were not used in the battle.[44]

The gunners in the forts complained that they could not see the enemy ships in the night. Fire rafts could have been placed across from the forts to serve as background lighting, but no one anticipated that Farragut's fleet would steam close to the forts. Most of the Confederate shots damaged only a ship's rigging, but not all of the shots were aimed high. The *Brooklyn* took fifteen shots, nine of them smashing through the hull. One of the shells that stuck in the bow was found to have a patch still over the fuse. Had the patch been removed the shell would have exploded, sending the ship to the bottom.[45]

Savez criticized the Confederate ships that did not fight. The *General Quitman, Defiance, General Lovell,* and *R. J. Breckinridge* were destroyed by their officers and crew. The unarmed tenders were also burned. The *Resolute* was abandoned. The captain of the *Defiance* was later found drunk. The *Jackson* was three or four miles upriver on her way to New Orleans. Incredibly, the Confederates sent her upriver because they were afraid that the Federals might invade through the bayous and "the jump."[46] Lack of coordination opened up the Confederacy to being cut in two.

The loss of New Orleans would be a blow to southern morale. The city was an arsenal, with powder mills, ammunition factories, foundries for casting cannon and shells, and machine shops for making small arms. The only other first-class foundry in the South was the Tredegar Works in Richmond. With the loss of New Orleans both Britain and France backed away from recognition of the Confederacy. Later, in his study of sea power, Alfred Thayer Mahan would shudder at what would have happened if Farragut had been stopped at the forts.[47] The Union victory at New Orleans was as important as its victory at Gettysburg.

Savez and the men of the *McRae* did not fight alone. The *Stonewall Jackson* and *Governor Moore* had pursued the *Varuna*. The *Governor Moore* even fired through her bow into the enemy to deliver the coup de grâce. The *Manassas,* besides chasing off the *McRae*'s attackers, had rammed the *Brooklyn.* The tug *Mosher* had pushed a blazing fire raft against the *Hartford*'s side until the *Hartford* sank the tug.

The *McRae* was in shambles. Everything topside had been cut to shreds by cannon fire. All the stays were carried away along with three-fourths of the shrouds. One shell had left a huge hole in the smokestack. What remained of the smokestack was riddled with holes from grapeshot. The hull had taken three hits—all at the waterline: one forward of the engines, another aft of the engines, and the third, amidships. Although the holes had been plugged, water seeped in. The ship miraculously remained afloat. The casualties amounted to four men killed and seventeen wounded. Savez was unhurt.[48]

Downriver the frightened crew of the *Resolute* had abandoned the ship with a white flag flying. Thinking the ship to be serviceable, Savez sent Lt. Thomas Arnold and some of the *McRae*'s crew over to inspect it.

Arnold lowered the surrender flag and checked the ship. Except for two shot holes in the hull and some damage to the upper works, the *Resolute* remained in good shape.

On the return trip, Arnold's boat passed the *Manassas* drifting in the river. A check of the damaged ram showed that her departing crew had cut the injection pipes, rendering her useless to the enemy. The proud ram was slowly sinking.

Savez, listening to Arnold's report of his findings, had an idea. He could take command of the *Resolute* and use her to raid the New England coast-line. Since there were guns, coal, and supplies, he could easily ready the ship for sea. He could ram one of the mortar fleet and, in the ensuing confusion, run past the rest.

A tug eventually arrived from the forts to haul the *McRae* off the mud-bank. Once back at the forts, Savez hurriedly made his battle report to Flag Officer Mitchell, then drafted his daring proposal. Mitchell replied that he would consider the plan.

The following day the Federals, noticing the activity aboard the *Resolute,* moved downriver and shelled her. One shot exploded below the main deck, wrecking the ship and Savez's plan.[49]

On the morning of April 26, Savez received orders to transport the sick and wounded, including Huger, up to New Orleans. With a flag of truce flying and a skeleton crew, he slowly took the damaged *McRae* up to the Quarantine Station. Farragut had moved most of his fleet to New Orleans. The *Mississippi* remained behind to prevent any Confederate ship from coming upriver. Since Savez needed permission to take the wounded to New Orleans, he boarded the *Mississippi*. The ship's captain approved but told Savez that he had to arrange the details of landing the wounded with Farragut.[50] While on the *Mississippi*, Savez met his friend from the Academy and the *Powhatan,* George Dewey. Years later after Manila Bay, Dewey would remember Savez's concern for his dying captain.[51]

For the seventy-five-mile trip up the Mississippi, the steam-driven donkey engine was started to drive the bilge pumps and dewater the ship. Once dry, the leaking *McRae* would soon take on more water and the pumps would have to be restarted. The boiler struggled to compensate for the holes in the *McRae's* smokestack. Savez also drove the ship slowly to alleviate Huger's pain. Frequent stops were needed to build up steam pressure, and the current slowed the *McRae.* Drifting wrecks made navigation difficult, but also foretold what lay ahead. Around noon on April 27 the *McRae* finally arrived at New Orleans. Savez anchored the ship close inshore off Julia Street.

The city still reeled from the shock of capture. The Confederates had torched everything they thought would be of use to the Union. The unfinished *Mississippi* had been burned. Huge piles of cotton smoldered on the wharves and riverboats. The charred hulks of burned ships cluttered the river. Mobs raged through the streets. The Union Navy sat in the river, with guns ready. Farragut's men were ashore negotiating the surrender of the city.

Savez boarded the *Hartford* and sought permission to talk with Farragut. Savez explained that he was under a flag of truce and only wanted to land the wounded. Farragut agreed to the request. He did, however, require Savez to sign an agreement that he would only land the wounded and the surgeon. Then by ten o'clock the following morning Savez must return to the forts taking back with him neither men nor equipment. To do this Savez pledged his word of honor.[52]

At anchor the *McRae* suffered another casualty. A towboat accidentally backed into the steamer. The shock of the impact knocked some of the shot plugs loose. The *McRae* began taking water.

When Savez returned, he found his crew had started the donkey engine to run the bilge pumps. Quickly, Savez moved the *McRae* down to the Canal Street levee and started transferring the passengers at once. The Federals even sent over a commandeered ferryboat to help.[53] Since Huger lived in New Orleans, Savez personally took him home late that afternoon.

By 6:00 P.M. Savez returned from Huger's home and found that the *McRae* had started to drag anchor. He let out the full fifty fathoms of anchor cable, but was unable to stop the ship. Savez had the anchor cast loose and attempted to move her across the river to Algiers and shallower water.

As the ship neared the shore, the *McRae,* catching an eddy current, swung around several times and plowed into submerged pilings. The *McRae* leaked from every seam; the steam-driven pumps were not enough to keep the ship afloat. Savez sent men ashore to get help to keep the hand pumps working. A police lieutenant and ten men returned. The Confederates worked the pumps all night, but the *McRae* had six feet of water in the hold at daybreak. Savez ordered the induction pipes cut to hasten the sinking, and then sent the crew ashore.[54]

Savez, remembering his promise to Huger, left the Confederate flag flying.[55] It did not go unnoticed. The Federals quickly sent a boat over to the *McRae* to haul down the flag.

Savez went back to the *Hartford* to explain what had happened. Since Farragut had gone ashore, he reported to the next in command. Savez was told there was no way of going downriver except by small boat and that it would be up to him if he wanted to go.[56] Savez went ashore.

When Farragut returned, the Union officer failed to report his meeting with Savez. Farragut, learning that Savez had scuttled the *McRae,* angrily protested Savez's conduct in a letter to Mitchell stating, "The written agreement upon the solemn promise of the commander, was signed by the pledge the vessel was to return in the condition in which she left by 10 o'clock the next morning of which at 8 A.M. she was discovered without the flag of truce flying abandoned and scuttled. All of which shows a regardlessness [sic] of the usages of civilized warfare! . . ."[57]

When Savez's actions during the battle were reported to Richmond, they impressed Mallory. The secretary of the navy later wrote that "the conduct of the officers and crew of the *McRae* . . . has rarely been surpassed in the annals of naval warfare."[58] Later in the war, the Confederate Congress would issue a joint resolution thanking Savez and the officers under his command.[59]

The following morning Savez walked into the mayor's office to get the flag of truce mail before starting downriver. There, to his surprise, he heard that the forts had surrendered and the *Louisiana* had been blown up. Since he had never surrendered, it seemed meaningless to stick to the original agreement. Savez believed he and his men were at liberty to go where they pleased.

After the fall of New Orleans, Savez took the train east to Richmond in hopes of getting duty someplace where the Confederates did not run from the fight. In the capital, however, the Navy told him to report to Flag

Officer Pinkney at Fort Pillow. Savez hurried back to the Mississippi River. Boarding a steamer at Memphis, he headed upriver.

Along the way, Savez heard much abuse of the old Hollins's Fleet. The squadron bore Hollins's name even though he had returned to New Orleans. Savez thought of resigning his commission and joining the army. Only the hope of getting his own command kept him from doing it.

Savez found Pinkney at Fort Randolph, Tennessee, a few miles below Fort Pillow. Pinkney had removed two guns from the *Polk* and *Livingston* and placed them in a battery ashore. Pinkney put Savez in command of the battery. After New Orleans, command of a gun battery was boring to Savez.

Confederate fortunes continued to ebb. On May 8, Farragut's fleet steamed up to Baton Rouge. The city's mayor refused to voluntarily surrender, but acknowledged that he did not have troops to defend the state capital. The landing party seized the arsenal and raised the American flag.

Admiral Foote's health had failed because of a wound he had received at Fort Donelson. His thrust down the Mississippi had stalled at Plum Point Bend, Tennessee, six miles above Fort Pillow. On May 9, he turned over command of the Western Flotilla to Capt. Charles Henry Davis. The next morning, to Davis's surprise, the Hollins's Fleet attacked. One Union ironclad was sunk on a sandbar and another beached to keep from sinking. Finally, Davis was able to drive off the Confederates.

After the disaster at New Orleans, the South did not have enough ships to parry Davis's and Farragut's thrusts. Unopposed, the Union navy continued upriver. Natchez yielded on May 13. Grand Gulf, Mississippi, was shelled on May 16. The Northerners steamed past the town and did not take it. On May 18, they arrived at Vicksburg and demanded that the city surrender. Unlike Baton Rouge, Vicksburg was built on a high bluff. Since only the mortars could reach the city, Vicksburg refused to surrender.

In the meantime, the Union army had laid siege to Fort Pillow. On the night of June 4, the fort was evacuated. Savez received orders to dismount his guns. He was told to send them down the Mississippi to the White River. The *Polk* and *Livingston* left and steamed up the Yazoo River. Savez was then ordered to Vicksburg to recruit men for Pinkney's boats.

At sunrise on June 6, the Western Flotilla arrived at Memphis. The Hollins's Fleet steamed out to meet the enemy. The townspeople lined the bluff and cheered. They hoped to see a repeat of the Plum Point battle.

Instead they witnessed a disaster. In a little more than an hour, the Yankees got their vengeance by sinking one ship, burning two, and capturing four. Only the CSS *General Earl Van Dorn* escaped downriver to join the *Polk* and *Livingston*. The city surrendered to Davis. With the battle of Memphis the Federals destroyed the Confederate forces on the Mississippi. The few ships left were up its tributaries.

Savez's luck suddenly changed. He learned of an ironclad, the CSS *Arkansas,* under construction up the Yazoo River. With a little maneuvering, Savez obtained orders to report to the *Arkansas.*[60]

CHAPTER FIVE

IRON WARRIOR

When Savez arrived at Yazoo City in June 1862, he found a beehive of activity aboard the *Arkansas.* Men worked around the clock as the Confederates tried to make up for lost time. They had started building the *Arkansas* at Memphis, but the fall of Island No. 10 forced them to move the incomplete ironclad up the Yazoo River to Greenwood, Mississippi. Unfortunately Lt. Charles H. McBlair, the commanding officer, tied the *Arkansas* to a pier in the rain-swollen river almost four miles from dry land. Work came to a halt. The hull had been built to about the main deck although the captain's cabin was unfinished. Machinery, guns, and supplies lay scattered on her decks. Part of the armor was at the bottom of the river.[1] The locals, annoyed with the lack of progress, telegraphed Richmond requesting a more energetic officer. Mallory replaced McBlair with Lt. Isaac Newton Brown.[2]

Brown had served in the Third Seminole and Mexican wars and had twice sailed around the world. At the beginning of the war, he worked on ironclads being built in New Orleans. He fled after Farragut passed the forts.[3] Once in command of the *Arkansas,* he immediately started to work. Brown found a diving bell to use in raising the iron armor. He then had the machinery, guns, and supplies dumped on board and ordered his unfinished ship towed 160 miles downriver to Yazoo City.

Before the war started, steamboats had been repaired at Yazoo City. Brown moored the steamer *Capitol* alongside the *Arkansas.* The steamer's drilling machines worked around the clock fitting the iron as armor. Brown used old railroad rails and boilerplate. The iron was shipped in by rail. The nearest railroad depot was twenty-five miles away, so the last part of the iron's journey was by wagon.[4] A commandeered sawmill cut lumber. The gun carriages had been growing trees ten days before.[5] He recruited laborers from military posts and off the city streets. Fourteen plantation owners furnished blacksmith's forges and men to run them. Two hundred men toiled to finish the ironclad.[6]

Savez later described the *Arkansas* as "a very pretty little gunboat."[7] The ironclad was 165 feet long with a beam of 35 feet and a draft of 11½ feet. The *Arkansas* looked like a ship cut down to the main deck. The bow section was narrow, and a heavy iron prow, which would act as a knife, extended underwater beyond the bow. The amidships section was flat-bottomed. The hull, though, did not flare outward like a steamboat, but rather curved inward with a slight tumble home. The stern section had somewhat of a hollow, on both port and starboard sides, to allow room for over six-foot-diameter twin propellers. Atop the main deck was a casemate made of one-foot-thick timbers covered with railroad iron.[8] Cotton bails were stuffed in back of the wood for additional protection. The casemate was a straight-sided box whose ends sloped backwards at thirty-five degrees. The top of the pilothouse and smokestack protruded from the top of the casemate. The casemate housed the *Arkansas's* armament. The ironclad carried a pair of 8-inch 64-pounders in her bow and two rifled 32-pounders astern. Both side batteries consisted of two 100-pounder columbiads and a rifled 32-pounder. Under the main deck was the second deck. Forward on this deck were crew berthing and the galley. The boilers and engines with their coal bunkers were amidships. Aft were the officers' quarters and wardroom. Magazines and storerooms were below the second deck.[9]

Savez reported to Brown, who was concerned that the Federals might come upriver looking for the *Arkansas.* Yazoo City was a mere sixty miles from the Union fleet. Halfway between the *Arkansas* and the enemy was Liverpool Landing. There the Confederates had stretched a barricade of logs across the river. The four guns mounted atop the river bluffs were the only fortifications between them and the Yankees.[10] The *Polk, Livingston,* and *General Earl Van Dorn* were anchored below the barricade. Brown told Savez to accompany him to Liverpool Landing to check the fortifications. Savez was also told to see to it that cotton bales were loaded on the steamer that Brown planned to take downriver. The bales would serve as makeshift armor for the *Polk* and *Livingston.* The *Van Dorn* had some light armor.[11]

At Liverpool Landing, Savez fortified the steamers. Savez informed the captains that Brown wanted them to keep steam up and ram any adventuresome enemy ships. Brown, in the meantime, sought out Flag Officer Pinkney, who had gone to Liverpool Landing after the fall of Fort Pillow. Pinkney told Brown he planned on leaving after Comdr. William F. Lynch arrived. Brown and Savez then returned upriver, satisfied that the *Arkansas* would be protected.

A day or two after their return to Yazoo City, Lynch arrived and inspected the *Arkansas.* He did not like what he saw and ordered Savez to go to Jackson and telegraph his findings to Richmond. Lynch's message stated: "The *Arkansas* is very inferior to the *Merrimac* [*Virginia*] in every particular; the iron with which she is covered is worn and indifferent, taken from a railroad track, and is poorly secured to the vessel; boiler iron on stern and counter; her smoke stack is sheet iron."[12]

By the time Savez got back to Yazoo City, he found the *Arkansas* ready to leave, even though Brown did not have a full complement of crew and the armor was not fully secured to the casemate. Brown had to move downriver before the hot summer sun caused the water to fall enough to trap the *Arkansas.* On June 20, some five weeks after Brown arrived at Yazoo City, the *Arkansas* got underway for Liverpool Landing.[13]

As the *Arkansas* steamed downriver, Brown learned from a passing steamer that the Union navy had been spotted coming upriver. He ordered full speed ahead, nine knots. Brown also had a bow gun fired occasionally to let Pinkney know help was on the way. As the *Arkansas* rounded the bend above Liverpool Landing, the Confederates could see that the guns on the bluff were not firing.

Suddenly someone yelled. Smoke could be seen coming from the *Polk* and *Livingston.* Pinkney had ignored Brown's instructions and let the steam go down. Without steam in the boilers the gunboats could not be moved. Pinkney had panicked and ordered them burned. Later it was learned that a river steamboat had come up to Satartia bar, five miles downriver. The inquisitive steamboat then retreated. Brown ordered his crew into the ironclad's boats to try to extinguish the flames. By the time the boats came alongside it was too late. Adding to the conflagration, burning ships drifted into the *General Earl Van Dorn* setting her on fire. Just like at New Orleans, Savez watched cowardly people rob the Confederates of ships.[14]

Brown also considered Pinkney to be a coward and traitor. The local correspondent for the *Mississippian,* the paper Savez worked for as a boy, dryly noted that Pinkney "did heroically manage to have taken ashore, without injury, a pair of pet chickens and a poodle dog."[15]

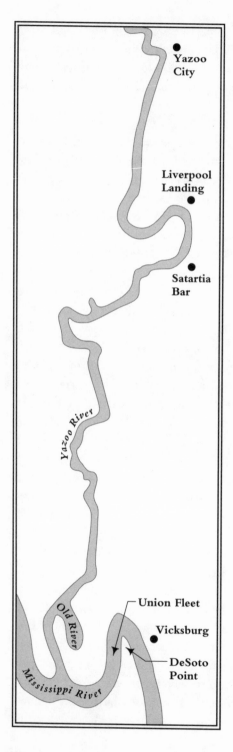

The next day Brown sent Savez with one of the pilots to sound the bar at nearby Satartia. Savez found plenty of water for the *Arkansas*'s draft. The pilot, however, warned that if the river level continued to fall, they would only have five more days to cross the bar. To complicate matters, the barricade at Liverpool Landing would have to be removed. The barricade's builder said it would take a week to remove it. Savez took the news back to Brown. Unconvinced, Brown ordered Lts. George Gift and John Grimball to go with Savez to inspect the barricade. They advised that it could be removed in less than half an hour.[16]

On the night of June 28, eight ships of Farragut's fleet ran past Vicksburg under heavy fire from the Confederate batteries on the bluffs. Rounding a peninsula called DeSoto Point, they dropped anchor. Porter's mortar schooners and three of Farragut's ships had been left below Vicksburg to provide covering fire. On July 1, Flag Officer Davis and the Western Flotilla joined Farragut. The two arms of the Union pincers had met.

YAZOO RIVER AND MISSISSIPPI RIVER— YAZOO CITY TO VICKSBURG

On March 1 the Confederates had controlled the Mississippi River from Columbus, Kentucky, to the Gulf of Mexico—nearly a thousand miles. Four months later their control had been reduced to the field of fire of the guns of Vicksburg. The loss of the Mississippi was one of the South's major defeats.

The Anaconda Plan was working. Beef from Texas and blockade supplies brought into Galveston were choked off. Few railroads had been built west of the Mississippi. Goods traveled by steamer downriver to the Mississippi, then to the railhead at Vicksburg. With the Federals at Vicksburg, even the rail line from Monroe, Louisiana, was cut off.

All 32,000 troops, the entire Trans-Mississippi Department, were isolated west of the river.[17] The South, always short of soldiers, needed to be able to shift troops from quiet fronts to active ones. Later in the war, the Confederates would rush McLaws' and Hood's divisions of Lt. Gen. James Longstreet's corps by train from Virginia to north Georgia to help Gen. Braxton Bragg fight the Battle of Chickamauga. None could be brought in from the Trans-Mississippi.

The North controlled the Mississippi River even though the South contested with formidable gun batteries. Union sailors could steam wherever they wanted. With control of the river, the Union army was ready to move troops against Vicksburg.

Savez, with all the other officers and crew, argued in favor of taking on the Federals. The most powerful Union fleet yet assembled on the river was hammering Vicksburg, but Brown was unsure. He felt the *Arkansas* could do little against so many ships. Several steamers remained up the Yazoo. Brown wanted to protect them so they could transport much-needed supplies. Brown finally decided to send Savez to Vicksburg to ask Maj. Gen. Earl Van Dorn for instructions.

Read saddled up at sunset on July 1 and set out for the threatened city. In the morning, after a fifty-mile ride, Savez met a friend, Col. William T. Withers. After breakfast they both went to see Van Dorn.

Although Van Dorn appreciated the importance of holding the Yazoo river, he felt that the falling water level would render the *Arkansas* useless. Van Dorn told Savez that his orders for Brown were to bring the *Arkansas* to Vicksburg. The *Arkansas,* like the *Virginia,* which had destroyed the *Cumberland* and the *Congress* and dueled the *Monitor* to a draw, should have been able to destroy the wooden ships of the enemy and hold its own against their ironclads. The *Arkansas* was to run past the Federals above the city and then drop downriver to attack the *Brooklyn*, two bluewater gun-boats, and mortar schooners. The *Arkansas* could then continue down the Mississippi, going out into the Gulf and on to Mobile. The *Arkansas*, in Van Dorn's view, could recapture the river. Van Dorn concluded by saying that Brown should move at once and act as his judgment should dictate.

Before returning to the *Arkansas*, Savez told Withers that he wanted to reconnoiter the Union Fleet above the city. Brown would need to know what lay in front of him before the *Arkansas* reached the safety of the guns on the bluffs of Vicksburg. After obtaining a guide from Withers, Savez rode to a site opposite DeSoto Point, where the Federal ships lay anchored. Dismounting, the two Confederates moved through the brush, vines, and briars, to a point overlooking the river.[18]

With field glasses Savez surveyed the *Arkansas*'s antagonists. Counting the fleet that came up from New Orleans and the one that came down from Cairo, there were thirty-three vessels.[19] On the opposite bank were the mortar scows and transports. The ironclads and rams were anchored on the near bank. The rams were designed to steam into southern ships and split them in two. Farragut's ships were spread out upriver from the flotilla.[20] In the heat of the late afternoon sun, the Northerners allowed the steam in their ships' boilers to go down to keep them as cool as possible. Without steam, they could not move out to meet the *Arkansas*. Savez noticed the large number "6" on the smokestack of the *Pinola*, the ship that fired the grapeshot that mortally wounded Huger, and vowed revenge. A small cut-ter left one of Farragut's ships and landed near Savez, but the thick brush prevented him and his companion from being seen.

Savez rode back until about two o'clock in the morning, slept until daybreak in the house of a planter, and then continued on to Liverpool Landing and the *Arkansas*.[21]

Upon returning, Savez found that Brown, anticipating the general's request, had prepared to leave. Brown had given Savez command of the twin stern rifles. The boilerplate armor on the stern had not been reinforced by railroad iron, a dangerous situation. Men from Pinkney's burned gun-boats made up for most of the crew shortage, with Jeff Thompson's Mis-souri cavalry providing the rest. Thompson had come to Mississippi after the fall of Memphis. All totaled, the *Arkansas*'s complement was 232.[22]

The *Arkansas* was moved below the barricade. On July 12 the ironclad steamed on to Satartia. Five hours steaming time separated the *Arkansas* from the Federal fleet.

There Brown gave his officers twenty-four hours to train their gun crews.[23] The ship's officers aligned the guns and marked their trunnions since the narrow gunports allowed little room for lateral training of the cannons. The Confederates could fire only when the enemy was directly in front of the gunports.[24]

Just then Lynch arrived from Yazoo City. Since the flag officer outranked Brown, Brown offered command of the *Arkansas* to Lynch, who then changed his mind about going. Before departing the *Arkansas*, Lynch told the ship's officers that he knew that they would do their duty and that he hoped that they would live to see their country free of invaders.[25]

On the cloudless morning of July 14, the *Arkansas* started downriver. About fifteen miles below the point where the Sunflower River runs into the Yazoo, an engineman explained to Brown that the boilers and engines were not tight, allowing steam to escape. As the steam condensed, the water ran down onto the second deck, where it drained down into the forward magazine, soaking the gunpowder. Brown stopped the *Arkansas* near the site of an old sawmill. The crew spread out the wet powder on tarpaulins to dry in the hot sun. All day long they turned and shook the powder to dry it. In the distance sounded the guns of the Union fleet.[26] By sunset the powder was dry and the crew was able to load it into the aft magazine.

Brown decided to make up for lost time by traveling at night. Near dark, Grimball, while standing watch topside, spotted a large tree overhanging the river just ahead of the *Arkansas.* Moving quickly, he grabbed a rope and jumped to a nearby tree. Then he tied the large tree out of the way. The ironclad came close to having its smokestack knocked over. Brown stopped the *Arkansas.* Lost time or not, a collision with a tree would destroy the smokestack and end the journey.[27]

During the night, two Confederate deserters made their way down the Yazoo in a stolen raft to the Union fleet. Aboard the USS *Hartford,* they told Farragut about the approaching *Arkansas.* Farragut did not believe them. Four days earlier he had written the secretary of the navy stating that he did not think that the *Arkansas* would ever come down the Yazoo. Davis, remembering the Confederate surprise attack at Plum Point Bend, was not so sure. Farragut finally decided to send a couple gunboats up the Yazoo to check. If the deserters had arrived a day earlier, the Federals would have found the *Arkansas* with her crew drying gunpowder ashore.[28]

At 3:00 A.M. on July 15 Brown ordered the officers and crew awakened. He wanted the *Arkansas* to run through the Union ships at daybreak when they were least likely to be on the alert. The *Arkansas* raised anchor and started downriver. Unfortunately one engine stopped, and despite the helmsmen turning the ship's wheel, the ironclad plowed into the riverbank.[29]

From his position in the pilothouse, Brown saw a plantation near the river. Desiring information on the enemy he sent Savez ashore while the *Arkansas* was maneuvered off the bank.

As Savez entered the house, the only person he found was an elderly black woman. When asked where everyone had gone, she would not tell. Savez assured her he was not a Yankee, but she replied she was certain he was a Yankee because "Our folks ain't got none dem gunboats!"[30] Savez returned to the *Arkansas*.

After an hour's work freeing the ship, Brown got the *Arkansas* underway again. The *Arkansas* approached the Old River section of the Yazoo, a lake to the left of the Yazoo. The air inside the ironclad grew sticky. Savez, like several of the other officers, removed his coat. His gun crew stripped off their shirts and tied their handkerchiefs around their heads to keep the sweat out of their eyes.

The men of the *Arkansas* cast loose the guns and loaded them with powder and solid shot to pierce the Union ships. Gunners pushed igniting primers down the cannons' vents. The gun captains pulled back the gunlocks and attached the firing lanyards. The crew stood at the tackle, ready to run out the guns. Others formed lines, ready to pass up powder, shot, and shell to the gunners. The pressure gauges on the boilers read one hundred pounds. All was quiet except for the thump-thump of the propellers.[31]

A gentle morning breeze blew off the low mist that hung over the water. Beyond the next bend in the river, smoke could be seen rising above the trees.[32] The enemy was coming.

Brown descended the ladder from the pilothouse and addressed his officers:

> Gentlemen, in seeking combat as we now do, we must win or perish. Should I fall, whoever succeeds to the command will do so with the resolution to go through the enemy's fleet or go to the bottom. Should they carry us by boarding, the *Arkansas* must be blown up. On no account must she fall into the hands of the enemy. Go to your guns![33]

As the *Arkansas* rounded the bend, the Southerners could see three Federals. The gunboat USS *Tyler* was in the lead, about a mile away. One-fourth mile astern of the *Tyler* was the ram *Queen of the West*. The ironclad *Carondelet* was a mile and a half behind the *Queen*.[34]

Brown decided to attack the *Carondelet,* telling the pilot to give the helmsman orders to steer toward the ironclad. Brown then ordered 1st Lt. Henry Stevens to have the bow gunners, Gift and Grimball, hold fire until the *Arkansas* closed with the enemy. Brown feared the recoil would slow the ship. The *Arkansas* charged toward the Union ships. Brown hoped to handle the *Carondelet* with the bow guns when he got within range. Should the smaller *Tyler* and *Queen of the West* decide to circle round to attack on the beam, he would use the *Arkansas'* broadside batteries to keep them at bay. If the *Arkansas* passed any of the Federals, Savez's stern rifles would take care of them.

The *Tyler* got off a wild shot, then came about and started downriver. The Confederates cheered as they saw the gunboat turn around. As the *Tyler* fled, the Federals fired their stern guns. Iron shot banged into the *Arkansas's* armor then bounced off. The armor on the bow bent under the blows, but held.

In the *Arkansas*, an Irish gunner stuck his head out a side gunport to get a better view. At that moment, a Union shot grazed along the side, decapitating him. The headless corpse fell back from the opening. Stevens, sensing that the crew might panic, ordered a sailor to help him throw the body over the side. "Oh, I can't do it Sir! It's my brother!" came the reply. The body was thrown overboard.[35]

The *Arkansas* charged on, gaining on the *Tyler*. Brown finally changed his mind and decided he would open fire on the *Tyler*. Gift got off the first shot from the port side columbiad. His cannon jumped off its carriage on the recoil, but the shot still made good. The 8–inch shell smashed into the stern of the *Tyler,* killing her pilot and bursting in the engine room. Grimball started firing with the starboard bow gun.

As the *Tyler* passed the *Queen of the West,* her captain, Lt. Comdr. William Gwin, hailed the *Queen* with his speaking trumpet, calling for her to ram the *Arkansas*. The *Queen,* however, was busy backing down to turn around. Gwin then bellowed his opinion to the *Queen's* captain.[36] The *Arkansas* fired her starboard guns at the *Queen* as she started to flee.

The *Carondelet* meanwhile blasted away with her guns as she quickly backed around and joined her consorts in flight. The *Tyler* slowed to take position off the *Carondelet's* port bow in an attempt to help the slower moving ironclad. The *Queen of the West* sped on downriver. The *Arkansas* charged on, yawing slightly so that the Union sailors could not get a good look at the weakness of her armor. The *Arkansas* then shifted its fire to the *Carondelet*.

Since all the action had taken place on the forward end of the gundeck, Savez had nothing to do. He impatiently watched in silence as the Union shots hit the *Arkansas*.[37] Savez suddenly heard the cries of the forward gun crew and saw Brown's limp figure.

To better direct the Confederate fire, Brown had climbed atop the casemate. In that exposed position he had drawn the *Tyler's* fire. A sharpshooter's minié ball had grazed his head. The shot, which knocked him out, had sent him tumbling down the open hatch. He was lucky, since the chief pilot had been killed and the Yazoo pilot wounded. Brown revived as the sailors started to carry him to the lower deck. He ordered his bearers back to their stations. Getting up, he returned to the pilothouse. As Brown returned to his position, the wounded pilot being carried below kept muttering, "Keep in the middle of the river."[38]

Gradually the *Arkansas* gained on the slower *Carondelet*. Gift, having gotten his cannon back in action, rejoined Grimball and sent shot after shot into the *Carondelet's* unarmored stern. The Confederates had shifted to solid shot in an effort to break the Federal's armor. They were successful. The *Carondelet's* casement split and the Confederate shots penetrated the ironclad.

Once, as the two ships were fifty yards apart, Gift saw a man standing outside the *Carondelet's* casemate loading a stern gun. Gift immediately fired his columbiad and when the smoke cleared the man, gun, and part of the *Carondelet's* deck had disappeared.[39] The Confederate shell smashed through the length of the ironclad, destroying the wheelhouse, the steerage cabin, and the captain's cabin. Steam pipes, gauges, exhaust pipes, and cold water pipes lay broken in the ship. The boats and davits were blown away and the steering gear cut. There was so much internal damage that Comdr. Henry Walke, the *Carondelet's* captain and Brown's former shipmate, thought that his ship had been hit in the bow before she turned.[40]

Yawing wildly, the *Carondelet* made for the mud flats and some willows that lay by the shore. The *Arkansas* followed cautiously since the Confederate ship drew five feet more water than the Federal. The *Carondelet's* flag was down and her guns silent. Seeing no sign of surrender, Brown called out to the ship. Getting no reply, he ordered a sharp turn so that the ship's roll would depress the guns and thus send the broadsides into *Carondelet's* waterline.[41]

Savez watched out the stern gunports for the enemy to come into view as the *Arkansas's* port cannons went off. He heard cheers as the *Carondelet* reeled under the impact of the shot and took on water up to the shield. When, at last, the *Carondelet* came into view, Savez barked the command to fire. Both guns roared, adding their smoke to the already hazy gundeck. As the gunners cheered wildly, Savez saw the *Carondelet*, clouded by escaping steam, drop astern as the *Arkansas* moved back into the river. White flags appeared out of the *Carondelet's* gunports. One Yankee used a pair of white drawers as a flag.[42] Brown decided not to press the attack further, since he did not want to risk grounding his ship. The *Arkansas* left the *Carondelet*, as Brown would later report to Mallory, "hanging in the willows."[43] It was 6:30 A.M.[44]

If Pinkney had not destroyed the *Polk, Livingston,* and *Van Dorn,* the Confederates could have used them to capture the *Carondelet* and take her back upriver to use in protecting the steamers on the Yazoo. Years later, Savez remembered this and wondered why the *Carondelet* could not have been stopped at Island No. 10 before she got to New Madrid.[45]

Ahead of the Confederates, the *Queen of the West* and *Tyler* fled for safety. The *Queen* was far out in front. The *Arkansas* closed to a little more than 500 yards from the badly wounded *Tyler* as the ships sped toward the Mississippi River.

Brown made the rounds to inspect battle damage. In the engine room, he discovered the temperature to be between 120 and 130 degrees. The breechings, the connections between the furnace and the smokestack, had been shot away during the battle, letting flames escape. He quickly organized relief parties since the engine room crew were starting to pass out. The relief crews could endure only fifteen-minute intervals. The steam pressure had dropped to twenty pounds, barely enough to move the ironclad.[46]

The *Tyler*, flying its signal flags, rounded King's Point and swung out into the Mississippi with the *Arkansas* in pursuit. By this time the *Queen of the West* had already reached the complacent fleet and her captain, shouting through his speaking trumpet, warned of the approaching Rebel ironclad. Amazingly, no one believed him. Just then the *Tyler* approached. Although the Union officers had heard the sound of cannon fire, they thought their ships were firing at shore batteries.[47] As the wounded *Tyler* ducked under the stern of the *Hartford,* the ironclad gave her a parting shot.

As the *Arkansas* approached closer to the Union fleet, the Rebels stared at a flotilla of steamships, ironclads, gunboats, river steamers, and mortars. Gift, peering through the gunport, thought they looked like chickens scampering about at the sight of a hawk. "Beat to quarters" could be heard through the still morning air. "Holy mother, have mercy on us! We'll never get through there!" exclaimed an Irish gunner upon seeing the Federals.[48] The *Arkansas*'s speed had dropped to about three knots. The ironclad would have to run the gauntlet to make it to Vicksburg. It was 7:15 A.M.[49]

The ram USS *Lancaster* had been moored upriver from the Federal fleet to serve as a picket. Upon spotting the *Arkansas*, the *Lancaster* slipped her anchor and turned downriver with the current to pick up speed. When the *Lancaster* was moving fast enough, she could turn to ram the approaching iron warrior.

Brown, noting the *Lancaster*'s maneuver, called to the pilot, "Brady shave that line of men of war as close as you can so the rams will not have enough room to gather headway in coming out to strike us."[50] Each Union ship captain might think he was going to be rammed. If the *Arkansas* could run close enough, the Federals, unable to completely depress their guns, would overshoot her.

As the *Arkansas* charged the Federals, an approaching powder boy told Savez that Gift wanted to see him. When Savez got to the open gunport, Gift pointed out the large number "6" on the funnel of the *Pinola*.[51]

As Savez returned to his guns, he heard the *Pinola* open fire. The first shot fell short and Gift returned fire. The *Arkansas* swung to port and gave the *Pinola* her port broadside as she passed the Federal. Savez saw the stack with the number "6" and called for the guns to be fired. With a roar the 32-pounders revenged Huger.

The *Pinola*'s attack started the battle. The cannons of the Federal ships erupted with shot, shell, grape, and canister. Union marksmen fired round after round at the Confederate intruder. Shots bounced off the *Arkansas*'s iron sides as she charged on.

The *Lancaster* then came around the *Richmond*'s stern and made for the *Arkansas*. When the attacker was about a hundred yards in front of the *Arkansas*, Gift fired a shell with a five-second fuse. The missile smashed through the enemy's hull and exploded in the boiler's mud drum, filling the ship with live steam and hot water. The crew, tearing off their shirts, leaped overboard.[52]

The Federals retaliated. The *Richmond* blasted 882 pounds of metal at the intruder. The cannon balls smashed into the port side of the *Arkansas*, knocking off a piece of her bow.

In return Savez fired both stern guns into the *Richmond*. The *Arkansas* dashed past the *Hartford* and *General Bragg*. The Confederate ironclad was hit repeatedly. A shot from the *Sciota* struck the *Arkansas* and bounced straight up in the air, exploding above the ship. If the Union gunner had cut the fuse a couple seconds shorter, the shot would have burst through the *Arkansas*'s hull.[53]

The *Arkansas*'s gundeck resembled a scene from Dante's *Inferno*. Blue-gray smoke from the Confederate guns hung thick in the air. The *Arkansas*'s iron plate rang when the Union shot hit. Timbers cracked, officers yelled, wounded Confederates screamed. The temperature on the main deck rose to 120 degrees.[54]

At the height of the battle, the *Arkansas*'s quartermaster took up a position next to the ladder to the berth deck. A husky sailor with one eye, he directed the powder monkeys as they passed shells up from the magazine, encouraging them to move quickly. When one had trouble getting a gun out, he grabbed the side tackle and hauled it out himself. Eyeing a wounded sailor, he asked, "Where are you hurt? Go back to your gun or I'll murder you on the spot—here's your nine-inch shell—mind, shipmate[,] the ladder is bloody, don't slip. Let me help you."[55]

The roar of the battle carried far beyond the river. Twenty miles to the northeast the thunder of the guns was heard at the Brokenburn Plantation in Louisiana. Kate Stone later recorded in her diary that she heard "continuous and heavy cannonading."[56]

Up forward a gunner, knocked down by the concussion of a striking shot, stood up announcing that shot never hit the same place twice. A minute later a shot exploded through the opening and killed him. When the smoke cleared, only Gift and one of his gun crew were left standing. Sixteen others were killed or wounded. The shell burst also set fire to the cotton bales used to back the armor. Stevens dashed to the engine room hatch, grabbed a hose, and hauled it back to extinguish the blaze.[57]

Union shot downed the *Arkansas*'s flag. Midshipman Dabney Scales crawled out on the casemate and hoisted the colors. Almost instantly, a Union shot carried the flag away again. Before the young officer could retrieve the flag, Brown ordered him below.[58]

As the *Arkansas* neared the end of the gauntlet, Brown called for the pilot to ram the USS *Benton,* which was attempting to raise enough steam pressure to move. In the excitement the *Arkansas* missed, but as they passed, the Confederates delivered their starboard battery into the enemy. When the *Benton* came into Savez's view, he poured shots into her stern. The *Ben-*

ton then turned and started to chase the *Arkansas* at a comfortable distance. The *Benton* finally slowed the chase as she came within range of the Vicksburg batteries.[59]

The *Arkansas* had passed through the mightiest fleet ever assembled on the Mississippi. The ironclad survived, but not without damage. Her boats were shot away and her smokestack looked like a nutmeg grinder. The steam pressure had dropped till the *Arkansas* hardly moved. The shot-up breeching leaked stack smoke and added to cannon smoke on the gun deck. Sixteen sailors were killed and seventeen wounded.[60] Blood lay in puddles while the surgeon worked below on the wounded. Gift nursed a broken arm. Savez again escaped unharmed.

Brown invited all his officers topside. Although not yet midmorning, the *Arkansas* had fought two battles. As Savez and the others started to congratulate Brown, a last shot from the Federals whizzed overhead.[61]

The battered *Arkansas* finally swung around DeSoto Point and Vicksburg came into view. From the bluffs, the townspeople cheered as the ironclad approached. The Confederates telegraphed word of the success to Richmond. General Van Dorn came down to congratulate Brown. As the well-wishers surged forward, the sight of the carnage on the gundeck stopped them short.

The unexpected arrival of the *Arkansas* panicked the Federals downriver from Vicksburg. They burned commissary stores, army transports, and the grounded mortar schooner USS *Sidney C. Jones.* The rest of the mortar fleet fled.[62]

At Vicksburg, the Confederates carried their dead, sick, and wounded ashore. The remaining crew washed down the deck, then broke for breakfast. Later the Missourians who signed on to bring the *Arkansas* to Vicksburg gratefully left.

Since getting to Vicksburg cost the *Arkansas* most of her coal, Brown ordered the ship moved to the coal depot.[63] As the crew loaded coal, the mortar fleet regained their courage, returned, and started shelling. Most of the shells fell short, although the *Westfield*'s shots came close enough to spray the crew and wet down the coal dust.[64] Savez lamented the fact that the *Arkansas*'s damaged condition kept her from attacking them. Savez also regretted Pinkney's destruction of the *Polk, Livingston,* and *Van Dorn.* With these three ships, the Confederates could have captured or destroyed the mortar fleet.[65] With coaling complete, Brown moved the *Arkansas* out of range. All during the day the officers and crew labored in the hot sticky weather to get their ship back in shape. Although Brown shared Savez's desire to attack the mortar fleet, the Confederates had too much work to do for a single afternoon.

The ironclad had caught Farragut off guard; he wanted her destroyed immediately. He had slept late that morning and when the *Arkansas* appeared he had to come up on deck in his nightshirt.[66] His fellow officers argued that a daylight attack under the guns of Vicksburg would be suicidal. Farragut reluctantly agreed to a night attack with his deep-sea fleet.

In the afternoon, the rising warm air formed thunderheads high over Vicksburg. At four o'clock the storm broke. By seven o'clock, the storm was over.[67]

Just before dark, the Confederates received word that the Federal ships were getting underway. After sunset, a range light was noticed across the river from the *Arkansas*. Since the Union ships would fire their broadsides when they were abreast of the light, Brown had the *Arkansas* moved a few hundred yards downriver.[68] The *Arkansas* was about to engage in her third battle of that day. The Southerners would have to fight from a damaged ironclad moored to the bank.

When the storm stopped, the Confederates heard the firing of the upper batteries. The *Arkansas*'s crew saw the *Iroquois* move up abeam of the range light and fire into the bluff.[69] They then opened fire with their bow guns and broadsided the *Iroquois* as soon as she drew abeam. Savez blasted the Federal with shots from his stern rifles.[70] The long line of Union ships came up one by one and unsuccessfully fired into the bluff. Two hundred feet overhead, the Vicksburg gunners sent round after round into the passing ships. The Union cannon started a fire ashore whose smoke helped obscure the enemy's view of the *Arkansas*.

As the *Hartford* arrived, the Federals spotted the flashes of the *Arkansas*'s guns. Farragut ordered the *Hartford* to fire in that direction, but the darkness and smoke obscured the *Arkansas* and most of the shots missed. A single 9-inch shot, however, did hit. It passed through the ironclad just above the waterline, wrecking the dispensary unit before exploding in the engine room, killing two men and wounding six others. One of the dead was a pilot; at dinner he had said he would not again pass through the ordeal of the morning for the whole world.[71]

The cannonading finally stopped. Farragut's fleet had passed. Again the Confederates had to carry their dead and wounded ashore, and repair battle damage; but their ship had survived. With the *Arkansas* the Confederates could dispute Union control of the river. That day the *Arkansas* earned herself a place in naval history, seeing more combat than the famous *Virginia* had.

The next day the Western Flotilla started a mortar bombardment. The Confederates continued the repair work despite the frequent showers of metal fragments from the bursting 13-inch shells. One shell, which brought up dead fish from the river, caused a sailor to remark, "Just look at that, will you? Why, the upper fleet is killing fish for the lower fleet's dinner!"[72] Brown frequently moved the ship in order to spoil the Union gunner's aim. The *Arkansas*'s rusty iron sides made her hard to see against the loess bluffs.

Brown worked to get volunteers to replenish the crew. At first, the new recruits were excited about serving on the now famous ironclad. Navy life appeared more glamorous than garrison duty. After they saw the shell holes and heard the stories about the rivers of blood, however, they developed acute cases of what Savez called shell fever and returned to their old commands.

Even the soldiers who remained were of dubious value. Stevens beseeched the volunteers on deck to stop playing cards and help move the ship. One sailor looked up and sneered, "Oh hell! We ain't no deckhands."[73]

The *Arkansas* lacked not only crew, but also officers, as both of the surgeons had taken ill. Brown telegraphed throughout the state for medical volunteers. A few days later the captain appointed a doctor from Clinton as surgeon. The officer of the powder division took the doctor on a tour of the ironclad. On passing the gun deck, the officer remarked that during battle, the wounded were carried below in a steady stream. At that moment the Union mortars opened up. The doctor spent the day standing on the companion ladder, ducking into his stateroom when he heard the whiz of the shells. After the shell hit he would return and watch for another. When the shells hit close by, he would groan, "Oh! Louisa and the babes!"[74]

Convinced his ironclad had been repaired enough to do battle, Brown ordered the *Arkansas* underway, because he was anxious to get at the mortar fleet. As the *Arkansas* started downriver, one engine broke down. With great difficulty the ironclad limped back to the wharf.[75]

The failure of the deep-sea fleet to sink the *Arkansas* forced Farragut to notify Washington, "that, not withstanding his prediction to the contrary, the ironclad ram *Arkansas* has at length made her appearance and took us all by surprise."[76] Farragut had just been promoted to the rank of rear admiral for his victory at New Orleans, the first officer in the history of the United States Navy to hold that rank. To not be able to sink one ironclad was unthinkable. Welles fired back his displeasure: "The escape of this vessel and the attending circumstances have been the cause of serious mortification to the Department and the country. It is an absolute necessity that the neglect or apparent neglect of the squadron on this occasion should be wiped out by the capture or destruction of the *Arkansas*."[77] Farragut consulted with the commander of the upriver fleet and devised a plan to finish off the *Arkansas.*

On July 22 the sound of the ship's drum beating to quarters woke up Read.[78] The enemy was again coming. On reaching the spar deck, Savez noted the *Arkansas* crew consisted of only forty-one men.[79] Union shells, sickness, and heat had taken their toll. Discounting the firemen below, there were not enough men to man Savez's stern rifles. Moving from gun to gun, the officers and crew would have to face the enemy while tied to the shore.

Savez did not have to wait long. The ironclad *Essex* came steaming into view amid a shower of cannon balls from the bluffs. Behind the *Essex* came *Queen of the West.*

Brown easily saw the Federal strategy. The *Essex* with her flat scowlike bow would shove the *Arkansas* against the shore, while the *Queen* with her sharp prow rammed her. The *Queen,* however, was not the only ship with a sharp bow. Brown intended to use the *Arkansas*'s ram to split the *Essex* in two as she hit. His crew undid the mooring lines from their bitts and played them out. Below deck the firemen threw pine knots into the boiler fire to raise the steam pressure. An engineer engaged the starboard engine and the *Arkansas* slowly swung out from the shore. When her ram pointed directly at the *Essex*'s flat nose, the Confederates opened fire. Shots hit the *Essex* and glanced off her as the ship charged on.

In command of the *Essex* was Cmdr. William "Dirty Bill" Porter, half-brother of the man in charge of the mortar fleet below Vicksburg. "Dirty Bill" refused to be stopped by Southern cannonballs. Again the Confederates fired and hit, but the *Essex* came on.

When the *Essex* closed to within fifty yards of the *Arkansas,* her two gun shutters went up and her cannons fired. A 10-inch shot hit the armor a few inches from the open gunport. The force of the impact shattered the armor and timber behind it. Everything flew through the open port diagonally across the gun deck. The shot finally stopped as it hit and broke the breech of the starboard aft broadside gun. By then eight men were killed and six wounded.[80] Again Savez was unhurt.

At the last minute, Dirty Bill ordered the *Essex*'s helm put over into a turn to avoid the *Arkansas*'s ram. The *Essex* hit the *Arkansas* with a glancing blow and slid along the Confederates' port side. As the *Essex* passed by, *Arkansas* fired a broadside. The *Essex* grounded on a mudbank.

The *Arkansas*'s gun crews hastily cleared the wreckage near Savez's stern rifles. The *Essex*'s first shot had carried debris all the way aft. The guns were loaded and run out as Savez moved into position to fire them. The *Arkansas* shook as the port propeller churned, swinging the ship around so the stern rifles could get off a shot. As the *Essex* tried to back off the mudbank, Savez fired. The *Essex* took the hit just as she worked loose. One of the shells penetrated the *Essex*'s casemate and exploded, killing one man and wounding others. One fragment grazed Dirty Bill's head.[81] The crippled Federal ironclad drifted off downriver to the awaiting fleet.

Brown ordered the *Arkansas* swung out again, as the *Queen of the West* bore down on her. The Confederates managed to load the guns in time to fire. The *Queen* struck the *Arkansas* aft of the bow, tearing a hole in the *Arkansas*'s port side and careening the ship. The hulls screeched as the *Queen*'s hull ground along the *Arkansas*. The Confederates fired a broadside. Unfortunately for them the *Arkansas*'s 32-pounder blew out its primer and thereby spoiled a shot that would have hit the *Queen*'s boilers. The *Queen* ran lightly into the bank. Savez got off a shot, though it hit the cotton bales on board and did no damage.

Once free, the *Queen of the West* returned upriver; the Confederates fired a broadside as she passed. When the *Queen* came in range of the *Arkansas*'s bow guns, Gift fired what he later described as his best shot of the day. The ball traveled nearly a mile, and skipped four or five times on the water, before striking the *Queen*.

After the attackers had gone, the Confederates found marbles among the debris. One of the *Essex*'s bow guns had fired a load of marbles in hope of using them like grapeshot.[82] Again the *Arkansas* survived.

After their failure to sink the *Arkansas*, the Federals resorted to long-range bombardment, but falling water and malaria forced Farragut to abandon the siege. On July 24 Farragut's fleet steamed toward New Orleans, leaving a rear guard to defend Baton Rouge. Davis led the Western Flotilla two hundred miles back upriver to Helena, Arkansas. The presence of the *Arkansas* precluded leaving even a token force behind. Supplies could now be shipped down the Red River and up the Mississippi to Vicksburg. Thanks in part to the *Arkansas*, the South had regained 400 miles of the Mississippi!

Sickness did not restrict itself to the Federals. Brown took four days leave to visit his family in Grenada, Mississippi. There he was taken ill.[83]

The war on the Mississippi continued. Gen. John Breckinridge, former vice president under James Buchanan and 1860 presidential candidate for the Southern Democrats, telegraphed Van Dorn requesting naval support for his coming attack on Baton Rouge. Farragut's ships protected the Federal troops holding the city.

Stevens, temporarily in charge, wired Brown, who sent word back not to move the ship until he arrived in Vicksburg by train. The sick Brown had to lie down on the mailbags. Stevens, faced with contradicting orders, wired the flag officer for a resolution. Lynch agreed with Van Dorn and the *Arkansas* left Vicksburg on August 4, 1862, at 2:00 A.M. Four hours later Brown arrived at Vicksburg.[84]

The next day Savez saw that war had come to his home state. Ashore were charred remains of homes. Their owners stopped poking through debris to cheer the *Arkansas*. The sight sickened Savez.[85]

When the *Arkansas* left, only thirty hours remained before Breckinridge planned to start his attack.[86] The chief engineer who had been on the ship during the trip down to Vicksburg was in the hospital, exhausted from overwork. His replacement, Eugene H. Brown, was unfamiliar with the machinery.[87] At the mouth of Red River, the engines were pounding loudly. Brown convinced Stevens that the machinery would hold up, so Stevens decided to go on.[88]

At one o'clock the following morning Savez stood the watch as officer of the deck. The *Arkansas* had gone about fifteen miles past Port Hudson when the starboard engine stopped. Savez ordered the ironclad rounded to and the anchor dropped. Brown and the rest of the engineers had different ideas about what should be done to fix the breakdown. Still not sure of how they were going to repair the broken engine, Savez ordered them to get to work.[89]

While awaiting repairs, Gift sent a party ashore to gain information on the situation at Baton Rouge. When they returned they reported that Breckinridge was due to attack at dawn and that the *Essex*, *Cayuga*, *Katahdin*, and *Kineo* were at Baton Rouge.[90]

Although the *Arkansas* was outnumbered, the Confederates still had a chance. The only ironclad was the *Essex*. Dirty Bill knew how hard the *Arkansas* could hit. Maybe he would be cautious. The *Essex* carried fewer guns than the *Carondelet*.[91] If the Confederates could cripple the *Essex*, they could scatter the wooden-hulled ships.

By daylight the engineers finished their repairs and the *Arkansas* got underway again. In the distance, the booming of Breckinridge's guns could be heard. As the *Arkansas* rounded the point, the *Essex* could be seen downriver. Now it would be the *Arkansas*'s turn to charge. Just then the starboard engine failed. With the port engine still moving, the *Arkansas*'s bow stuck hard in the cypress stumps on the bank, turning her stern downriver. The Confederates dropped the anchor and the engineers went to work. Ashore people gathered to watch the impending fight. In the afternoon, Stevens got a message from Breckinridge stating that his troops had driven the Federals back through the town to the protection of the *Essex* and her consorts.

At sunset the engines were working again. Stevens, realizing that the *Arkansas* was low on coal, decided to go back upriver a couple of miles to a landing to refuel the ship. On the way the starboard engine broke. Stevens ordered the ship secured to a bank with her bow pointed downstream. The crankpin on the shaft was broken; the blacksmith worked at the forge that night to repair it.[92]

Around 7:00 A.M. the *Essex* and the rest of the squadron came upriver. This is what the Confederates hoped would happen. Dirty Bill waited until the *Essex* came within a quarter mile of the *Arkansas* before he opened fire.

The repairs had just been finished. Stevens rang for full speed ahead and the *Arkansas* moved out toward the *Essex*. Savez smiled as the crew cheered.[93]

Wishing to get a longer run before he rammed, Stevens ordered the *Arkansas* into a turn. This time the port engine broke. The helmsman turned the wheel in vain. The rudder would not hold the *Arkansas* in a straight line. The starboard engine swung the ironclad completely around, sending the ship into the bank.[94] The *Arkansas* grounded on tree stumps. Savez's rifles now faced the *Essex* and he opened fire.

Stevens knew all was lost. The ship could not be repaired and freed again to fight. It would not take long for the *Essex* to shoot through the thin armor plating on the stern. With tears in his eyes, Stevens ordered the *Arkansas* destroyed before she fell into Union hands.

The crew filed ashore as the officers prepared to destroy the ship. They axed the engines, opened the magazines and scattered about cartridges and placed shells on the gundeck between the cannons. Savez loaded his rifles and ran them out. The Confederates cut open the cotton on the bulkheads between the guns and set it afire. After torching the bedding in the wardroom, they left the ship.[95]

Stevens had to be helped ashore. The lieutenant burned his hands badly when a charge went off as the engines were being destroyed.[96] Climbing the bank the officers and crew escaped with their side arms and the clothing they wore.

The current worked the *Arkansas* lose from the tree stumps. The ship, ablaze from bow to stern, drifted down on the *Essex*, which turned and left.

Without the *Arkansas's* help, Breckinridge failed to take Baton Rouge. A Union naval observer positioned himself in the tower of the statehouse and by signals directed his ships' gunfire. When Breckinridge learned of the *Arkansas's* fate he withdrew and turned his troops north to occupy and fortify Port Hudson.[97]

The *Arkansas* had lasted twenty-three days since she left Yazoo City. Lack of reliable engines, not Yankee cannon balls, had defeated her. In a sense, the blockade beat the *Arkansas* because the blockade prevented the importing of engines.

After his escape Savez started walking down the road with the others, slowly twirling a firing lanyard, the only thing he saved from the *Arkansas*. Ahead he saw a small group of women. One was talking to a sailor while the others quietly cried as they watched the *Arkansas* burn and explode as the shells went off. The woman who had talked to the sailor called Savez's name and said, "You won't recognize me, but I am Jimmy Morgan's sister!" Dressed in rough sailor pants, boots, an old straw hat, and a thin gauze undershirt Savez felt he was not properly dressed to greet an old shipmate's sister.[98]

That night, Morgan's sister confided in her diary that she knew she had embarrassed Savez. She tried not to take note of his clothing. She was; however, glad she did not originally meet him dressed the way he was dressed that day.[99]

As Savez walked along the road he heard a loud explosion. It was noon on August 6.[100] The fire had reached the *Arkansas's* magazine. Again Savez found himself without a ship. He and the others went to Jackson where they joined Brown. At Jackson Savez got orders to go to recently fortified Port Hudson to help man the guns on the bluff. There he had the pleasure of firing on the *Essex* as she passed by on the night of September 7.

Brown went on to command another ironclad, the CSS *Charleston* in Charleston, South Carolina. Gift served on and commanded several ships: the *Chattahoochee*, *Baltic*, *Gaines*, *Ranger*, *Savannah*, and *Tallahassee*. Both men went on to write about their wartime experiences. Stevens was killed in battle on January 14, 1863.[101]

The months of hard work and heavy fighting started to catch up with Read. On the way to Atlanta to see about ordnance stores, he became ill. He gave the duty to another lieutenant and returned to Raymond, Mississippi, for rest.

While in Raymond, he learned that Brown had gone to Yazoo City. After Savez recovered, he started toward the train station ready to report to Brown when a messenger delivered him a telegram. Savez had orders to go to Mobile and report to John N. Maffitt, captain of the CSS *Florida*.

The *Florida* and Maffitt had already achieved legendary status. The ship, originally named *Oreto*, was built in Great Britain as a commerce raider over the objections of the United States consul, who maintained that British neutrality forbade the building of warships for the South. The Confederate naval agent John D. Bullock had sent the *Oreto* to Nassau, shipping the cannons and ammunition separately. Maffitt slipped past the USS *Cuyler*, which had been sent to catch him. At a deserted island named Green Cay, Maffitt rendezvoused with his supply ship. After christening the *Oreto* "*Florida*" he discovered all the implements to train and fire the cannons had been left behind. Even worse, yellow fever had incapacitated the officers and crew. Maffitt sailed to Cuba, but the authorities in Havana refused to allow him to recruit crew members or replace his missing equipment. Maffitt, himself sick with yellow fever, left Cuba for the Confederacy. He sailed the *Florida* on September 4, 1862, through a hailstorm of Union blockaders' cannon fire into Mobile Bay. The guns of Forts Morgan and Gaines kept the Yankees from following him.[102]

Read immediately exchanged his ticket for one to Mobile.[103]

Photo 1: Charles W. Read, Naval Academy Photograph.
U.S. NAVAL HISTORICAL CENTER PHOTOGRAPH

Photo 2: U.S. Naval Academy, Annapolis, Md. View shows (L-R) the Old Chapel, the Mess Hall, and the Recitation Hall.
U.S. NAVAL HISTORICAL CENTER PHOTOGRAPH, COURTESY OF CAPT. C. C. MARSH

Photo 3: USS *Plymouth*. U.S. NAVAL HISTORICAL CENTER PHOTOGRAPH

Photo 4: USS *Powhatan*. U.S. NAVAL HISTORICAL CENTER PHOTOGRAPH

Photo 5: Lt. Thomas B. Huger. U.S. NAVAL HISTORICAL CENTER PHOTOGRAPH

Photo 6: CSS *McRae*. U.S. NAVAL HISTORICAL CENTER PHOTOGRAPH

Photo 7: Midshipman James Morgan, C.S.N., at age fifteen.
U.S. NAVAL HISTORICAL CENTER PHOTOGRAPH, *RECOLLECTIONS OF A REBEL REEFER*

Photo 8: Battle at the Southwest Pass—the ram *Manassas* attacking
the *Richmond*. U.S. NAVAL HISTORICAL CENTER PHOTOGRAPH

Photo 9: Pope's Fleet under attack by Hollins's Fleet of fire ships at the Head of the Passes. U.S. NAVAL HISTORICAL CENTER PHOTOGRAPH

Photo 10: Union mortar boats bombarding Island Number 10.
U.S. NAVAL HISTORICAL CENTER PHOTOGRAPH, *HARPER'S WEEKLY*

Photo 11: USS *Richmond*. U.S. NAVAL HISTORICAL CENTER PHOTOGRAPH

Photo 12: Farragut's fleet passing the forts. U.S. NAVAL HISTORICAL CENTER
PHOTOGRAPH, *LIFE OF DAVID GLASGOW FARRAGUT*

Photo 13: Federal fleet at New Orleans. U.S. NAVAL HISTORICAL CENTER PHOTOGRAPH

Photo 14: USS *Mississippi*. U.S. NAVAL HISTORICAL CENTER PHOTOGRAPH

Photo 15: USS *Hartford.* U.S. NAVAL HISTORICAL CENTER PHOTOGRAPH

Photo 16: Lt. Isaac Newton Brown.
U.S. NAVAL HISTORICAL CENTER PHOTOGRAPH

Photo 17: CSS *Arkansas* running through the Union fleet at Vicksburg.
U.S. NAVAL HISTORICAL CENTER PHOTOGRAPH, LINE ENGRAVING FROM
BATTLES AND LEADERS OF THE CIVIL WAR.

Photo 18: Destruction of the CSS *Arkansas.* LIBRARY OF CONGRESS

Photo 19: Lt. John N. Maffitt.
U.S. NAVAL HISTORICAL CENTER PHOTOGRAPH

Photo 20: Destruction of the *Jacob Bell*. U.S. NAVAL HISTORICAL CENTER PHOTOGRAPH

Photo 21: British 32-pounder rifled cannon on the Blakely pattern from the CSS *Florida*, Willard Park, Washington Navy Yard, Washington, D.C.
PHOTOGRAPH BY AUTHOR

Photo 22: CSS *Florida* and CSS *Clarence* part company.
MAINE HISTORICAL SOCIETY LIBRARY, PHOTOGRAPH FROM *THE RUDDER*

Photo 23: CSS *Tacony* leaving the *Kate Stewart* and the burning *Clarence* and *M. A. Shindler*.

Photo 24: CSS *Tacony* among the fishing fleet.

Photo 25: Burning of the CSS *Tacony*. MAINE HISTORICAL SOCIETY LIBRARY,
PHOTOGRAPH FROM *THE RUDDER*

Photo 26: Blowing up of the cutter *Caleb Cushing*. MAINE HISTORICAL SOCIETY
LIBRARY, PHOTOGRAPH FROM *THE RUDDER*

Photo 27: Confederate Prisoners at Fort Warren. Read is seated on the
right end of the bench in the front—ninth from the left.
U.S. NAVAL HISTORICAL CENTER PHOTOGRAPH

Photo 28: A 10-inch columbiad at Battery Semmes on the James River.
LIBRARY OF CONGRESS, BRADY COLLECTION

Photo 29: James River Squadron at the Obstructions in the James River.
U.S. NAVAL HISTORICAL CENTER PHOTOGRAPH

Photo 30: Burning of the CSS *Webb* below New Orleans.
U.S. NAVAL HISTORICAL CENTER PHOTOGRAPH

Photo 31: Charles W. Read, 1868.
MR. AND MRS. JOHN MAYNARD,
NAVAL HISTORICAL CENTER PHOTOGRAPH

Photo 32: Charles W. Read,
shortly before his death.
MR. MALLORY READ

Photo 33: Read's tombstone. PHOTOGRAPH BY AUTHOR

CHAPTER SIX

ABOARD THE CSS <u>FLORIDA</u>

On November 4, 1862, Read boarded the CSS *Florida* and reported to Capt. John Newland Maffitt. "This last lieutenant," Maffitt recorded in his journal:

> I personally applied for. He had acquired a reputation for gunnery, coolness and determination at the battle of New Orleans. When his commander T. B. Huger was fatally wounded he continued gallantly to fight the *McRae* until she was riddled and unfit for service. I am sorry to say the Government has not requited him. He seems slow—I doubt not but he is sure. As military officer of the deck he is not equal to many—time will remedy this.[1]

The *Florida,* a 191-foot-long screw sloop of war, had been modeled after the British warships. She was a wolf, designed for speed.[2] The *Florida's* naval architect had given her a narrow bow to slice through the waves. Her rigging and aft-racking masts showed that she was British built. The huge fore-and-aft gaff sails on the foremast, mainmast, and mizzenmast meant her best points of sailing would be from a wind abeam to close-hauled.[3] The *Florida* would tack to windward faster than the Naval Academy training ship *Plymouth.* But, when running before the wind, a square sail ship would have an advantage. The topsails and topgallants on the foremast and mainmast plus the mainsail on the foremast would help offset this handicap. The *Florida's* steam engine would also lend speed.

Despite the Union Navy's blockade, Savez felt that the *Florida* had been in Mobile Bay too long. Confederate blockade runners were able to get in and out the mouth of the bay.[4] To Savez, every passing squall made for the ideal conditions to run the blockade. Maffitt even noticed Savez's impatience.[5]

Disgruntled citizens of Mobile had written to Mallory and complained that Maffitt had not put to sea. If Semmes was sinking Yankees with the *Alabama,* why should the *Florida* be at anchor in Mobile Bay? Maffitt's critics ignored the fact the *Florida's* machinery needed repairs. Because of the shallow channel, the *Florida* had to anchor off Dog River, twenty-eight miles from Mobile.[6] Machinery had to be disassembled, moved by boat to Mobile for repair, and then returned. Three months were needed to get the ordnance supplies for the cannons.[7] But Maffitt's critics had not forgiven him for his part in an incident that had happened just before the war started.

Maffitt, then in command of the USS *Crusader,* had refused to turn the ship over to an unruly Mobile mob. He had felt that the ship must be returned to the government before he could resign his commission. Maffitt had been prepared to destroy his ship rather than surrender it.[8]

By December 6 repairs were finished and ordnance supplies were stowed. A full complement of officers and crew, including the *Arkansas's* engineer, Eugene Brown, were on board. The *Florida* steamed down the bay and anchored near Fort Morgan. The Confederates waited for the right weather to run out through the blockaders.

Nine days later Savez, as officer of the deck, was called upon to administer punishment. A seaman had pulled a knife on the master-at-arms. Insubordination could not be tolerated, because officers relied on the petty officers to carry out their orders. Any hesitation on a sailor's part in battle could lose the ship. Savez had the sailor "spread eagled" on the ship's grating for the day.[9]

On Christmas Eve Maffitt, desiring to give the crew gunnery practice, got the ship underway. Passing Fort Morgan, he stopped the *Florida* just short of the bar. Just ahead, on the other side of Sand Island, was a perfect target. The USS *New London* was steaming on a westwardly course. The *Florida's* guns roared. *New London* returned fire, but missed. Three of the *Florida's* shots appeared to hit the target. Later a report in the *Mobile Evening News* said that shot and shell "dashed the water upon the Lincolnites' decks."[10]

On December 30 Savez learned that Mallory had ordered Maffitt relieved of command because of his reluctance to leave the harbor. Maffitt invited his friend, Adm. Franklin Buchanan, aboard the *Florida,* where Buchanan assured the ship's officers of his confidence in Maffitt's bravery. The admiral then defended Maffitt in a long letter to Mallory, as a good choice for captain. Buchanan also visited President Davis, who happened to be in Mobile at the time, and told him of the injustice. Mallory withdrew the order.[11]

On January 10, 1863, Maffitt decided to run the blockade. The ship's hull had been painted gray with a mixture of lampblack and whitewash, because gray was harder to spot at night than black.

Winter had brought a northeasterly gale. When Maffitt informed his officers that he was going to take the *Florida* out to sea, they wholeheartedly supported the decision.[12]

Just as the ship got to the mouth of Mobile Bay, the storm blew over. As the skies cleared, the lookout counted thirteen Union ships just beyond the bar and out of range of the guns of Forts Morgan and Gaines. The blockaders, anchored in an arc around the main channel, waited for the *Florida* to come out. Maffitt anchored the ship.

Three nights later, a harbor pilot came on board. Maffitt wanted to take the *Florida* on a reconnaissance mission down to the bar to check out the channel and to judge the alertness of the blockaders. Slowly the Confederates eased their way past two blockaders; a third appeared to be anchored in the channel. No one spotted them, but Maffitt brought about the *Florida* and started back into the bay.

The Confederates had removed the channel lights to keep the Federals from trying to run into the bay. Near Fort Morgan the pilot accidentally ran the *Florida* hard aground. The anchors were run out and the crew manned the windlass; the *Florida* would not budge. Lightening the ship took two days of labor, unloading guns and coal onto steamers. Even so, two tugs were needed to break the *Florida* free.[13]

On the night of January 15, storm clouds moved in out of the west. By midnight, a gale was blowing. In the *Florida's* wardroom, the officers discussed the weather. It was ideal for escape. Lookouts on Federal ships would be straining to see in the inky darkness. The Confederates could barely see Fort Morgan; Fort Gaines on the other side of the entrance to the bay was not visible. On the deck the guns had been secured for heavy weather. Overhead, double reefs had been set in the topsails and balanced reefs in the fore and main trysails. The topsails had been tied aback with small, light rope-yarns. A pull from the sheets and halyards would set the sails free without sending the crew aloft.[14] In the engine rooms, steam hissed from the valves.

Maffitt knew the Federals would be waiting. Before taking command of the *Florida,* he had commanded the blockade runners *Cecile* and *Nassau*.

For five months he had skippered his ships through the Union blockade at Wilmington, North Carolina. He had been successful because he did not do what the Union Navy thought he would do.[15]

By two o'clock, the storm abated. The wind shifted around to west-northwest, breaking up the cloud cover. The stars started to come out and a light mist hung low over the bay. Out behind the bar a heavy sea was running. The January night turned bitter.[16]

Maffitt figured that the Federals would have expected the *Florida* to come out during the storm. Now they would be turning in for the night. Those left on watch would be under cover because of the cold.[17] A swift stroke would set the *Florida* free.

"All hands on deck!" came the cry from topside. Seconds later Savez and the other officers were in their lookout positions: one every twenty feet along the ship's railing. The crew stood by the halyards and sheets. Maffitt gave the order to get underway and the bell in the engine room rang. Coal heavers shoved anthracite coal into the fires in the dual boilers. The hard coal, brought in from Great Britain by blockade runners, was ideal, because it burned without much smoke. An engineer opened a steam valve and the steam hissed through the pipes to the twin steam engines, which could develop one hundred horsepower.[18] On deck, the ship's anchor was raised and secured to the cathead.

The *Florida* shuddered as she picked up speed. Savez could just make out the grass growing on the sod atop the five-sided brick Fort Morgan. Clearing the fort, the *Florida* headed down the channel. A leadsman cast the sounding lead and yelled out the water depths.

Soon they were past the covering fire of the fort. Ahead, seven anchored blockaders rolled and pitched in the heavy swells. The channel at the bar was less than a mile wide.[19]

One blockader appeared to lie dead ahead, inside the bar. The helm was put over. Distances were deceptive at night, but still it was wise to give the Federal warship as wide a berth as possible. The watch was not on deck. Even Comdr. Robert B. Hitchcock, the blockade station commander, had gone below after midnight to work on his reports.[20] To starboard lay Sand Island, small and low, barely visible. The channel ran beside the island. Another anchored blockader was passed without the alarm being sounded.

The *Florida* slowed as the helmsman followed the line of breakers to the bar. With precision, the leadsman called out the soundings. The ship's speed had slackened a little at the bar so that the leadsman could take measurements. Once past the bar, Maffitt rang up the engine room for full speed ahead.[21]

In the engine room, they were out of anthracite; only bituminous coal remained. Tiny burning embers of the soft coal swirled up the twin smoke funnels. Hitting the cold night air, the embers glowed like a thousand fireflies.

Seconds later a rocket rose from among the blockaders. Across the water the beating of drums could be heard. Coston signal lights flashed. The Federals were preparing to give chase.

Maffitt ordered the sails set. Quickly the Confederates pulled the halyards and sheets. The sails snapped loose from their ties and were set in the wind.[22] The *Florida* lunged forward through the middle of the blockaders. Under sail and steam the *Florida* bounded along, making fourteen and a half knots.[23]

Sound of cannon fire was heard, but the splashes could not be seen as the *Florida* sped through the blockaders. More rockets streaked upward as the Union Navy started in pursuit. It would take time for the blockaders to get speed up. On through the night the *Florida* raced southward toward the Yucatan Channel, leaving her foes behind.

Just before daybreak, Maffitt released hands from quarters only to have to call them back when a sail was sighted ahead. It was the *Brooklyn*. For fifteen minutes everyone on deck watched as the *Florida* gave the Federal a wide berth. The *Brooklyn* flashed a light, then sailed on mistakenly thinking the *Florida* was a Union gunboat.[24]

With the dawn, the sails of one ship could be seen twelve miles astern.[25] Their pursuer was the *Cuyler*. The previous August, after Maffitt slipped past this ship leaving Nassau, it cost the *Cuyler's* captain his command. The new captain, Comdr. George F. Emmons, was determined not to repeat his predecessor's mistake.

Savez stood his watch, occasionally stealing a glance astern to try to catch a glimpse of the *Cuyler*. The only good views occurred on those brief moments when both the *Florida* and the *Cuyler* rode up in phase on wave crests. Even then the *Cuyler* was hull down and Savez could only see the ship's masts. On through the day they ran, the lone wolf pursed by a single hound.

Under the heavy strain of the chase, the *Florida's* fore topsail yard sprung loose toward evening. A loose yard could tear sails apart, so all hands were sent aloft. The sail was unbent and the yard lowered to the deck for repairs. The *Florida* slowed down. When at last the damage was fixed, and the yard and sail replaced, the *Cuyler* had come within three miles.

As night approached, Maffitt decided to use one of his blockade-running tricks. He ordered all sails taken in and the engine stopped. The *Florida* with her low freeboard and bare spars would be difficult to see against the darkening sky and rolling seas.[26] The Confederates watched anxiously as the *Cuyler* closed on them, then passed on toward Mexico. The ruse had worked.

Emmons's orders were that if he lost sight of the *Florida* in darkness he was to keep steaming in the direction he was heading.[27] Later, Emmons would write that he was "fancying himself near promotion in the morning, but gradually dwindled down to a court of inquiry at dark, when I lost sight of the enemy."[28]

The *Florida* sailed off into the night on an eastward course. The next day no sail was in sight. Maffitt opened his sea orders from Mallory. Since the blockade prevented sending captured ships back to the South, the Union ships were to be burned. Foreign-owned ships were not to be harmed. By 1863, the Northern merchants were selling their ships to foreign shipping companies to protect them. If Maffitt had doubts about the ownership, he could require the master of the vessel to sign a bond guaranteeing payment to the Confederacy after the war was over and then set the ship free. Prisoners were to be treated humanely. The prisoners' baggage was to be preserved from pillage; however, Maffitt could resupply the *Florida* from his captures. Chronometers, sailing directions, charts, and flags could be taken from captured prizes. He was not to battle Federal ships and only fight if it could not be avoided. The instructions were, as Maffitt would later write," brief and to the point, leaving much to the discretion but more to the torch."[29]

On January 19 the *Florida* was steaming seventy miles northwest of Cuba toward the Straits of Florida. A current of a knot and a half ran through the straits, eventually joining the Gulf Stream north of the Bahamas. Northern merchant ships frequently used this passage, taking advantage of the current, even though the homeward trip meant a beat to windward. As the sun rose the lookout called out that two sails were in sight: one off the lee bow and the other to windward off the stern. The two ships were hull down with only their topgallants in view. Their mainsails, topsails, and hull were below the horizon.

Chasing the one to leeward would allow the *Florida* to run up to her with a broad reach, one of the *Florida*'s better points of sailing. Steaming would be unnecessary and that would save coal. To take the one to windward by sail would mean spending the day close-hauled, running a longer distance tacking back and forth. If the *Florida* did not make the capture by nightfall, they might lose sight of the Yankee at night. Saving coal was important. The coal bunkers were low since the *Florida*'s escape from Mobile Bay. Although the one to leeward could be overhauled faster, ahead lay the western end of Cuba, where she could take refuge inside Cuban territorial waters. Maffitt ordered the helmsman to steer to windward. The coal supply would have to be replenished in Cuba.

By 2:00 P.M. the *Florida* approached a brig. The two-masted, square-rigger looked Yankee built; still the Confederates wanted to be sure. When the Confederates were about three miles astern, they ran up the American flag. The brig hoisted the American flag as well. In the quasi-fairplay world of commerce raiders, you could make the approach flying the enemy's flag, as long as possession of his ship was taken under your own flag. Otherwise, you were a pirate. All hands were called to quarters. When the *Florida* closed to within 500 yards, a shot was fired across the brig's bow—the universal sign to stop. It was hoped that the prey would think the *Florida* was a Union navy gunboat patrolling for blockade runners. The brig clewed up the sails and hove to. Two of the *Florida*'s boats were lowered for the boarding party.[30] A sailor started to raise the Confederate flag.

After a short while, one of the boats returned with the master of the vessel, Capt. John Brown, and the brig's papers. The Confederates were in luck; the brig was the New York-built *Estelle*. Her manifest showed she was bound from Santa Cruz, Cuba, to Boston with a cargo of sugar, honey, and molasses. The *Estelle* was on her maiden voyage. The brig and her cargo were valued at over $130,000.[31] Maffitt condemned the *Estelle* to be burned. John Brown, despite his famous namesake, pleaded in vain to save his ship, saying that he was not an abolitionist. He was half-owner of the *Estelle*. Brown and his crew were allowed to remove their personnel belongings. The boarding party took the *Estelle*'s flag, chronometer, charts, and part of the cargo to supplement the ship's mess.

That evening the smell of burning honey and molasses drifted across the water as the flames leaped from the *Estelle*'s deck into the rigging. Maffitt ordered the *Florida* to get underway, because the burning ship would surely attract other ships. Key West was just to the north and it was home port for the Federal cruisers.[32]

The next afternoon the alarm rattle called the crew to quarters. Off in the distance lay the port of Bahia Honda on the island of Cuba. Just ahead, off the port bow, was a warship.[33] If the *Florida* could hold her off, the

Confederates could reach the three-mile territorial limit and safety of Cuban waters. There the Union navy would not attack them, thus avoiding trouble with Spain.

Reaching the forward pivot Savez ordered the big rifle swung around on its races and loaded. The hinged gunports were swung open and the 7-inch Blakely moved forward. They tightened down the recoil compressor. Maffitt announced that she probably was the *Susquehanna.*

Savez ordered the elevating screw given one turn. The stranger was about 800 yards away. Looking across the trunnion sight, Savez satisfied himself that the first shot would hit her just at the waterline. Stepping back he pulled the lanyard taut for Maffitt to give the order. Just then the lookout called that the steamer had raised Spanish colors. Savez let the lanyard go slack.[34]

On the evening of January 20 the *Florida* steamed past Morro Castle and into Havana harbor. Although Maffitt should have sought permission before anchoring, the pro-Confederate Spanish government pressed no objections when he went ashore to make amends the next morning. The crew of the *Estelle* were sent ashore. Arrangements were made to replenish the *Florida's* coal supply.[35]

The Cubans wildly welcomed the Confederates. Bands played the "Bonnie Blue Flag" and hundreds of small boats swarmed around the *Florida.* Savez was astonished at the Cubans' enthusiasm.[36] Maffitt, feeling the ship had not been at sea long enough, refused to allow shore leave.

The United States consul Robert Schufeldt protested to the Cubans for allowing the raider admittance and sent a message, by express steamer, to Key West for Federal cruisers.[37] Schufeldt tried all his tricks to hold the *Florida,* informing Maffitt that according to international law a belligerent could not sail out until twenty-four hours after the adversary's ship had sailed. Schufeldt went on to say that there would be one U.S. ship leaving every day for some time to come. Schufeldt assailed the Cubans authorities, insisting that the *Estelle's* cargo had been Spanish property. His efforts failed when the *Florida* was allowed to finish coaling and leave. At 6:00 A.M. on January 22, the Confederates headed eastward.[38]

Twelve hours later, the USS *Wachusett* steamed into Havana harbor. Her captain, Acting Rear Adm. Charles Wilkes, had been patrolling off the Yucatan coast searching for the *Alabama* when he got word that the *Florida* had escaped from Mobile. The crew of the *Florida* were fortunate that Maffitt had fooled the *Cuyler;* otherwise, the *Cuyler* would have chased them into the guns of the *Wachusett*. Guessing that Maffitt would head for Havana, Wilkes ordered his ship to steam for Cuba. Wilkes had been given command of a West India Squadron: the *Wachusett, Dacotah, Cimarron, Sonoma, Tioga, Octorara,* and *Santiago de Cuba.* Nicknamed the "flying squadron," they cruised the Bahamas and the West Indies, searching out and destroying commerce raiders. Upon learning that he had just missed the *Florida,* Wilkes stayed in port and issued orders for his incoming squadron—deciding not to take out the *Wachusett* in pursuit.[39]

If the Federal cruisers appeared as the *Florida* steamed along the Cuban coast, Savez could appreciate his captain's cunning. She could move toward the island to hide in an inlet. Inside the three-mile limit the Federals could not attack without provoking the Spanish government, which might then recognize the Confederacy. The Confederates could meanwhile pounce on any Union merchantmen outside the territorial waters.

Territorial water protection worked both ways, however. The first ship spotted by the *Florida*'s lookout was the bark *La Coquena.* Maffitt ordered the pursuit; the Confederates fired a shot as they closed on the bark from Portland, Maine. The Downeaster just managed to make it to safety inside the three-mile limit.[40] If the *Florida* took a prize in Cuban water, the Spanish might close their ports to Confederates. The *Florida* steamed on.

At 1:00 P.M. that afternoon, the Southerners saw the brig *Windward* coming out of the port of Matanzas.[41] Sightings were taken; the *Florida* was four miles from shore. The British flag was raised. The Confederates also relied on their ship's "British" appearance. The *Windward* grew suspicious and came about. At Maffitt's order, Savez put a shot across the *Windward*'s bow. The *Windward*'s master, Capt. Richard Roberts, later complained that the Confederate flag had not been raised until after his ship had been boarded. The brig was bound for Portland, Maine, having just departed with a cargo of sugar. Her crew elected to row back to Matanzas rather than be held prisoners on the *Florida.*

Later that afternoon, the *Florida* captured the brig *Corris Ann* as she awaited a pilot boat to go into Cardenas. Capt. Frederick H. Small, like Roberts, complained that the *Florida* had the British flag flying until the Confederates came aboard.[42] The brig from Machias, Maine, was loaded with a cargo of barrel staves she had gotten at Philadelphia. The blazing *Corris Ann* drifted into the harbor at Cardenas after the Confederates torched her.

Maffitt decided to leave Cuban waters, but engine trouble caused him to turn back. Sailing around a small spit of land known as Pointe de Hicacos, the Confederates dropped anchor in the harbor of Cardenas.[43] The captives were put ashore and the engineers started to work on the engines.

As the *Florida* rode at anchor, a warship approached out of the north. The *Florida* lay tucked behind the point, palm trees casting a shadowy backdrop as the sun set. The Union ship steamed on without coming into the harbor.

Hiding, another trick Maffitt had learned as a blockade runner, impressed itself upon Savez, who found that his captain could also be his mentor. At nine o'clock, with the engines repaired, the *Florida* left.[44]

At sea on the morning of January 23, Maffitt told his officers to inspect the coal they had gotten in Havana. It did not take them long to confirm the engineers' complaint about its poor quality. The boilers could not carry more than five pounds of steam pressure, which meant that under steam the *Florida* could only make five instead of nine and a half knots. Only three days worth of coal from Mobile remained in the bunkers. The officers recommended throwing the Havana coal overboard and running to the nearest English port for more coal. Dirty work lay ahead for the crew.[45]

Three ships had been burned. The Northern press screamed for blood. Secretary Welles was furious. Northern merchants pressured him to provide protection for their ships from the *Florida* and *Alabama*. Withdrawing ships from the blockade to provide protection meant more blockade runners would get through. He reluctantly ordered the *Rhode Island*, *Lackawanna*, and *Monongahela* to sea to search for the "pirates." In Havana the captains of the "flying squadron" picked up their orders. Comdr. Thomas H. Stevens's orders told him to take the *Sonoma* to Cardenas, then to Nassau by way of the Tongue of the Ocean.[46]

The *Florida* crossed the Salt Key Banks. Ahead lay the Bahamas, a 750-mile-long archipelago with treacherous coral reefs, many just below the surface. It was night and Maffitt slowed the ship so as not to arrive before morning. When the ship motion changed, Maffitt ordered soundings taken. The leadsman yelled that they were in only four fathoms of water; Maffitt had the anchor dropped.[47] Savez learned to sense the signs of danger even in the dark.

At daylight the anchor was raised. Staying beyond the shoals south of Andros Island, Maffitt waited until he was near the Channel Rock, then turned northward. The water darkened in color as the *Florida* passed the sandbar at Queen's Channel into the deeper Tongue of the Ocean.

At 2:00 A.M. on January 26, the lookout called out that the Nassau Light on New Providence Island had come into view. At daybreak the Confederates rounded the point and steamed into Nassau harbor flying the Confederate flag on the gaff and the Confederate war pennant from the main.[48] Once more Maffitt had to apologize for not asking permission to enter the harbor. The oversight did not matter, since as in Havana, blockade runners—there were more than a dozen in the harbor—were making money for Nassau merchants. Coal was loaded, but not without protests from the American consul.

The townspeople warmly welcomed the Confederates, and visitors were permitted on board. While in Nassau, twenty-six of the sailors deserted, although only two of them were any good. Although British neutrality allowed Maffitt to reprovision and coal the *Florida*, it did not allow signing on sailors. With a little gold, Maffitt engaged the services of a black crimp who dealt in shanghaiing. The crimp supplied the Confederates with new "recruits" after the *Florida* had steamed out of British waters. The new men, who had been enticed into taking a fishing trip, found out that they would instead be fishing for Northern merchant ships.[49]

The Confederates sailed down the Tongue of the Ocean and made for Green Cay, the island where the *Florida* had been christened. At anchor off the small island, the ship was scraped and painted. Maffitt wanted to remove the last of the lampblack and whitewash.

At 4:30 A.M. on February 1 the *Florida* steamed southward through Queen's Channel.[50] The lookout sighted a steamer to starboard. Savez, who had the morning watch, notified the captain, who pronounced it an English packet bound for Nassau. He informed Savez that there was no need to raise the colors.

Savez continued watching the oncoming ship. Soon she was hull up; she was a double-ended side paddle wheel gunboat. As he watched, the stars and stripes ran up to each masthead. There was a muffled bang of a cannon fired.[51]

All hands were called to quarters; the ship was cleared for action. Maffitt ordered the *Florida* to be brought about and run back up the Tongue of the Ocean.

Maffitt told his assembled crew that Mallory's orders told him to avoid battle. "The loss of a single ship would be nothing to the enemy," said Maffitt, "but very serious to the Confederacy. Our mission is to drive the enemy's commerce off the sea, and besides, we have no port we can put into to repair any damage. But if we are overhauled we will turn and fight him."[52]

Two of the 6-inch smoothbore cannons used for firing broadside moved aft to fire through the stern ports. The aft 7-inch rifle was trained astern. The dinghy was taken inboard and the wheel unshipped to provide a clear field of fire. Auxiliary steering was rigged on the second deck.

The gunboat was now in plain view, her side paddles churning. Savez heard Maffitt say he thought she was the *Santiago de Cuba* with ten guns.[53] They watched the Federal ship move in and then fall off, to keep out of range of the *Florida*'s stern guns.

Throughout the day the *Florida* raced; past Green Cay, past Nassau and New Providence Island, and through the North East Providence Channel. Into the night the Federal, apparently hoping to run across another cruiser before moving in, hung on in the chase. Maffitt tired of the game. He informed the engineer that "the first thing we know we will fall in with another one of those fellows and they will double bank us. Now I want no more fooling, let her go."[54] The engineer opened the throttle; all sails were set. When the Confederates sped past Hole in the Wall on Abaco Island, out into the Atlantic Ocean, the Federal was hull down with only her masts showing.[55] By the next morning, no sail was in sight.

Later the Confederates learned that their pursuer was the *Sonoma* with only four guns. Maffitt was sorry then he had not gone against orders and attacked. The *Sonoma*'s captain wrote in his report that machinery kept breaking down, preventing him from getting close enough to open fire.[56]

The *Florida* sailed eastward, then picking up the Gulf Stream, turned northward toward New England. Maffitt wanted to give the Yankees "a small appreciation of war troubles."[57] Because of the Union blockade of southern ports, Maffitt kept the *Florida* well out to sea.

Off Cape Hatteras a gale blew in from the northeast. The *Florida* clawed her way northward. The ship's launch was wrenched loose from the davits and lost. As the *Florida* pitched downward, the propeller rose clear of the water. Briefly freed from the resistance of the water the twin blades spun rapidly. The upward pitch submerged the propeller and the drag of the water slowed the blades sending shudders through the ship. The repeated shocks would eventually snap the propeller off the drive shaft. Maffitt ordered the helmsman to steer southward and eastward—back toward the flying squadron. The thought of raiding to the north was, for the time being, relinquished.[58]

Once clear of the storm, the Confederates resorted to sail alone, to save coal. Since the propeller would add to the drag and slow the ship, the British designers had come up with an ingenious solution to the problem. They had encased the propeller in a frame. The propeller in its frame could be decoupled from the drive shaft and raised with a hoist into a stowage well within the ship.[59]

Around 8:00 P.M. on February 5, the lookout spotted a steamer longer than the *Florida* through the mist. The stranger changed course and headed for them. Maffitt reached into his bag of blockade-running tricks. The twin funnels were lowered and all lights were put out except a single outboard lantern. The *Florida* turned head-on toward the approaching steamer. With luck the intruder would be fooled into believing the *Florida* was a West India trader. The stranger turned out to be the USS *Vanderbilt*, with fourteen guns;[60] her bow alone was enough to sink the *Florida*.

Hailed and asked if she had seen a steamer go by, Maffitt answered, "Yes and going at great speed right astern."[61] There was no reply. The *Vanderbilt* finally picked up speed and charged off into the darkness. Savez learned from Maffitt what quick thinking could do.

Maffitt set a course farther into the Atlantic as he headed toward the Windward Islands. The time was used to repair the damage from the storm.

Three days later the lookout sighted a fore-and-aft schooner. As the *Florida* approached, the schooner hoisted the British ensign and saluted them. Disappointed, the Confederates sailed on.[62]

On February 12 the first bell of the forenoon watch had just sounded when the lookout sighted sails off the lee beam. The *Florida* came about and gave chase. All hands were called aloft. Booms were run out the yards and the starboard-studding sails spread. By midmorning only the ship's royals could be seen by the lookout. The propeller was lowered and the steam engine was started. The *Florida* at last closed on the ship. The Confederates were going to capture a prize on Lincoln's birthday.[63]

The quarry was a clipper, flying the American flag. When the *Florida* closed to within three miles, Savez fired a shell with a thirty-second fuse. The shot splashed one and a half ship's length astern on the port side.

The clipper clewed up and backed the yards. As the *Florida* approached, Maffitt ordered the Confederate flag raised. He then hailed the clipper asking where she was bound and ordered her to strike the colors. When she did not reply, Maffitt had Savez fire a second shot. The clipper lowered her flag.[64]

Savez was told to lead the boarding party. The ship's cutter was lowered; Savez took his place in the stern and ordered his charges to make for the prey.[65]

The name above the carved trail boards read *Jacob Bell*. The clipper was a medium rather than sharp model, yet capable of good sustained speed, having previously made the run from New York to Bombay, India, in seventy-eight days.[66] The *Jacob Bell* had set sail from Foochow, China, bound for New York with 1,380 tons of tea and 10,000 boxes of firecrackers, matting, camphor, and cassia. The cargo was valued at one and a half million dollars, the most expensive prize captured by any Confederate raider during the war. The owners of the cargo were A. A. Low and Brothers of Brooklyn Heights, well-known for their radical abolitionist views.

The Confederates started moving the *Jacob Bell's* forty-one crew and passengers to the *Florida*. A heavy sea slowed the transfer. Once on deck, the captives were shackled, since that many prisoners might try to seize the *Florida*.

Not everyone from the *Jacob Bell* came up the ladder. The *Florida's* block and tackle boom hoisted a wide rattan chair out of the ship's cutter. In the chair were two women passengers: the pregnant wife of the captain of the *Jacob Bell,* Mrs. Charles Frisbee, and Mrs. H. Dwight Williams, the wife of a customhouse officer in Swatow, China. Mrs. Williams, who had a falling out with Mrs. Frisbee and was not speaking to her, denounced her captors as pirates. Maffitt gave the women the use of his cabin and wrote in his diary that Mrs. Frisbee seemed pleasant enough, but Mrs. Williams was something of a tartar.[67]

Mrs. Williams handed Maffitt a list of the baggage she wanted brought aboard the *Florida*. Maffitt told her that if he took all of her things his sailors would not have room to work the guns. He finally did allow some boxes to be brought aboard.

The transfer extended into the following day. Maffitt also allowed his officers and crew to help themselves to the *Jacob Bell's* cargo, since it would otherwise be burned. They brought back silver, china, India sweetmeats, cases of claret, and spools of thread. Savez decided that his bunk could use some cotton sheets, and the wardroom could also use the table linens and a cake basket. When Mrs. Williams recognized her things, she glared daggers at him.

Mrs. Williams later wrote a book in which she scathed Maffitt for allowing the pillage of her property. Savez was the only officer mentioned by name.[68]

By two o'clock flames shot up the rigging of the *Jacob Bell*. Sails bursting into flames tore loose from their spars. The 10,000 cases of firecrackers
exploded, making the dying ship sound like a floating Fourth of July. Savez
lamented the destruction of a beautiful ship.[69] Everyone silently watched
the *Jacob Bell's* death.

When the Yankees learned of the loss of the *Jacob Bell,* they demanded
that the Union navy catch Maffitt and hang him from a yardarm.[70] Northern merchantmen were feeling the bite of the raiders. Insurance rates skyrocketed. American ships were being sold or transferred to foreign registry.

Aboard the *Florida* a cry of "sail ho" sent the Confederates to quarters.
The chase proved fruitless; the ship turned out to be the French brig *Leonce
Lacoste.*

On February 15 another sail was sighted. The *Florida* chased the ship
the whole day, into the night. With darkness the prey eluded the gray wolf.
The *Florida* finally overhauled the Danish bark *Morning Star.* The Danes
were bound for St. Thomas and willing to take the entire party from the
Jacob Bell.[71]

The capture of the *Jacob Bell* had proven the necessity for coal. The
Florida, now low on fuel, had last coaled in Nassau and by British regulations could not take on more coal from a British port for three months.
That meant going to the Danish port of St. Thomas or French Martinique.
Maffitt surmised Union ships would be watching both ports and decided to
try his luck in the British port of Bridgetown, Barbados. He guessed right
because the *Oneida* and *Cuyler* were headed for Martinique. Admiral Wilkes
was in St. Thomas having transferred his command from the *Wachusett* to
Vanderbilt. Upon the arrival of the *Morning Star,* Wilkes left Puerto Rico.
Next, he planned to steam to Barbados.[72]

At Bridgetown the crew of the *Florida* loaded coal all that day and into
the next. Maffitt had convinced the governor James Walker that most of the
coal he had gotten at Nassau had been used during the storm. Since the
storm was an act of God and not the Yankees, he should be allowed at least
enough coal to enable the *Florida* to move well to windward of the Federal
cruisers.

The United States consul Edward Throwbridge protested to the British
government. He also wanted the *Florida* detained until the two American
merchant ships could leave. The British allowed the Confederates time to
finish coaling, but did make the Confederates stay twenty-four hours to
allow the merchantmen a chance to escape. On February 25 the *Florida* left

Bridgetown on a southerly course. Unknown to the authorities, ten men joined the *Florida*'s crew in violation of British neutrality.

While Maffitt had been ashore he had hinted that he wanted to capture a California steamer bound for New York from Panama with gold. The trick worked. When Wilkes arrived he took the bait and ordered the flying squadron off in the wrong direction.[73]

On the *Florida* one morning Isaac White crawled out beyond the bulwark onto the cathead to unshackle the cable from the anchor. The *Florida* pitched up and down; suddenly White slipped, screamed, and fell into the water. Unable to swim, he sank before he could be rescued.[74] Everyone was stunned; White was the first man lost on the voyage.

Encountering strong head winds and heavy seas, Maffitt turned the *Florida* northward to run with the wind and sail along fifty-four degrees west longitude. This course would take her across the shipping lanes that came up from Cape Horn and Cape Hope. The Confederates would also stay to the east of the patrolling Union cruisers. With good wind the *Florida* picked up speed. During one day's run the Confederates logged one hundred and thirty-seven miles.[75]

Savez was still learning from Maffitt. To survive as a raider meant you not only had to stay a jump ahead of the Yankees, but you had to go where the picking was good.

On March 6 the *Florida* captured a clipper called the *Star of Peace* bound from Calcutta to Boston. The *Star of Peace* was carrying a cargo of saltpeter for powder mills, destined to be used against Southern soldiers. Once burning, the ship was used as a gunnery target. After the drill was over, the *Florida* sailed off. At nine o'clock that night, the flames reached the saltpeter. Even though the *Florida* was at least twenty miles away her sails were illuminated by the fire's light.[76]

On March 12 the *Florida* turned eastward. The Confederates, sighting a ship, put on more sail, only to discover their target was an Englishman. But the day was not a loss. A schooner was later sighted and when the *Florida* raised the British flag, the *Aldebaran* hoisted the American flag. The *Aldebaran* had sailed out of New York for Marenham, Brazil, with a cargo of flour, beef, pork, hams, live lobsters barreled in ice, brandy, rum, whiskey, wine, and clocks—Yankee "fixins" as Maffitt would later record. Savez chuckled when he heard that the master of the vessel, Capt. Robert Hand, had protested, saying he was a true Southern Democrat who thought the war was to battle for the Negro and not the Union. The cargo improved the ship's mess. That night the *Aldebaran* died a fiery death.[77]

The *Florida* turned and ran eastward. From the noon time sextant observations, Savez realized that the *Florida* was north of the homeward track of the *Plymouth*. The *Florida* sailed through the Sargasso Sea. Mats of olive-colored clustered seaweed floated on the surface. Ancient mariners feared this area, thinking their ships would become entangled in the sea-weed, never to be released. Ghostly wrecks of galleons and pirate ships were thought to lie just below the surface of the remarkably clear deep blue water. With steam propulsion the *Florida* moved on, oblivious of the dense seaweed and ghosts.

To break the monotony of the daily routine of drill, swabbing deck, scraping, and painting, Maffitt would occasionally "splice the main brace." The crew appreciated the grog. Sometimes they entertained their captives with a rousing chorus of "I wish I had a Bowie knife to kill old Lincoln and his wife."[78]

Every ship stopped was European owned. Since the *Florida* had become crowded with manacled prisoners, the Confederates needed a ship to remove them. The English brig *Runnymede*, bound from Pernambuco, Brazil, to Grennock, Scotland, took eleven prisoners. The master of the *Larra Mara* refused to take anyone to Liverpool.

On March 25 the *Florida* stopped an Austrian bark belonging to the Cunard Royal Mail Steamship Line. The bark was bound for New York with a load of coal. Maffitt closely inspected the ship's papers. With some misgivings, he decided that the coal was British property. He suspected that northern merchants were transferring registry of their cargoes to foreign shipping lines. Maffitt released the bark after three prisoners were put on board with some provisions and water.

During this time two of the prisoners from the *Star of Peace* decided to enlist as crew of the *Florida*.[79] Besides being released from their shackles, there was a good reason to enlist: money. After the war, crews of the raiders could claim a share of the prize money from the Confederate government amounting to the value of the captured ships. In any event, sailors in the mid-nineteenth century were citizens of the world rather than a country.

When the *Florida* was three hundred and forty miles south-southeast of the Azores, Maffitt decided he had gone far enough eastward. Ahead lay Madeira and the Canary Islands, where the Union navy might be steaming.

After a three-hour chase, the *Florida* overhauled the Federal bark *Lapwing* on March 28. The bark was bound from Boston to Batavia on the island of Java. Her cargo consisted of furniture, lumber, provisions, and sixty tons of anthracite coal.

Maffitt decided that rather than burn the *Lapwing,* he would use the bark as a raider. With her square-rigged fore and mainmast, plus the fore-and-aft mizzen, the *Lapwing* looked New England built. First Lt. Samuel W. Averett was given command. The bark was renamed the *Oreto II* and a 12-pounder boat howitzer with ammunition was provided for armament. Maffitt instructed Averett to stay close to the *Florida.* If the ships became separated, however, two rendezvous locations were given. Savez, the assistant surgeon, a midshipman, and fifteen men were sent over with Averett to the *Oreto II.* Coaling the *Florida* was postponed until the next day.

The next day, after supervising the coaling, Savez returned to the *Florida* and the *Oreto II* sailed off. At 4:00 P.M. on March 30, the *Florida* got a signal from the *Oreto II* that a ship was ahead.[80] The *Florida* steamed past her consort and overhauled the bark *M. J. Colcord.* The officers had been taking turns leading the boarding party; the bark was Savez's turn.

When Savez went aboard the bark, her master handed him a roll of newspapers and asked his steamer's name. Savez lied that it was the USS *Iroquois* and asked for the latest news of the war.

The man replied that Gen. Ambrose E. Burnside had been shipped out of his boots at Fredericksburg, and that Southerners fought like devils. Their privateers were running Northern ships off the ocean. He'd heard of a mate to the *Alabama* called the *Florida,* but he thought he was far enough to the southward to be clear of her.

Savez thanked the captain for the news and papers and informed him that he and his crew were now under the guns of the *Florida.*[81] The captain's face dropped as he saw the Confederate flag being run up on the privateer.

The bark was loaded with flour and bacon from New York and bound for Cape Town. Since night had fallen, her destruction was put off until the next day. In the morning, while the Confederates were unloading the *M. J. Colcord,* the Danish brig *Christian* sailed up. Maffitt sent off all his prisoners, giving the Dane liberal provisions. Since the *Christian* was bound for Santa Cruz, California, it would take time for the North to find out the *Florida* was headed toward the South Atlantic.

The first two weeks of April were exasperating. The *Florida* lost sight of the *Oreto II* after the *M. J. Colcord* was burned. All the ships hailed were foreign owned.

Just before noon on April 12 the *Florida* came upon Saint Paul's Rocks, the rocky islet extending fifty feet above the surface. Maffitt sent a boat over to take sextant sightings so he could correct the ship's chronometer, but the sea was too rough to land.[82]

Two days later the *Florida* came across the *Oreto II,* which had also had bad luck. Maffitt was happy because the *Florida*'s coal bunkers were almost empty.

The *Florida* started coaling, a task that required manhandling buckets of coal out of the hold of the *Oreto II* and up to the deck. The buckets were then lowered into the ship's boats and rowed over to the *Florida*. There they were hoisted up on board and taken down to the bunkers. The Confederates spent two days at the Equator hauling coal.[83]

On April 17 the *Florida*'s gunners fired a shot at the clipper *Commonwealth,* which clewed her sails and hove to. She had left New York for San Francisco with $60,000 worth of cargo for the Federal government. Maffitt took what he could use, then torched the ship. Part of her cargo was sailors' clothes destined for Mare Island Navy Yard, California. Savez and his shipmates exchanged uniforms courtesy of Gideon Welles.

Six days later, the Confederates captured the Baltimore bark *Henrietta.*[84] The bark's manifest showed her to be loaded with 3,250 barrels of flour, 600 kegs of lard, and thousands of candles, all for delivery to Rio de Janeiro. The master of the vessel was a Downeaster named George Brown, who proclaimed that the Bible approved slavery and that he strongly supported southern rights. As greasy flames roared, Brown dryly remarked, "Doesn't she burn pretty? She belongs to Mr. Whitridge. He is a great Union man."[85]

On April 25 the *Florida* pounced on the clipper *Oneida,* bound for New York from Shanghai with a million dollars worth of tea and cargo.[86] Jessie F. Potter, the *Oneida*'s New Bedford master, protested to no avail that the *Florida* was flying the British flag when he was stopped. Maffitt gave each member of the *Florida*'s crew two bolts of Chinese silk.

The *Florida* was proving her worth. Maffitt wrote a letter to John D. Bullock saying that the *Florida* had done six million dollars worth of damage. The expenditures for the *Florida* were £45,628. Insurance rates skyrocketed. Cargo was sent in foreign ships while American ships were either sold or left at anchorage in port.

As the *Oneida* was still burning, the *Florida*'s lookout spotted another sail. This proved to be the French bark *Bremontier* bound from Bordeaux to New Caledonia. With some reluctance the bark's master, Captain Destremeaux, agreed to take prisoners to Pernambuco.[87]

The *Florida* dropped anchor off the island of Fernando de Noronha on April 28. There, the Confederates learned they had missed the *Alabama* by six days. Semmes had cruised the same waters as the *Florida*, which accounted for the absence of Northern ships. Part of the crew was given shore leave while the rest worked on overhauling the machinery and cleaning the boilers. The *Florida*'s stay at the island was shorter than Maffitt wished. On May 1, a Brazilian warship arrived with a new governor. The old governor had been too generous to the *Alabama*. Since Brazil was doing a good trading business with the United States, the *Florida* was ordered to leave. On the way out, the *Florida* met the *Oreto II*. Maffitt instructed Averett to go eighty miles to the west and meet him at the uninhabited island of Rocas. After coaling, the two ships parted.[88]

On the night of May 5, the *Florida* was heading toward Cape San Roque. Maffitt struck up a conversion with Savez, who was taking his turn on watch. Maffitt asked Savez what he thought of going to the East Indies. Savez could not see how burning ships in a remote ocean would affect the war. He said he'd rather resign and join the army.[89]

Maffitt changed his mind about going to the East Indies. He confided that although he hoped to go north in the *Florida*, believing much damage could be done there in a short time, he hated to abandon the southern cruise at the present time.[90] Savez told his captain about his plans. Maffitt finally agreed to give Savez the first small ship captured.

When the morning broke, the lookout sighted a sail to leeward heading north. The *Florida* gave chase and soon was within cannon shot. The brig *Clarence* hove to and Savez went on board.

Savez examined the ship's papers in the captain's cabin and found that the cargo was coffee being taken from Rio de Janeiro to Baltimore. The *Clarence* was about 250 tons and stoutly built with a black hull, little sheer, a half elliptical stern, and a short bowsprit. Her rigging was a hermaphrodite: half schooner, half brig—with no sails above the main topmast staysail. The main boom did not extend past the taffrail. The *Clarence* was what Savez wanted for a raider. Grabbing a blank page and a pen, Savez wrote a proposal to Maffitt, proofread it, and corrected a few mistakes. Taking the brig's papers and captain back to Maffitt, he there presented his proposal:[91]

> *C.S.[S.] Steamer "Florida"*
> *At Sea, May 6, 1863*

Sir: I proposed [sic] to take the brig which we have just captured and with a crew of twenty men to proceed to Hampton Roads and cut out a gunboat or steamer of the enemy.

As I would be in possession of the brig's paper and as the crew would not be large enough to excite suspicion, there can be no doubt of passing Fort Monroe successfully. Once in the Roads I would be prepared to avail myself of any circumstance which might present for gaining the deck of an enemy's vessel. If it was found impossible to board a gunboat or merchant steamer, it would be possible to fire the shipping at Baltimore.

If you think proper to accede to my proposal, I beg that you will allow me to take Mr. E. H. Brown and one of the firemen with me. Mr. Brown might be spared from his ship as his health is bad and you could obtain another engineer at Pernambuco.

> *Very respectfully*
> *your ob't serv't*
> *C. W. Read*
> *2d Lieutenant, C.S.N.*[92]

Returning to the *Florida*, Read handed his letter to his captain and reminded him of his promise. Maffitt told the first lieutenant to call all hands and ask for volunteers for a crew. The entire crew volunteered, so Savez had to pick. For officers besides Brown, Savez selected John E. Billups, Nicholas B. Pryde, and J. W. Matherson. The recruiting was interrupted temporarily when a sail was sighted to windward. The *Florida* gave chase, but the ship proved to be the *Oreto II*. By the time they had returned to the *Clarence*, Savez had a crew of twenty-two in all.

Maffitt also gave Savez a 12-pounder boat howitzer with its ammunition, rifles, pistols, cutlasses, and provisions. He then wrote a commissioning letter to keep Savez from being held as a pirate if he was captured:[93]

> *C.S.[S.] Steamer "Florida"*
> *At Sea, May 6, 1863*

Sir: Your proposition of this date has been duly considered—under such advisement as the gravity of the case demands. The conclusion reached is that you may meet with success by centering your views upon Hampton Roads. The Sumpter *(a Cromwell steamer) is now a kind of flagship anchored off Hampton Bar and at midnight might be carried by boarding. If you find that impractical, the large quantity of shipping at the Fort or in Norfolk could be fired and you and your crew escape to Burrell's [Burnell's] Bay, thence making your way safely to the Confederate lines.*

The proposition evinces on your part patriotic devotion to the cause of your country, and this is certainly the time when all our best exertions should be made to harm the common enemy and confuse them with attacks from all unexpected quarters. I agree to your request and will not hamper you with instructions.

Act for the best and God speed you. If success attends the effort, you will deserve the fullest consideration of the Department and it will be my pleasure to urge a just recognition of the same.

Under all circumstances you will receive from me the fullest justice for the intent and public spirit that influences the proposal.

I give you a howitzer and ammunition that you may have the means of capture if an opportunity offers in route.

Wishing you success and a full reward for the same,

I am yours very truly,
J. N. Maffitt C.S.N.
Lieut. Commd. C.S.S. Florida[94]

Savez thanked Maffitt and told him that he was going to officially rename the *Clarence* "Confederate States Corvette *Florida No. 2.*" The men and supplies were transferred to the *Clarence.* Once on board Savez had the crew line the rail, tip their hats, and give three cheers. As the *Clarence* sailed past the *Florida,* she dipped her flag, then sailed southward and westward.

Savez watched until the *Florida* was hull down. Thirteen days before his twenty-third birthday, he had his own command. Savez was the youngest man to command a commerce raider. With a handful of men and a small ship, he, like his mentor, was determined to give the North "a small appreciation of the war's troubles."[95]

CHAPTER SEVEN

RAISING CAIN AND
THE PRICE OF FISH

As the lookout struck the ship's bell at noon, Savez peered through the sextant's telescope. Turning the sextant to one side, he looked at the instrument's reading. He did not need the chart to tell him the *Clarence* sailed slowly on a northwesterly course toward the Caribbean. Somehow in the excitement of getting his own command he had misinterpreted the ship's log. Even with thirteen knots blowing, the *Clarence* lumbered along, her bottom fouled from barnacles and her copper plating working loose. With all sails set and a half gale of wind astern, the *Clarence* would take all day to pass a drifting bunch of seaweed.[1]

The crew had started to grumble: A. L. Drayton wrote his complaints in his diary. The *Clarence,* having been outfitted in Baltimore, had poor provisions. The ship's hold held only two barrels of pork, a barrel of bread, two barrels of flour, and a large tank of water. The *Florida's* boarding crew had made off with the pots and pans.

Savez had not told anyone where he was taking the *Clarence.* Some thought Barbados; some were sure it was the coast of Brazil to capture a steamer; and some were convinced they were returning to the Confederacy.[2] One night Savez heard one sailor ask another if he had any idea where they were going. The sailor spat tobacco juice to leeward and replied, "Damn me, if I don't believe we're carrying the mail!"[3]

To keep the crew busy, Savez had put them to work making Quaker guns. Spare spars were cut and painted black to look like guns. Carriages were built for the wooden cannons. Gun ports were cut in the bulwarks. When finished, the *Clarence's* new "armament" consisted of two Parrotts, a nine-pounder on the quarterdeck, two 24-pounders amidships, and two

32-pounders in the waist. According to Drayton it was "Quite a formidable battery, all wood."[4]

Savez then ordered pistol practice for the crew. A target was set up on the anchor. Since the anchor was secured on the cathead, the shots would go over the side and not into the ship. At least that was the theory. The Confederates had had little practice and the *Clarence's* gentle rolling did not help their aim. One sailor hit the foresail. Another hit the anchor's fluke; the ball ricocheted back bruising his shipmate on the shoulder. Drayton concluded that some of them could not hit a barn door.

Eighteen days after leaving the *Florida,* the *Clarence* finally sighted a ship that she was able to overtake. Savez had the crew called to quarters. As the bark drew near, Savez could see the name on the transom: *Forrester.*[5] He then ordered a blank cartridge fired. The bark ran up the Union Jack and kept on going. Savez next ordered a shot put across her bow, after which the Englishman hove to. Savez put Brown in charge of the boarding party and sent them over to the bark.

As soon as Brown climbed over the rail of the bark, the master of the English vessel challenged their firing on the Union Jack. Brown pointed to the American flag flying from the *Clarence* and claimed to be a master of the ocean.

Brown then offered to buy or exchange cabin stores. When the Englishman refused, Brown begged for help for his scurvied crew. The master again refused and started to get his ship out of the stays and put her back on course.

Brown asked to be allowed to safely leave. When the master replied that he could go, Brown signaled Savez, who had the American flag lowered and the Confederate flag raised.

When the master saw the Stars and Bars, he threw his arms around Brown and offered him the "whole damned ship!" He then called the steward to break out the stores.

Brown said that was not necessary; he wanted only newspapers to catch up on the war. After the captain got the newspapers, Brown offered him a bag of coffee for every day of the year for his courtesy, if he would send over his cutters to the *Clarence.*

The British captain was so pleased with the coffee he reciprocated with two barrels of "'alf and 'alf" with the advice to drink it in moderation, and a packet of temperance tracts. As the *Clarence* sailed on, the British ship dipped her colors and bade them Godspeed and success to the Southern cause.[6]

Savez set a course for the Windward Islands. The cry "Land Ho!" came from the masthead. As the *Clarence* sailed closer, the lookout spotted a sloop of war, flying the American flag, at anchor. Savez hoisted the Stars and Stripes and kept on sailing. The flying squadron was still around.

Leaving the Windward Islands behind, the *Clarence* continued her northwest course until she was off the Southern coast. Savez then headed northward. Like Maffitt, he stayed eastward of the Union blockaders. When the wind shifted around to the north, the *Clarence* tacked back and forth, beating to windward. All the sails sighted were southbound. Savez would order the chase to no avail.[7]

The crew continued guessing the *Clarence's* destination. Brazil and Barbados had been replaced with Liverpool, England. Someone had it on good authority from the quartermaster that they were going to rendezvous with the *Florida.* Drayton continued complaining in his diary about his shipmates, Savez, and being homesick.[8]

On the night of June 6, under clear skies, Savez saw a flickering light to the northwest, the Cape Hatteras Lighthouse.[9] Since Union troops had captured and occupied Hatteras Inlet in 1861, the North had to keep the lighthouse lit to warn mariners of the dreaded Diamond Shoals. Underwater sandbars, extending from the lighthouse nine miles out to sea, had caused shipwrecks since the sixteenth century. The Outer Banks deserved the name "Graveyard of the Atlantic."

At dawn Savez sighted eight sails on the horizon, all except one to leeward. Savez had a chance for the one upwind. He ordered the helmsman to bring the ship up a point, which brought the *Clarence* toward the approaching bark.

"All hands to quarters!" rang out through the *Clarence.* Under the command of Nicholas Pryde, captain of the gun, the gun crew pulled the tarpaulin off the 12-pounder howitzer. The tompion was removed and the barrel was sponged and loaded.

Savez noticed the Yankee, like the *Clarence,* carried a hermaphrodite rig. That meant she could maneuver quickly and she was running with the wind. Savez plotted the intersection of the two courses. He had to bring his ship to just off the Yankee's bow. If the bark would not heave to when fired upon, she would be forced to turn to avoid collision and turning would slow her down. The bark would have to continue to turn about to maintain her southerly course. In the meantime, the *Clarence* would fall off the wind and need to turn and run parallel to the prey. Savez would then have the Yankee in howitzer range. Savez knew if he miscalculated the intersection, the bark would sail past him as he came about. If the Yankee had a green crew, the ships would collide.

Savez had the Confederate flag hoisted up the gaff. Without taking his eyes off the rapidly closing bark, he told the helmsman to hold the wheel steady. Savez ordered Pryde to fire. The howitzer's one-pound powder charge did not make an impressive noise. As the gun's white smoke swept away to leeward, the bark's crew started to clew up the sails to bring their ship about.

Savez's crew braced the headsails around and let out the mainsail's sheet. The helmsman turned the wheel, and the *Clarence's* bow swung to port. The oncoming waves now broke on the ship's starboard side and then on the stern as the Confederates ran before the wind.

The bark's crew were setting the studding sails; she was going to run for it. Savez called to Pryde to fire again. The two ships were less than forty feet apart. This time the cannon ball crossed over the bark's bowsprit. The bark clewed up the headsails and hove to.

One month after leaving the *Florida,* Savez had made his first capture. The bark proved to be the *Whistling Wind,* bound for New Orleans from Philadelphia with $14,800 worth of coal for Farragut's squadron. The bark's crew, papers, and nautical instruments were removed, and then the ship was burned.[10]

The following day Savez captured the schooner *Alfred H. Partridge* out of New York bound for Matamoros, Mexico. The schooner's papers showed she was loaded with arms and clothing for the Confederate forces in Texas. Some Yankee merchantmen were running around their own blockade to neutral Mexican ports to sell supplies to the Confederacy. Savez let the ship go, but took a bond from the master of the vessel for $5,000 to deliver the cargo to the citizens of the Confederate States. The schooner's master did deliver to Matamoros, probably with more of a desire to make money than fear of paying a bond.

On June 9 a sail came down on the *Clarence.* The brig *Mary Alvina* was soon afire. She had been bound from Boston with a load of commissary stores that were destined never to be delivered to New Orleans.[11]

Savez continued sailing northward. He needed to clear the Outer Banks because the Federal navy steamed through these waters going to and from their blockading stations. A burning ship would attract the warships.

The next night Savez allowed the captured crews up on deck. A warship loomed up from windward. Savez softly called out instructions: Dismount the howitzer and Quaker guns and tumble them into the hold; take the log of the *Mary Alvina* and make an entry for the day; place a guard by the prisoners and order them to remain quiet.

The steamer came abreast of the *Clarence,* but Savez could not make out her name when the stranger hailed. He identified his ship as the American brig *Mary Alvina,* bound from Boston for New Orleans with stores for the blockading fleet.

Savez whispered to quartermaster Billups to take the prisoners below deck. Savez then dashed down to the captain's cabin. After hiding his carpetbag, he put on oilskins and a sou'wester jacket to hide his faded uniform.

An officer and ten armed sailors boarded. The officer asked to see the ship's papers. Savez escorted the officer to the cabin and brought out the log and manifest. The officer, one of Savez's Annapolis classmates, seemed more interested in the log than Savez, who had grown a goatee and bushy mustache since leaving the Academy. To distract him from the last entry, Savez offered him a glass of sherry.

Satisfied that all was in order, the officer apologized to Savez for delaying the delivery of Admiral Farragut's supplies and left. Savez was glad the boat crew had not passed by the brig's stern, where the name *Clarence* was written across the transom.

That night Savez examined the newspapers he had taken from the *Whistling Wind* and *Mary Alvina.* Savez discovered that it would be impossible to sail into Hampton Roads. No ships were allowed in unless they were carrying supplies for the U.S. Government and then only if they were boarded and searched. Sentries were on guard on the wharves. Ships at the docks, under the guns of Fort Monroe, were also guarded by a gunboat. The news corroborated what he had learned from his prisoners. Unable to carry out the type of raid he had planned, Savez decided to take the *Clarence* northward and look for a faster ship with which he could meet up with Maffitt, if the *Florida* came north.[12]

The search meant that the prisoners had to stay on board until Savez got his new ship. It would be days before the three ships he had burned would be missed, giving him more time to raid without the Federals looking for him. Once the prisoners were released to another ship, the Union navy would come out in force.

On the morning of June 12, the *Clarence* lumbered along about forty miles off Capes Henry and Charles. Beyond the capes lay Hampton Roads and the Gosport Navy Yard, the largest naval base in the country.

A smoky fog hung just above the water. Coming through the mist to stern was a black-hulled bark with a rusty-colored set of sails. By her appearance, she was New England built. The quickness of her approach showed she was a faster sailor than the *Clarence* and her captain might try to run for it. The howitzer had a range of less than three-quarters of a mile and the cannon ball was the size of a softball.

Savez had an idea. The Yankee would not pass him by if the *Clarence* was in distress so he ordered the American flag hoisted upside down. The ruse worked; the bark came up to the *Clarence* and hove to.

The *Clarence*'s boat was launched. Savez pushed the tiller over as the crew rowed toward the bark. She was three-masted and about 400 tons—a good-sized replacement for the *Clarence*. The copper plating on her bottom could be seen as well as the name *Tacony* written across her stern.[13]

Savez told the bark's master, Capt. William G. Munday, that he was fifty-five days out of Rio de Janeiro, bound for Baltimore, and entirely out of water. Saying he would assist in passing it to the boat, Savez waited until Munday started to take off the aft hatch, then pulled his revolver, leveled it at the captain's head, and told him he was a prize of the Confederate States Navy.[14]

A check of the log showed she was six days out of Port Royal, South Carolina, bound for Philadelphia under ballast. The *Tacony* had gone to Port Royal to deliver coal to the Federal navy. The log showed the *Tacony* had made one hundred and eighty miles on one day's sail. Savez decided to replace the *Clarence* with the *Tacony*.

Leaving part of the boarding party, Savez returned to the *Clarence*. When a schooner was sighted, Savez ordered Pryde to point the howitzer at the approaching ship. The schooner's master yelled that he would surrender.

The intruder was the *M. A. Shindler* who, like the *Tacony*, had delivered coal to Port Royal and was in ballast, bound for Philadelphia. Savez decided to burn the schooner and then returned to transferring his command to the *Tacony*.[15]

First to be moved was the howitzer. Tackle was rigged and a sling was fitted around the gun. The lifting whip and steadying lines were hooked to the sling. Under the eye of Boatswain's Mate James Matherson, the cannon was hoisted up and swung out over the bulwark. The crewmen on the whip line lowered the gun, while those on the steadying lines tried to prevent it from swinging. The trickiest part came as the 760-pound cannon reached the boat alongside, where waves rose and fell three feet. If the gun came down too slowly, its swing could smash a boat crew against the ship's hull. Too fast and the gun would plummet through the bottom of the boat, sinking it. When the gun was a few feet above the boat, Matherson raised his arms and clinched his fists to signal the crew to stop lowering. Just as the boat started to rise on the wave he gave a thumbs-down. After securing the howitzer, the boat crew started rowing for the *Tacony*.

Savez turned his attention to a nearby schooner, which had changed course and was heading his way. Savez knew he would have to rely on a Quaker gun and ordered the gunner to run out a wooden cannon. He motioned him to hold the firing lanyard up in the air so the schooner's master would be sure to see it.

The master jumped to the cabin top, waved his arms and screamed, "For God's sake don't shoot! I surrender!" Savez ordered him to come aboard with his papers.

As he came on board he was astonished when he saw the cannon. "Yes, it doesn't take but a wooden gun to catch fools such as you, captain," said Savez. "Your curiosity has done you in. You were a good six miles to windward before you altered course, but now you've run into the lion's mouth and will have to take the consequences!"[16]

The schooner *Kate Stewart* was in ballast bound for Philadelphia from Key West. Savez had captured three Philadelphia-bound ships before noon.

Savez had taken about seventy-five prisoners; some from the *Kate Stewart* were women. Neither the *Tacony* nor the *Clarence* was big enough to keep all of them. He also did not have enough food for everyone. Since the *Kate Stewart* was in the poorest shape, he decided to use the schooner to get rid of his prisoners. First, Savez had the schooner's master sign a bond for $7,000 payable to the president of the Confederacy thirty days after the signing of a peace treaty.

After transferring his men aboard the *Tacony* and his prisoners onto the *Kate Stewart*, Savez set fire to the *Clarence* and the *M. A. Shindler*. Once released, the *Kate Stewart* sailed off on a port tack for Cape Henlopen and Delaware Bay. The schooner headed home to Philadelphia rather than going the shorter route to Hampton Roads, which bought the Confederates more time before they were discovered. Savez ordered a northeast course set and renamed the *Tacony "Florida No. 2."*[17]

Savez read Maffitt's instructions to the crew and cautioned them that they might be taken prisoner to keep them vigilant. Drayton would write, "The plan as laid down was a bold one, but I must say a reckless one, and I cannot approve of it; was impossible for any one to conceive it, and had we been successful the Yankees would have opened their eyes and thought h—l was certainly broke loose."[18]

The sails of a brig were sighted to starboard. The chase was on again. As the *Tacony* neared her prey, the Confederates had a scare. A Union sloop of war passed close by with the ship's officers eyeing the *Tacony* suspiciously, then sailing on.

Later, when the *Tacony* had overtaken the brig, Savez ordered the captain aboard. Savez later wrote that the captain was the maddest man he ever met.

The captain asked Savez if he had seen the man-of-war that just passed; to which Savez replied that he had, but it was the captain's brig he was after.

The captain responded: "When that man-of-war swab hears that you have captured me he'll come here, and if you don't go away he'll catch you sure. But if you go twenty miles from here he'll never find you!"[19]

The brig was the *Arabella* bound from Aspinwall, Panama, to New York. Since the cargo was neutral, Savez was forced to release the *Arabella*. Savez made the master write out a bond payable for $30,000 thirty days after peace.

That night Savez made an entry in the *Tacony*'s log. If another cruiser stopped them, he might not have a chance to make false entries. He carefully copied the penmanship, hoping any Federal officer would not notice the slight difference.[20]

In twenty hours Savez had captured four ships, replaced the *Clarence* with a fast bark, picked up more navigational charts, and gotten rid of his prisoners, all within forty miles of the armada of Federal ships at Hampton Roads.

Welles's day was ruined. The Saturday had started out well enough. He had taken a break from his schedule to go to a concert by the Marine Band in Lafayette Square, across from the White House. At 5:00 P.M. the telegram arrived:[21]

Philadelphia, June 13, 1863

The pirate *Clarence* captured within sight of Cape Henry yesterday morning, brig *Shindler,* schooner *Kate Stewart,* and bark *Tacony* of this port. They are using the *Tacony* for pirating further.

E. A. Souder & Co.

After Captain Munday had put the *Kate Stewart* into port in New Jersey, he boarded the train to Philadelphia and rushed to his company's office. The shipowners in turn fired off a telegram to Washington.

Welles had the largest navy to date in the United States' history at his disposal, but he had to act fast before the newspapers picked up the story. He would notify Hampton Roads, Philadelphia, New York, Boston, everywhere to catch the pirate.

Telegraph messages went out to charter or seize any fast vessels that could be sent to sea within forty-eight hours to search for the *Tacony* for two weeks. Up and down the coast, commanders, captains, and flag officers jumped. Orders were quickly drafted; ships prepared to go to sea. Telegrams were sent back to Welles.

From Acting Adm. S. Phillips Lee, Hampton Roads:

Young Rover ordered to cruise south of Cape Henry to Hatteras, *Commodore Jones* between the Cape of Virginia, *Western World* . . . north of Cape Charles. All within the Gulf Stream. *Sumpter* [*sic*] . . . on general cruise.

From Rear Adm. Hiram Paulding, commandant Navy Yard, New York:

The *Tuscarora, Seminole, Dai Ching,* and *Adela* are ready and will proceed tonight to sea. We hope to send the *Virginia* and *Kittatinny* off tomorrow.

From Comdr. Cornelius K. Stribling, commandant Navy Yard, Philadelphia:

Have procured three steamers *Suwanee, Tonawanda,* and *America* to search for the pirate.

From Comdr. John B. Montgomery, commandant Navy Yard, Boston:

The *Montgomery* will be dispatched to her cruising ground tomorrow evening.

As the days passed, more ships were sent to sea: the *Jacob S. Whedon, Cherokee, Amee, Herbert Mantor, Sarah Burton, Young Turk, Montgomery,* and

Trinity from Boston; the *United States, Sabine, Blackstone, Marion, Cumbria,* and *Curlew* from New York; and the *William Bacon* and *Matthew Vassar* from Hampton Roads. The yacht *America,* winner of the *America*'s Cup, was drafted for the hunt. By Sunday President Lincoln got into the act, by ordering the secretary of the treasury to "cooperate by the revenue cutters under your direction with the Navy in arresting rebel depredations on American commerce and transportation and capturing the rebels engaged therein." Even the *Kate Stewart* was chartered and sent back out.

As the United States Navy was starting out after Savez, he captured the brig *Umpire* on June 15. The prize was taken off the Delaware coast. The brig had been bound for Boston from Cardenas, Cuba, with a cargo of sugar and molasses. By evening, the Confederates left the *Umpire* in flames.[22]

Savez set the *Tacony* on a northeasterly course. Enough time had passed since he had released the *Kate Stewart,* carrying the prisoners, for the Federals to mount a search for him. Off Nantucket he would cross the path of packets leaving New York for Europe, as well as fall in with New England fishing fleets. He also might rendezvous with the *Florida.*

The *Tacony*'s escape was aided by bad weather. On June 16 the wind swung around to the north. Savez knew the upcoming storm would make it hard for the Union navy to catch him. At 5:00 A.M. Savez had the crew take in the topgallant sails and later furl the mainsails. The next day the wind was blowing a fresh gale. Double reefs were set in the fore and main topsails. The pumps were worked every four hours to keep the hold dry. By June 19 the supply of fresh water started running low. Savez put everyone on short allowance, one-half gallon a day.[23]

A passing Union man-of-war hailed the *Tacony,* asking if anything had been seen of a "pirate brig." Savez yelled back that he had sighted a ship earlier chasing an East Indian to the northwest. The heavy seas prevented the Federals from coming aboard and they steamed off. Later that day a Federal gunboat asked the same question and Savez sent him southeastward.

Confined to their quarters because of the storm, some of the crew resumed grumbling. One man said that he wished that a Yankee warship would capture them. Savez had the man placed in irons, and the grumbling stopped.[24] At last on June 20, the storm started to abate.

Later that day, as the *Tacony* sailed through the Nantucket Shoals, Savez saw a packet ship approaching. In the middle of the fore topsail was a large black circle. When the packet hove to she proved to be the *Isaac Webb* of the Black Ball Line. The prize was a huge ship with a length on deck of

185 feet and a beam of over thirty-eight feet. Her main deck was sixteen feet above the water. The top of the main mast towered 172 feet above the main deck. The *Isaac Webb*'s 1,800-ton displacement was more than four times that of the *Tacony*. The blunt-shaped packets were designed to carry cargo, yet make the passage from Liverpool to New York in sixteen days.[25]

Savez put Billups in charge of the boarding party. When the Confederates returned with the vessel's master, he threw the ship's papers on the cabin table and roared, "You had better burn the ship!"

Packet captains, Savez had heard, were rough, hard-driving men used to being instantly obeyed. These were men whose orders were enforced on their crews by chief mates with brass knuckles and belaying pins. The crews nicknamed "packet rats" were dredged from the waterfronts of the world.

Looking over the papers, Savez was horrified to see that the *Isaac Webb* was carrying 750 Irishmen. The *Tacony* could not possibly hold so many people.

Leaving Billups and most of his crew on board, Savez ordered the *Isaac Webb* to accompany the *Tacony*. Savez wanted to find the mackerel fishing fleet in hopes of transferring the passengers and burning the Yankee's ship. Savez did not find the fleet and finally gave up and bonded the packet for $40,000.

Later that day Savez did capture a fishing schooner, the *Micawaber*. When the schooner's crew came aboard, their captain asked if they could have two of the ship's boats. The fishermen wanted to take their chances rowing over forty miles to land. Savez agreed; the fewer prisoners he had the better. Savez sent them off with three gallons of water and a few pounds of bread. Twelve hours later, the fishermen reached the South Shoal Light Ship. In the meantime, the Confederate torchmen had made quick work of the schooner.[26]

The *Tacony* sailed on toward Georges Bank. During the morning of June 21, a clipper was sighted coming through the mists. Savez ordered the American flag hoisted and had the howitzer fired, but without shell, to conserve shots. The clipper continued sailing, so Savez ordered a shell fired and yelled for the ship to heave to. The clipper clewed up and stopped.

When the *Tacony*'s boat pulled alongside, the mate on the clipper said, "For Lord's sake give us a rest about that Rebel bark, we have been heaving to all night to hear about her!" Later Savez learned that warships warning that the *Tacony* was in the vicinity had overhauled the clipper four times that night.

The clipper was the *Byzantium* bound from London for New York. Her cargo was coal. Thirty minutes after the capture, the clipper was in flames.

Around noon on the same day Savez captured and burned the bark *Goodspeed* bound for New York from Londonderry, Ireland, in ballast. The *Goodspeed*'s captain was depressed over the loss of his ship until he came aboard the *Tacony*. Recognizing a friend of his, the captain of the *Byzantium,* his spirits perked up.[27]

Welles's ships were returning empty-handed. Each captain filed reports stating where he had been, how hard he had searched, and how many ships he had stopped. The captain of the *Commodore Jones,* an armed ferryboat, complained that his ship, bouncing like an India rubber ball, had thrown spray fifty to sixty feet ahead and to the side. The *Seminole*'s captain reported so many leaks that he had been forced to use the main pumps and donkey engine to stay afloat. Even then he had fourteen inches of water in the hold. The yacht *America* had lost her jib stays and bobstays in the bad weather that had hid the *Tacony*. The yacht returned to port in a crippled rig. The school ship *Marion* had gone out manned by midshipmen, only to return with nearly all of them seasick. In the panic of sending ships out, some captains were told to look for the *Clarence*.

More ships were ordered out; those returning were sent back; more ships were chartered and sent out. The chartered side-wheeled steamer *Ericsson* eventually came across the *Florida*. Maffitt by then was heading north. The *Ericsson*'s captain, realizing he was outgunned by the *Florida,* turned and ran. Maffitt pursued and opened fire, eventually striking the Federal. The *Ericsson* finally escaped into a fogbank.[28]

Newspapers gave the raiders front-page coverage. The *Baltimore Sun* ran statements from the captains of the ill-fated ships. "MORE DESTRUCTION BY REBEL PIRATES" screamed the *New York Tribune.* Later the editor, Horace Greeley, attacked the navy with: "This Rebel cruiser *Tacony* in a few hours makes her appearance under the very nose of the Yankees and frightens them half to death." The *New York Herald* fired another shot with:

When the news first reached the Navy Department they should have ordered the chartering of every available steam vessel and sent them to sea, if need be with volunteer crews shipped for a cruise of twenty days. Every available steam vessel! After one little cruiser![29]

The owners of the *Isaac Webb* joined in with a letter to Welles decrying the fact that the navy's ships were returning empty-handed. The pirate, they said, was armed with only two wooden guns and a brass one. They suggested the government put a price on the pirates and grant commissions to individuals for their capture and destruction. Our glorious flag, the letter concluded, was gradually disappearing from the ocean.

The citizens of New York panicked. The Chamber of Commerce asked the navy to provide convoys to protect American ships. New York Sen. Edwin D. Morgan asked that the navy use the frigate *Roanoke* for the defense of New York City. The answer was no.

The New York mayor then telegraphed the same request and got the same answer. Maj. Gen. John E. Wool joined the argument, stating: "This great emporium from which you are supplied with money and almost everything to carry on the war against the Rebels must be protected."[30]

Gov. John A. Andrew of Massachusetts sent a letter to Welles claiming that "a Rebel vessel, manned by as daring a crew as that of the *Tacony*, might burn half the towns along Cape Cod. . . . The ignorance of the Rebels as to our defenseless condition is our most effective protection in the absence of action by the Navy Department . . . the Navy . . . cruisers . . . were not sent until the *Tacony* had rioted along Vineyard Sounds for four days." Welles fired back a telegram telling Governor Andrew that cruisers were sent out thirty minutes after the department received word of the *Tacony*.[31]

In Boston, the insurance underwriters offered a $10,000 bounty for the capture of the *Tacony*. The city fathers of New Haven and Provincetown pleaded for protection from the "pirate."

Welles got a request to protect the railroad ferry at Havre de Grace, Maryland. The locals feared the Confederates would raid their town and burn the ferry, thus cutting the rail connection on the eastern seaboard. Welles ordered a gunboat plus two 32-pounder cannons for the ferry sent to the town.[32]

People flocked to the coast to look for the pirates. There was a report that ministers led their congregations to the seashore, where they prayed that the Lord would deliver them from the fury of the Confederate "Vikings."[33]

Welles confided to his diary that he had sent out over twenty vessels in search of the pirate *Tacony*, and that had she been promptly taken, he would have been blamed for such a needless and expensive waste of strength; now he was censured for not doing more.[34]

To add to the confusion, Gen. Robert E. Lee was marching toward Pennsylvania. Would the Confederates turn and attack Washington?

On June 22 the *Tacony* crept through the thick fog on Georges Bank. Savez could hear the fishing boats ringing their bells in hopes that passing steamers would alter course. Savez realized he could cripple the fishing fleet.

As soon as the fog cleared, Savez had a boat in the water. Hundreds of fishing boats appeared to be on the banks. The Southerners steered for the nearest schooner. Once they captured their prize they moved on for the next one and then the next. In all he bagged five schooners: the *Marengo, Florence, Elizabeth Ann, Rufus Choate,* and *Ripple*. Seventy-six fishermen stood on the deck of the *Tacony*. By then some schooners, suspicious at the sight of a bark, started to slip their anchor cables and leave.[35]

Upon seeing the fisherman leaving, Savez ordered the Confederate flag raised and fired a few shots to scare them. As the shells splashed harmlessly in the middle of the fleet, the anchor chains were quickly dropped into the water and sails rapidly went up. Savez later wrote that he not only "raised Cain, but also the price of fish."[36]

To dispose of his captives, Savez picked the oldest schooner, the *Florence*. After bonding it, he loaded on board all the fisherman and had the schooner set sail for Gloucester. The Confederate torchmen burned the other schooners.

The newspapers the fishermen had carried reported that the *Florida* was headed north. Maybe Savez could rendezvous with Maffitt.

On June 23 Savez caught two more schooners, the *Ada* and *Wanderer*. Both were burned. The *Ada*'s owner had worked twelve years to make enough money to buy a schooner.

That night a steamer approached. A Federal gunboat was almost alongside; a faked log would not work now. There was no way to convince a boarding party that a Philadelphia-bound bark had been blown this far off course.

When hailed, Savez answered that he was on the bark *Mary Jane* from Saquala Grande bound to Portland. The captain of the gunboat replied that there was a Rebel privateer cruising along the coast burning merchantmen and that he had better keep a sharp lookout.

Savez thanked the captain and the warship steamed northward. Savez and his crew stood speechless.

Savez realized it was time to "change the program." He told his crew that he wanted to capture a fast schooner, switch ships again and burn the *Tacony*.

At six o'clock in the morning of June 24, the fog lifted. Another packet was sighted and boarded. She was the *Shatemuc* bound from Liverpool to Boston with 350 immigrants and a cargo of iron plates. The passengers, Savez discovered, had agreed to enlist in the Union army—no doubt substitutes paid by the patriots who stayed at home. Savez wanted to burn the *Shatemuc* because he felt the iron plates were destined for use in Union ironclads. He finally gave up and bonded the packet for $150,000.[37]

Hardly had the *Shatemuc* departed when the lookout spotted a sail to the southeast. The *Tacony* gave chase, but the wind died down. Determined not to let a prize get away, Savez ordered a boat lowered. He and the boat crew rowed the three miles to the fishing schooner the *Archer*.

Once alongside, the Confederates climbed over the low bulwark. Savez saluted the captain and his men and then informed them that they were prisoners of the Confederate States. Leaving the fishermen on deck, the Confederates went below and ate the fish chowder the *Archer*'s crew had prepared for supper.

The *Archer*, Savez decided, was just what he needed to continue raiding. After supper he set sail for the *Shatemuc;* the packet had not sailed far in the light wind. All the fishermen, along with some provisions, were transferred and the *Shatemuc* was sent off again. Savez then went to the *Tacony* and took off the gun, booty taken from the prizes, some stores, and the rest of his crew and their effects. After midnight the *Tacony* was torched. When the bark had burned to the waterline, Savez ordered the helmsman to steer west by north, then went below.

The *Tacony*, however, did not sink. The hulk, awash, drifted northward. In July 1863 it was found and towed into Cape Cove, Nova Scotia.[38]

With the capture of the *Archer*, Savez had caught and burned or bonded twenty ships in eighteen days. Maffitt had captured twenty-one ships in four months.

Before turning in for the night, Savez made an entry in his notebook:

The latest news from Yankeedom tells us that there are over 20 gunboats in search of us. They have the description of the *Tacony* and overhaul every vessel that resembles her. . . . The schooner *Archer* is a fishing vessel of 90 tons, sails well and is easily handled. No Yankee gunboat would even dream of suspecting us. I therefore think we will dodge our pursuers for a short time. It is my intention to go along the coast with a view of burning the shipping in some exposed harbor [and] cutting out a steamer.[39]

At first light on June 26, the *Archer* sailed through the waters of the Gulf of Maine toward the coast. He had put the schooner on a beam reach. The lookout sighted an island that looked like the back of a great whale, Monhegan Island. Savez, wanting to raid more than an island, left Monhegan Island to starboard.[40]

As the Confederates drew closer to the Maine coast, numerous islands came into view. Beyond the islands lay the fishing village of Boothbay Harbor.

Later in the morning, four bells rang out, marking the midpoint of the forenoon watch. Just ahead, a small spritsail double-ended lapstrake-built ketch glided along. In the boat two fishermen were hauling in their trawl. The fishermen were eight miles southeast of Damariscove Island.

When Savez ordered them to come alongside, the fishermen answered that they were under trawl. When they would not cut it, Savez ordered his men to bring the fishermen on board. The Confederates hoisted a ship's dory over the side. When they came up alongside the fishermen's boat, they climbed in. With drawn pistols, Savez's men told the fishermen that they were Confederate prisoners. The trawl was cut and the Confederates rowed both boats back to the *Archer*.[41]

Savez had both fishermen taken below to the captain's cabin. Albert Bibber and Elbridge Titcomb of Falmouth, Maine, were questioned separately. Knowing that Falmouth was near Portland, Savez asked his captives what warships were in the harbor. Remembering that the Federals searched incoming ships at Hampton Roads, he asked if returning fishing vessels were searched. Savez offered them drinks of brandy, cigars, and twenty-dollar gold pieces to make them think he was a smuggler. They told him that the revenue cutter *Caleb Cushing* was the only armed ship in Portland. Fishermen were not boarded upon entering the harbor. From a newspaper they gave him, Savez learned of the arrival and departure times of the coastal steamers. One, the *Forest City,* was due the next day.

Satisfied, Savez got up and walked out of the cabin saying, "All I want of you is to take this vessel in and out of Portland."[42]

Later Bibber gave a deposition claiming that he had not helped the Confederates. He also said he had not believed that they were Confederates, since Savez wore a black frock coat and blue or black pants. He thought they were drunken fishermen on a frolic.[43]

With the assistance of the fishermen, Savez sailed the *Archer* westward through Casco Bay. Below deck Drayton concludes his diary with "if Mr. Read is not promoted to a Captaincy no man in the Navy deserves it."[44] Off Portland Head Light, Savez brought the *Archer* about. The white-painted rubblestone-and-brick lighthouse marked the entrance to the Ship Channel, up which Savez took the *Archer* toward Portland Harbor. After passing Cushing Island to starboard, Savez passed two forts, Fort Preble on the mainland and Fort Scammel on House Island. Only one fort remained, Fort Georges on a small island in Diamond Island Roads. The *Archer* safely anchored in Portland Harbor off Fish Point as the sun set.[45]

Savez and the other Confederate raiders sent one hundred and seventy-six Northern ships to the bottom of the ocean. The impact of the raiders extended beyond the cost of lost cargo and ships. Read's sinking of the schooners amounted to less than two percent of the fishing fleet. More schooners than that could be sunk during a stormy fishing season. The real damage occurred when the insurance rates on American ships were increased, making the total American shipping rates higher than foreign rates. Since neutral ships were not burned, the merchants transferred their cargo to foreign shippers for not only lower costs, but also to assure delivery. The few American ships that hauled cargo handled small shipments. Ships were laid up or sold. A Boston financier, R. B. Forbes, wrote Secretary Welles on July 8, 1863, that 146 of the 180 vessels in New York were foreign owned. The raiders were the South's most successful use of sea power. By the end of the war, Great Britain surpassed the United States in cargo carried. The American merchant marine would not recover until World War I.[46]

CHAPTER EIGHT

IN OLD ABE'S DOMAIN

On Sunday, June 28, 1863, Savez and his officers found themselves confined in a ground floor room of the Fort Preble guardhouse. His crew were in the room across from his. In the passageway between the rooms, a double guard of soldiers was stationed. Listening to the crew's off-key refrains of "Way Down in Alabama," Savez decided they were better sailors than they were singers.[1]

Savez went back to reading the book he had gotten after he gave an interview to Charles Brown, an author who used the pen name of Artemus Ward. Savez appreciated the gallon of whiskey Brown gave him as much as the book. Only a day had passed since his capture, and Savez had been besieged by reporters and townspeople wanting interviews.[2]

Now a group of reporters accompanied by Capt. Nathaniel Prime entered his cell. The spokesman for the group introduced himself as Mr. Berry of the Associated Press. Berry told Savez that the grand master of the state, William P. Preble, wanted to know if any of his officers were Free Masons. Read said no. Berry then asked Savez if he would volunteer details of his cruise since leaving Mobile. The information, he said, would be as interesting to Savez's friends as to the Northerners, and his friends would probably get it about as quickly.[3]

Savez realized that Berry's statement was right. Since the ships he bonded and released had had enough time to reach port, the Yankees knew of his captures; besides, they had his journal. The important thing was not to let the reporters know where the *Florida* might be.

Savez gave the reporters a carefully worded account of both his cruise and that of the *Florida*. Brown interrupted, adding details such as their firing the Dutch Cheese at the Portlanders.

Later, Savez sent a grocery list into town with one of the guards. He ordered sardines, soda biscuits, and other delicacies for his crew to supplement the meager prison fare. The order was paid for with the gold he had brought in his carpetbag. Savez also sent a note to a local tailor for clothing samples. The people of Portland had seized the few clothes the Confederates had left on the *Archer*.[4]

Somehow after the surrender, John Billups, Robert Hunt, and an English boy nicknamed "Buttons" had separated from the rest of the Confederates. The three were hauled off to the jail in Portland, where the townspeople wanted to hang them as pirates. "Buttons," the youngest, was flogged for being sassy. The three managed to smuggle word of their treatment to Savez, who forwarded their letter to the Federal government and got them transferred to a military prison.[5]

The previous night, the city marshall Mr. Heald and most of the police department visited Fort Preble. They wanted to take the Confederates to the town jail. The fort's commander, Maj. George Andrews, refused, insisting the Confederates were prisoners of war. The Portlanders returned to the city, where Heald informed Mayor McLellan that the Confederates could not escape.

About 3:00 A.M. on June 29, Portland's bells rang out. Someone sighted a Confederate gunboat. Men were being landed on Cape Elizabeth to rescue Savez and his men. The gunboat turned out to be the *Tiger*, the tug used to bring the 7th Maine to Portland. The armed guard posted during the chase of the *Caleb Cushing* was still on board the tug.

Confederate ships were reported off Cape Sable and in the Bay of Fundy. Welles telegraphed McLellan and asked if he was certain all the Rebels were captured. The mayor said he was sure all the Confederates were in prison.[6]

Lt. Comdr. Richard W. Meade Jr., of the USS *United States*, filed a cruise report to Secretary Welles. Meade was sure that his ship's course would have intercepted the *Caleb Cushing* had Savez gotten away from the Portlanders. If he had captured the Confederates, Meade stated, they "would scarcely be prisoners of war in Fort Preble." In response Jefferson Davis swore he would hang ten Federal officers of the highest rank, if a hair of Savez's head was harmed.[7]

After the war, David D. Porter, by then an admiral, wrote: "This was a remarkable raid and showed great gallantry on the part of Lieutenant Read . . . although the presence of a single Federal gunboat, under an intelligent captain, would have nipped the whole scheme in the bud."[8]

While in Fort Preble, Savez learned of the capture of the Confederate ironclad *Atlanta*. The ship had grounded in Wassaw Sound near Savannah, Georgia, and was unable to break free before the Union monitors arrived. Aboard the *Atlanta* was Lieutenant Barbot, who had served with Savez on the *Arkansas*. Barbot had been imprisoned in Fort Lafayette, in Brooklyn, New York. Savez sent Barbot a letter saying he had been "bagged, and nicely closeted, in a well built fort in Old Abe's dominions." Savez went on to say that he expected to be sent to a prison in Boston or New York in a few days, but not for long, as he expected to be exchanged and sent to Dixie.[9]

Andrews, meanwhile, was concerned about his prisoners escaping. Half his troops were up every night guarding Savez and his men.

Andrews's request for a transfer of his prisoners was approved. On the night of July 27, Savez and his men were secretly put on a Boston steamer. Andrews sent Captain Prime and thirty-five soldiers from the fort to accompany the Confederates. The master of the vessel was not told the identity of his passengers. At Boston the Confederates were transferred to a tug and taken to one of the harbor's outermost islands, Georges Island—the site of Fort Warren under the command of Col. Justin Dimick. At three o'clock in the morning, Savez was logged in on the fort's muster roll.[10]

The star-shaped, five-sided brick-and-granite Fort Warren occupied about twelve of the island's thirty-five acres. The fort had been completed in 1857, and its cannon protected the main ship channel into Boston Harbor and was the principal defense against any Confederate naval attack on the city.[11]

The Confederates were held in the "dungeon" which, despite its name, was above ground. The cells were a series of granite block casemates with brick-vaulted ceilings. These casemates were fifty by eighteen feet and interconnected by a central corridor. The prisoners could pass from cell to cell. The cells were built into the southwest bastion. The light came through narrow rifle-slot embrasures in the outer wall. Charcoal braziers provided the only heat.[12]

On July 30, 1863, Savez wrote a report to Secretary Mallory outlining his cruise. Savez also asked for money to purchase clothing for his men. The food and new clothes he had gotten at Fort Preble had cost him most of his money. His letter was forwarded to the Confederacy.

Among the prisoners, Savez found a friend from North Carolina, Lt. Joseph W. Alexander, who had graduated from Annapolis three years ahead of him.[13] Like Barbot, Alexander had been aboard the *Atlanta*. Savez discovered that he had two things in common with Alexander: small stature and a craving to escape.

During the day, the prisoners were allowed to walk on the parade ground in the center of the fort. The soldiers even permitted the Confederates, a few at a time, to go on top of the ramparts. Savez used this opportunity to explore.

To escape Savez needed to know all the details of the fort and surrounding area. The wall with the main entrance had a pair of doors with "Fort Warren 1850" carved in high relief in the keystone block above them. The doors were large and too heavy to be moved in a hurry. A guard stood in a sentry box to the left of the gate. Bribing the guard would take money, and Savez was broke. The granite walls were too thick for tunneling. From the top of the wall it was a thirty-foot drop to the ground. It might be possible to tie together scrap pieces of rope. A dry moat and sloping earthen glacis surrounded the fort. From the bottom of the moat to the top of the glacis was a scalable six feet. The glacis extended down to the seawall and was covered with grass in which he could hide. Sentries patrolled the island, but they could be avoided. The nearest land was Lovell Island, a half-mile north, across the channel. A large wooden gunnery target lay on the seawall directly across from the island. The soldiers launched the target and moored it out in the channel whenever they drilled with the fort's cannons. During a night escape, the target would serve as a landmark to make sure he headed toward the island. On Lovell Island, Savez noticed a house, which meant people and a boat.[14] Not being a good swimmer, Savez would have to construct a raft to get to the island. But first, he had to figure out how to get to the fort wall.

Alexander solved Savez's problem. Savez's friend explained how he had gone to the pump room to take a bath. The pump room, like the "dungeon" cells, had rifle slots in the walls. When the guards were not watching, Alexander examined the rifle slot. The opening was V shaped, narrowing from three feet wide on the inside to seven and a half inches at the outside. The fort's architect had intended that riflemen be able to train their rifles left and right while presenting only a narrow target to an advancing enemy. Alexander climbed into the slot and discovered that he could squeeze through the outside opening.[15]

Savez and Alexander knew that they would need help getting off the island. They also knew that anyone going with them would have to be thin enough to get through a rifle slot. They asked James Thurston and Maj. Reid Saunders to join them. Thurston was a first lieutenant in the Confederate marines and a shipmate of Alexander's. Saunders was an army quartermaster.

The four collected the material they would need for escape. Working at night when the guards were out of the cells, they prepared their equipment. Savez discovered that none of his companions were strong swimmers. They made a raft out of two-gallon demijohns and corked them shut to serve as floats, lashed together with canvas. A half dozen cans of milk and oysters were added. Since everything had to go through the rifle slot, final assembly would have to wait until they were in the water. Sea chests and carpetbags were searched for scraps of rope. These were tied together, but the line was not long enough to reach the ground from the rifle slot. Fortunately the rifle slots were only about fifteen feet from the ground. They would have to jump the last few feet. A large stick was smuggled in from the parade ground. The stick would be placed across the inside of the slot and serve as a brace for tying the rope.

On Sunday, August 16, all was ready. A northwest wind brought drizzle and an overcast sky, perfect conditions for escape. Never again, Savez vowed, would he answer "here" to any Federal officer.[16] The others in the cell agreed to help although they could not fit through the opening. At nine o'clock the stick was wedged in place and the rope was tied on to it, then lowered out the opening. To be as skinny as possible, shirts were removed. The first one out gathered the raft parts as they were lowered.

Sixty feet away was the main sally port and a guard. The howl of the wind muffled any sounds the Confederates made climbing out. The dark, misty night obscured the guard's vision.

When everyone was out, the four quickly dressed, gathered up their makeshift raft, and climbed up the glacis. Crawling and sliding through the grass they made their way down the slope.

On the sea wall, two sentries paced. With shouldered rifles, the sentries would walk toward each other then turn and walk away only to pivot and return.

The escapees waited until the Federals were walking away from each other. One by one the Confederates dashed across the top of the seawall then dropped over the side. The noise of the wind-driven waves drowned out the Confederates' footsteps. Every one landed on the beach and missed the rocks.[17]

The four stayed close to the seawall and worked their way toward the gunnery target. There they assembled their raft and waded into the mounting surf. Once in the cold water, the Confederates discovered that they were swimming against a knot-and-a-half flood tide.[18] The wind blew spray in their faces and they lost sight of Lovell Island. After about a half an hour, the escapees allowed the wind to blow them back to Georges Island.

The four took apart their raft and climbed back over the seawall. Dodging the sentries, they made their way back to the fort. The rope had been left out in case they would have to return. After finding a board in the moat, they propped it against the wall, stepped on it, grabbed the rope, climbed up and squeezed through the rifle slot. The last man knocked the board over as he ascended.

Savez, Alexander, Thurston, and Saunders had told few prisoners of their plans. Now most refused to believe the four had been outside. One midshipman finally noticed that their clothing was wet. Tasting the water, he found it salty. Doubts vanished.[19]

The four left some parts of their raft on the beach. Later that day guards spotted the demijohns tied to canvas, but did not report their discovery. Colonel Dimick had no idea that the Confederates could leave the fort.

Savez and the others needed strong swimmers to cross the channel to Lovell Island to capture a boat and return for the others. Savez suggested his gunner Pryde. The group also recruited Thomas Sherman, a sailor from the USS *Santee,* imprisoned for speaking out against the United States.

At nine o'clock on the night of August 18, the group tried again. Pryde and Sherman would go out first. If anything happened to prevent the rest from getting out, the strong swimmers might be able to swim to freedom. Again the rope was thrown out. Reaching the ground, Pryde and Sherman climbed up the glacis and waited for the others.

Next, Alexander climbed up into the rifle slot opening. His foot brushed a bottle sitting near the edge of the opening. It crashed on the granite floor.

Outside they heard the cry of the sentry. The rope was pulled back inside. Lights could be seen through the rifle slot. After about fifteen minutes the Confederates realized that the wind was blowing toward them so the sound of the bottle would not have carried out to the sentry. The lights came from the lantern of an officer returning to the fort from the boat landing.

The remaining four climbed out and joined Pryde and Sherman. Everyone made their way through the weeds to the seawall. After going over the seawall, they passed within forty feet of a sentry to make their way to the gunnery target. Pryde and Sherman swam into the cold water. The others settled back by the seawall and waited.

As before, the wind pushed the waves onto Georges Island. The four waited in vain. Somewhere offshore the dark water claimed the lives of the two swimmers.[20]

The four finally realized that their friends would not return. Alexander and Thurston were chosen to swim the channel using the gunnery target as a raft because they were the better swimmers. Savez and Saunders would wait until the other two came back with a boat.

The target was on the seawall. Waiting until the sentries were walking away from them, the Confederates pulled the target off the wall and into the water. Before Alexander and Thurston could get away, the sentries turned around and started back toward each other.

When the sentries were above the Confederates, they noticed the target was missing. The Confederates huddled next to the sea wall under their jackets. Walking over to the edge of the wall, one sentry spotted the dark unrecognizable shape of Savez's jacket and dropped stones on it. The sentry then leaned down and shoved his rifle toward Savez's jacket. The bayonet on the rife stopped on Savez's chest. Savez froze.

The Federal decided he was not going to stick his bayonet into salt water and pulled back his rifle. The two continued talking about the target's disappearance, concluding that the "spirits had taken it away." Years later Alexander would write that Savez's coolness was the bravest thing he saw in the war.[21]

Savez and Saunders helped the other two push the raft out into the water. They then waited until dawn. Even if their friends had made it to Lovell Island, they could not make it back before daylight. Savez and Saunders decided to return to the fort.

This time Savez was not as careful crossing the seawall. He turned toward the startled sentry and raised his arm as though he had a knife. The sentry panicked and jumped over the wall. Others, however, took up the Federal's cry. Within seconds the alarm spread.[22]

The two Confederates ran back to the fort. There was no need for hiding in the grass. They jumped into the ditch and raced toward the rope and safety.

Grabbing the board, Savez shoved it against the wall and stepped up to grab the rope. The board snapped with a loud crack. Savez toppled back to the ground.

"Halt!" shouted the guard at the sally port. Saunders bolted back over the glacis. As Savez jumped back up, the guard rushed up with his rifle leveled. Savez raised his hands and was marched inside the fort, where Colonel Dimick put him in close confinement.

Saunders's escape was short-lived. Ten minutes later he was caught near one of the buildings on the grounds. Saunders joined Savez in close confinement.

The guards searched the cells to find out how many Confederates escaped. All the missing were noted except Thurston. He had fooled the guard by stuffing extra blankets under his blanket. In the light of the guard's lantern the Federals thought Thurston was asleep like the rest of the officers. Thurston's escape was discovered later in the day.

Dimick signaled the first passing steamer and sent word of the escape to Boston. The news was telegraphed to other towns. Somehow, though, the Boston-based Revenue Cutter *Morris* was not sent out after the Confederates.[23]

Alexander and Thurston made it to Lovell Island. Drained by their long swim in the cold water, they barely dragged the raft ashore. They had put their clothes on the raft to enable them to swim more easily, but the waves had washed their pants overboard; all they had to wear was their hats, drawers, and shirts. Fortunately, what money they had was kept in one of the shirt pockets. The two found a small sailboat pulled up on the beach. Pulling the bow anchor out of the sand, they unsuccessfully tried to push the boat into the water. They then discovered a second anchor off the boat's stern. The line was cut and the boat launched.

By then, dawn had broken. Setting sail, they steered toward Georges Island to get Savez and Saunders. There they saw the sentries, but not their friends. Alexander and Thurston then sailed up the coast hoping to reach New Brunswick, Canada.[24]

By afternoon the pair landed their boat just east of Rockport on Cape Ann, Massachusetts. On the beach were some boys playing in the sand.

When the escapees asked for food, the boys ran off. The Confederates set sail again.

By sunset they had reached Rye Beach, New Hampshire. They hailed a man, standing outside his house, and asked him to come to their aid. When the man rowed up to them, the Confederates told him they had sailed out of Portsmouth for a lark, gone swimming, and their clothes had blown overboard while they were in the water. The stranger returned with old clothes, food, tobacco, and a small bottle of cherry brandy. Alexander was certain that the man recognized them, but was so frightened he helped them anyway.

The two Confederates set sail again, hoping to make Eastport, Maine, and the Canadian border by morning. Unfortunately, the wind died.

The next day the Revenue Cutter *James C. Dobbin* out of Portland stopped and searched them. Jedediah Jewett had sent the cutter out to look for them. Finding Confederate money, the Federals took Alexander and Thurston to Fort Preble. On September 7, 1863, Alexander and Thurston were returned to Fort Warren and placed in close confinement.[25]

Savez and his friends' escape attempt alarmed the Bostonians. The city fathers ordered a telegraph line run from the statehouse out to Georges Island so they could learn of any future escapes. Eleven miles of cable were laid out, six miles of which were underwater.[26]

When Savez and his fellow escapees were allowed out of close confinement onto the parade ground for exercise, no one was permitted to speak to them without a guard's permission. While they were outside, their cell was searched to look for any evidence of another attempt to escape. Although the escapees refused to give their word that they would not try to escape, the Federals eventually let Savez and the others return to the other Confederates.

On their return, they found that some changes had been made to the rifle slots. The Federals had embedded three heavy iron bars across each rifle slot opening.[27]

Savez had been optimistic in Portland when he wrote his letter to Barbot. Unfortunately both sides had stopped exchanging prisoners. By 1863 the Union army was using former slaves as soldiers. The South refused to recognize the slaves as soldiers and returned them to servitude. Secretary of War Edwin M. Stanton, with Lincoln's support, refused to exchange prisoners until the Confederates included the former slaves.

On September 15 Savez retrieved a package that cost him $5.75 in postage. Inside he found $500 in gold and a letter from the Confederate Navy Office of Provisions and Clothing, instructing him to divide the amount among his men according to their rank and rating. Savez was also to forward duplicate receipts, one to the paymaster and the other to Robert Ould, Confederate Agent of Exchange.[28]

Prison life was hard to endure. Savez's friend Alexander felt he could kill a Yankee every day of his life; even that would not repay him for the mental agony he suffered.[29] There was nothing for Savez to do except walk the parade ground and ramparts and wait to be exchanged.

Savez and the others were allotted a daily half-pint of soup, fourteen ounces of bread, and eight ounces of cooked meat. They occasionally got two potatoes and some beans or hominy. Edward A. Pollard, a Confederate editor who had been captured on a blockade runner, called the food "diaphanous slices of bread and bits of fat pork." Sutlers came to the fort to sell food, sugar, and coffee. Savez was able to use some of the Confederate gold to supplement the meager prison fare.

At night Savez's casemate was filled with the snoring of prisoners, which obscured the sound of scampering rats. A story was told about one Union soldier who had returned from leave in Boston with his hair greased with barber's oil. During the night, the soldier dreamed countless mosquitoes attacked him. In the morning he discovered the rats had eaten his hair. His head was as smooth as if he had shaved it.[30]

The days dragged on, each one like the day before, except for Sundays when the Confederates received one mail delivery instead of two. Savez, nevertheless, managed a half smile for the Yankee photographer who photographed the Rebels.

By January 1864 Savez's hopes for exchange faded. Grant, soon to be in command of all Union armies, opposed prisoner exchanges because the North had more men than the South. The North could replace its missing soldiers with immigrants from Europe. From the ramparts Savez saw them debark onto Lovell Island. The recruits were trained there and then shipped south to fight without ever going to the mainland.[31]

Savez was lucky to be at Fort Warren. In other prisons, both north and south, men died of battle wounds, malaria, pneumonia, dysentery, and the guards' bullets. During the war, of the more than a thousand men confined at Fort Warren, only thirteen died.[32]

On June 2, Savez, without his knowledge, was raised to the rank of first lieutenant in the Provisional Navy. The Provisional Navy, created by the Confederate Congress, was Mallory's way of allowing rank to be based on merit rather than the strict navy system of seniority.[33]

Savez, as well as others, never gave up his idea of escaping. The cabin boy from the *Atlanta* made three attempts to break out. His inspiration came from a book he was reading, Alexandre Dumas's novel *The Count of Monte Cristo.*[34]

Savez and Alexander inspected the bricked-up fireplace in their casemate. The chimney joined with the one from the adjacent casemate so that the two flues were side by side. Only the hole for a stovepipe came through the bricks. The flues were not large, but together they presented an escape route.

The two searched for digging tools. Friends provided pocketknives, which had been overlooked when the guards searched the incoming prisoners. A rusty ice pick was found in a crevice in one casemate.

The pair started to dig away at the mortar to remove the bricks. William T. Morrill, an engineer from the *Atlanta,* helped. Taking turns they worked quietly at night. Once through the fireplace opening, the Confederates found there was only room enough for one man to work at a time. Savez stood on his friends' shoulders until he had worked his way up high enough to get a foothold. After the partition between the two flues was removed, the bricks were beaten into dust and either carried out with the slops in the morning or hidden under prisoners' bunks. Before morning the opening was rebricked using bread as mortar, then whitewashed. The effort took months.

Working in the small opening, Savez frequently had mortar fall into his eyes. Although the lime in the mortar caused him pain, he could not go to the Union army surgeon. His right eye became permanently damaged.

Savez finally reached the chimney cap. The mortar around the cap was chipped loose. After the sentries passed, Savez pushed the cap aside and climbed out.

Savez quietly called back for Alexander, who was a little bigger than Savez. He wiggled and squirmed, but could not go up or down the chimney. The other Confederates stood on each other's shoulders and pushed Alexander up the chimney, tearing off both skin and clothing. Neither Morrill nor any of the other prisoners decided to follow.

The cap was replaced and both men made for the scarp of the fort. Since they had no rope, they jumped into the dry moat. Crawling through the weeds, they avoided the sentries patrolling the grounds. This time the escapees went to the boat landing, where just offshore they saw a small fishing boat. The fort's officers used it for sailing.

Savez and Alexander hid under a pile of old sailcloth. When two guards approached, one noticed the pile of sails and poked the sailcloth with the bayonet on his rifle. The blade ran into Savez's thigh, missing bone and arteries. The other soldier observed that since the dunnage was wet his companion would have a rusty blade to clean in the morning.

"It's wet," remarked the first soldier as he ran his fingers across the bayonet, not realizing that it was dripping with Savez's blood.

After the soldiers left, Savez bound up his wound. He and Alexander then swam to the boat. Despite the pain Savez climbed into the boat and helped Alexander to raise anchor. The two set sail for Canada where they planned to make their way to Halifax. There they could get passage on a steamer to Bermuda and pick up a blockade-runner to go back to the Confederacy.

By morning, they had left Fort Warren behind and were in the midst of several hundred fishing boats. As they sailed through the fleet, Savez saw several steamers coming from the direction of Boston. He told Alexander that they should stay with the fleet during the day and move on at night. There were too many boats, Savez felt, for the Federals to search in one day.

The pain from his wound bothered Savez. Alexander begged him to lie down and sleep. Savez agreed, but told his companion to watch the other boats and do exactly as the fishermen did. Savez insisted that Alexander do nothing to draw attention to them.

After Savez dozed off, Alexander let go of the tiller and moved forward to see what was wrong with the jib sheet. He misjudged the boat's quick weather helm and the wind's force on the mainsail turned the sailboat directly into the wind. The jib and the mainsail flapped uselessly in the wind. When Alexander got back to the tiller, a steamer approached.

Soon Savez found himself on a Federal ship. He knew the officer in charge, but hoped the officer would not recognize him.

When the officer asked their names, Savez and Alexander explained that they were "poor harmless fishermen."

The officer looked at Savez and remarked, "I thought you were my old shipmate Savez Read and I was going to treat you like a gentleman, but as you are only a common fisherman, into the brig you go in double irons, until further orders!"

This was too much for Savez, who said, "Sam, you are not going to treat an old shipmate that way, and me badly hurt too?"

Savez was sent below. The ship's doctor tended to his leg wound and treated his eye.[35] Savez and Alexander were then returned to Fort Warren.

Civilians, both North and South, had objected to the edict permitting no exchange of prisoners. On August 25 Saunders's mother wrote Jefferson Davis, requesting that her son and Savez be placed on a list of prisoners to be exchanged. She referred to Savez as "my dear son's companion in this escape through the loop-hole of the fort." Although Secretary of War James A. Seddon wrote her that the efforts for exchange had failed, he was premature in his assessment. The Union and Confederate navies finally agreed to exchange their prisoners. On October 1, 1864, Savez and the other naval prisoners were loaded on a steamer. They were bound for City Point on the James River. Unfortunately for Mrs. Saunders the exchange was too late; her son died on September 3.[36]

CHAPTER NINE

ON THE JAMES RIVER

A cold rain pelted the Union steamer as she rounded Newport News Point heading up the James River, leaving Hampton Roads astern.[1] Aboard the steamer were the prisoners from Fort Warren. Savez was once again in the South, even though it was territory controlled by the Federals.

The channel cut close to the shore; the steamer's wake splashed on the beach. On March 8, 1862, in these waters the Confederate ironclad *Virginia* sank the *Congress* and the *Cumberland*. The next day the *Virginia* fought the *Monitor*. In little less than two months hence, the Union navy would scuttle the captured *Florida* off Newport News Point.

Following the channel, the steamer moved to mid-stream and passed Burwell's Bay. Maffitt, in his response to Savez's request to take the *Clarence*, had suggested Burwell's Bay as a way of getting back into the Confederacy just over a year earlier. As the river snaked back and forth, the shore to starboard was Union-held territory, the shore to port was a no-man's-land behind Northern lines.

Seventy-two miles upriver from Newport News Point, the steamer finally pulled into City Point, Virginia. The little town, located where the Appomattox River flowed into the James, had been transformed into a giant supply depot for the Union army. Twelve miles up the Appomattox River near the city of Petersburg, Grant's and Lee's armies fought each other from their trenches.

Savez and the others were put ashore and into a makeshift prison. They found themselves embroiled in a controversy; the problem was Maj. Gen. Benjamin Butler.

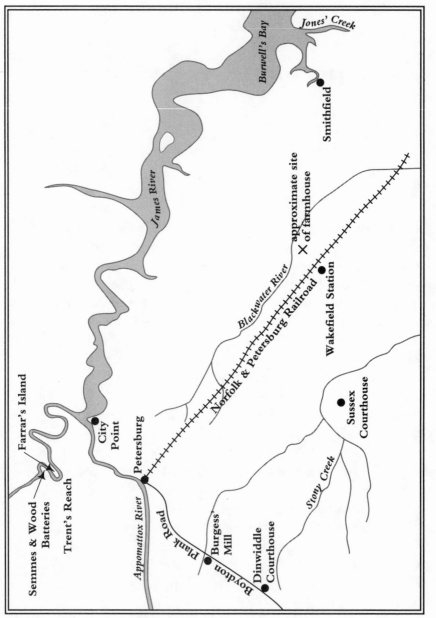

Jones' Creek

Burwell's Bay

Smithfield

James River

approximate site
of farmhouse

Blackwater River

Wakefield Station

Norfolk & Petersburg Railroad

Sussex
Courthouse

Farrar's Island

Semmes & Wood
Batteries

Trent's Reach

City
Point

Petersburg

Stony Creek

Appomattox River

Plank Road

Burgess'
Mill

Boydton

Dinwiddie
Courthouse

JAMES RIVER AND SOUTHEAST VIRGINIA

Butler had created for himself a post as special agent for exchange. From his headquarters at Fort Monroe near Newport News, Butler had a say in all prisoner exchanges held on the James River. The Southerners were outraged.

Butler had acquired their wrath from his earlier activities at New Orleans. After Farragut had taken the city, Butler had been placed in charge of its occupation. New Orleans' women had been insulting Federal troops by spitting on them and dumping chamber pots as they walked under balconies. To stop the insults Butler issued Order No. 28, which stated that "when any female shall by word, gesture, or movement insult or show contempt for any officer or soldier of the United States she shall be regarded and held liable to be treated as a woman of the town plying her avocation."[2] Butler became known as "the Beast."

The Confederate commissioner of exchange was Col. Robert Ould. At first Ould refused to meet with Butler and negotiated only with Butler's assistant. By October 1864, though, the Confederates were meeting with Butler.

To complicate matters, Butler had insisted that former slaves be included in the exchange of naval prisoners. Just exchanging naval prisoners would be unfair to the soldiers.[3]

Secretary Welles, wanting an exchange of all naval prisoners, argued that the Confederates had previously exchanged all their black naval prisoners. Mallory, his counterpart, also wanted an exchange. After Butler sent a telegram to Lincoln, Lincoln and Welles met with Stanton, Secretary of State William H. Seward, Maj. Gen. Ethan A. Hitchcock, and Chief of Staff Henry W. Halleck. As a result, Lincoln wrote Grant telling him to go ahead with the exchange.[4]

Butler did not know that Savez had command of the *McRae* when the ship sank at New Orleans. After the war Butler wrote that the sinking was a flagrant violation of a pledge of honor to surrender the ship. Not knowing that the *McRae* had struck underwater pilings, Butler claimed Confederates deliberately bored the holes in the hull. He noted that "they took care to keep themselves out of New Orleans after I came. If I had found them there, they would have been deprived of future opportunity to do any more rascality, and by the most effectual means."[5]

On October 18, 1864, Savez and eighty-nine other naval officers and men were herded down a pier. There they boarded the flag-of-truce steamer *New York*. The Confederates, steaming under a white flag, were finally on their way to be exchanged.

The steamer stopped at a bend in the river known as Trent's Reach where the Federals had built barricades to prevent the Confederate James River Squadron from coming downriver to attack City Point. Chains and a spar boom had been stretched across sunken hulks. The Federals pulled the spar boom aside and the *New York* passed through the opening. The steamer eventually pulled ashore to a makeshift pier at the small clearing in the tree-lined riverbank known as Cox's Landing. It was there that the exchange was held.

According to a previously established accounting system, the prisoners were traded. If equal ranking officers were not available, the ordinary seaman was used as the common denominator. An admiral would be traded for an admiral or sixty seamen, a flag officer for forty, a commodore for twenty, a captain for fifteen, a commander for ten, a lieutenant or master for six, a master's mate or ensign for four, a midshipman or warrant officer for three, and all petty officers for two.[6]

Twenty-two months had passed since Savez had been in the South. With the fall of Vicksburg and Port Hudson, the Union controlled the Mississippi River. Farragut had his fleet in Mobile Bay. In the Carolinas Charleston and Wilmington were heavily blockaded. The Anaconda Plan was slowly strangling the South.

At Richmond, Savez, still limping from his bayonet wound, walked up the gangplank and boarded the CSS *Patrick Henry*. The ship served as a combination receiving ship, guard ship for prisoners, and schooling ship for midshipmen. Savez was delighted when he saw his old friend Jimmy Morgan. That night, as a guest of the ship's officers, Savez sat in the wardroom and told of his escape attempts. Morgan later wrote of the incident and recalled how Savez's eye still bothered him and how emaciated and disheveled he looked.[7]

Savez then reported to Flag Officer John Mitchell. After the surrender of Fort Jackson and Fort St. Philip in 1862, Mitchell had been captured and sent to Fort Warren. Exchanged in August 1862, Mitchell went on to become chief of the bureau of orders and detail and then commander of the James River Squadron.[8] With this came promotion to flag rank.

The James River Squadron was composed of three ironclads, Mitchell's flagship the *Virginia II*, *Richmond*, and *Fredericksburg*; four gunboats, the *Hampton*, *Nansemond*, *Drewry*, and *Beaufort*; the steamer *Torpedo*; and three small steam launches, the *Wasp*, *Scorpion*, and *Hornet*.[9] Obstructions, however, at Trent's Reach and the Union navy kept the squadron bottled up at Richmond.

Since the Confederacy suffered from a shortage of ships, Mitchell did not have a ship assignment for Savez. Instead, he gave him the command of a pair of gun batteries on the James River: Battery Semmes and Battery Wood. Accompanying Savez were two of his master's mates from the *Clarence-Tacony-Archer* raid, Billups and Matherson.

On October 28, 1864, Savez took charge of the gun emplacements. Battery Wood's powder magazine was covered only with loose earth. Worse yet, the doors opened facing the Federal batteries across the river. An enemy shell could have hit the magazine and blown up the battery. Even the drainage ditch had been dug improperly. Water drained into rather than away from the magazine. Savez dashed off a report to Mitchell and then set about correcting the deficiencies.[10]

The James River curved back and forth in a series of loops. Savez's batteries were located on the west side of one of these curves, upriver from the obstructions at Trent's Reach. They were located below Battery Brooke and above Battery Dantzler. On the other shore was a peninsula known as Farrar's Island.

Butler was trying to connect the curves by digging the Dutch Gap Canal across the land and thereby bypassing the obstructions. Butler wanted a passage for the Union ironclads to steam upriver. For laborers he used captured Confederate soldiers and blacks, justifying their use by stating that the Confederates had used Federal prisoners to dig fortifications at Charleston under Union fire.

The Confederates cannonaded the canal even though their own men came under fire. General Lee doubted whether the Federals would remove their ironclads from protecting City Point; but he could not afford to be wrong. The north might try crossing the river above Confederate gun batteries to come around the back of Petersburg. Grant had taken Vicksburg in such a maneuver. Since Battery Semmes was in line with the canal, Savez bombarded it daily. To Savez the sound of 10-inch columbiads hurtling the 127-pound shells was "music in the air." He later wrote that Lee said that Battery Semmes made a bowling alley out of the canal.

The Federals returned the fire. Although the exploding Union shells chewed up the protecting earthen parapets, neither the Confederates nor any of their cannons were hit. At night Savez set engineers to work shoveling dirt to repair the damage. The firing finally diminished to a few shots a day, with no firing at all on some days.[11]

Shooting at a canal two miles away became too tame for Savez. He reasoned that he could lead a raiding party of dozen men if he had a small boat and a mule-drawn wagon to carry it. He would take his raiding party far enough west to pass around the flank of the Union troops at Petersburg, then double back to the river and launch the boat. His prize would be the captured ironclad *Atlanta*, which was anchored off Fort Monroe. The Union navy had brought her to Hampton Roads after her capture near Savannah. Savez would use the boat to capture a tug. Once on the tug, he would rig a long pole with a small bomblike device called a spar torpedo off the tug's bow. Approaching the ironclad unsuspected in a tug, he would stick the torpedo under her hull. With one pull on the lanyard, he would then explode the bomb and sink the *Atlanta*.

The plan was risky, but Savez was convinced he could succeed. Everyone knew that Maj. Gen. Wade Hampton had successfully "rustled" 2,400 head of Union cattle and captured three hundred prisoners behind enemy lines. Besides, this was the way his old Annapolis classmate, Lt. William Cushing, sank the Confederate ironclad *Albemarle* at Plymouth, North Carolina.

In November 1864, Savez got Mallory's approval for the raid. The territory south of the Union lines was a wooded, marshy lowland with few roads and few inhabitants. It was a no-man's-land. Savez arrived at the river having bypassed Smithfield. The Confederates camped on the banks of a tributary called Jones' Creek. Fort Monroe lay twenty miles downriver.

That night they rowed down to Hampton Roads, but Savez could not find a tug. There were no tugs on the river the following night either. On the third night, as they were returning to their camp, the Confederates came upon a sutler's schooner that had moved in during the night. No watch had been posted. Without resistance, the schooner was taken.

The sutler had a general store's worth of merchandise: tobacco, candy, canned food, fish, wine, razors, cheese, and myriad items. The starving Confederates had not seen such goods since the start of the war, but the schooner would have to be destroyed.

Just then, a tug pulling a barge filled with hay steamed upriver. The tug came to within a half mile of the schooner, then dropped anchor. Savez decided that he would have to capture the tug. The black cavalrymen and their white officer put up a fight. One soldier was killed and two were wounded before the Federals surrendered. Besides the cavalrymen, a Union paymaster and a gang of laborers were also on the tug. Together, Savez had thirty prisoners.

Savez took the tug over to the schooner and then put all his prisoners except the tug's engineer and firemen on the barge. He then cut the barge adrift and torched the schooner. Federals, who had heard the shots during the capture of the tug, would come upriver to investigate. Savez had the tug run ashore and scuttled. Leaving the engineer and fireman on the beach Savez led his men back to Southern lines.[12]

Back in his gun batteries, Savez grew excited when he heard that torpedo boats were being built at Charleston, South Carolina. The prototype was named the CSS *David*. Armed with a spar torpedo, the *David* had attacked and severely damaged the USS *New Ironsides*. The plan was that a flotilla of boats was to steam out and attack the Union blockaders. Although the *David* sank after the attack, Savez requested that he be considered as commander of one. His request was in vain.[13] The boats were built, but they never had the opportunity to attack the Federals.

In his boredom, Savez pondered his earlier raid. Since the tug he had captured had stopped, he could probably capture one. This time instead of going for the *Atlanta*, he would attack the twin-turreted monitor, the USS *Onondaga*. He had seen her near City Point.

Savez got another spar torpedo, a wagon, mules, and eight men. To help him approach the monitor without alarming the Union sailors, he obtained blue shirts. Savez knew dressing like Federals was risky. If caught, they could be hanged as spies; returning to their own lines, Confederate pickets could shoot them.

Just above Jones' Creek at Burwell's Bay, Savez seized a tug that night. No shots were fired. The torpedo was rigged to the end of a long pole, then stowed on the bow. Savez ordered the tug's captain to get underway for City Point.

Shortly before dawn, the tug rounded a bend in the river and came upon three schooners loaded with hay for Union horses. If Savez passed them, the Federals might suspect that something was wrong. They could easily go ashore to sound the alarm. If he captured the schooners, the ensuing fight would alert any nearby Yankee.

As he pondered his choice, Savez looked downriver. A column of black smoke rose above the treetops. That meant a Federal gunboat was approaching. Since sinking the *Onondaga* was out of the question, Savez decided to burn the schooners.

The schooners were taken without trouble. Soon flames were licking their way through the hay bales. Savez then beached the tug, torched it, and set it adrift. While the Federals investigated the burning schooners and tug, Savez and his crew escaped into the brush.

Toward evening of the next day, Savez heard the sound of horses' hoofs. He ordered his men to hide in some bushes by a rail fence. Half of a Confederate cavalry patrol had ridden by when a scout spotted the blue shirts and rifles. Some soldiers surrendered; others fled. As the Confederate colonel rode back, Savez had an idea. Realizing that he had been mistaken for a Yankee, he asked the colonel if he had any extra horses.

Savez called his men as the horses were brought up. Eight men came out of the bushes and mounted up. Then Savez asked the colonel the name of his regiment. After the colonel answered, he asked Savez who he was. Savez identified himself and said that he only wanted to escape back to Richmond.

Savez made it back through the lines without incident. That night he wrote a report documenting his capture of three schooners loaded with hay, one tug, and a regiment of Confederate cavalry. The colonel challenged Savez to a duel, and Savez accepted the challenge. Higher officers heard of the proposed duel and prevented it.[14]

By late December 1864 Atlanta and Savannah had fallen. The Federals were bombarding Charleston. Fort Fisher was under attack by the largest Union fleet ever assembled during the war. If the fort fell, the port of Wilmington, North Carolina, would be closed to blockade runners. Since the Federals held the Mississippi, most of Lee's supplies came through Wilmington.

About all that remained of the Confederacy was parts of Mississippi, Alabama, Georgia, and the land west of the Mississippi River. Virginia also still hung on, barely. Come spring, Grant was sure to extend his lines westward from Petersburg. He had the men to do it and Lee lacked the men to prevent it.

The night of January 15 was cold and dark. Recent rains had caused a freshet, which raised the level of the river. The high water broke the ice and washed away the obstructions at Trent's Reach. Savez sent Billups and Matherson out in the river in a dugout to take a closer look.[15]

The schooner that had been sunk on the south side of the old channel was moved downriver several hundred yards. The wreck on the north side had washed ashore. Two other wrecks had their bows under water. The north channel was clear.[16] Savez's sailors reported that there was fourteen feet of water through the obstructions at a point where the river was eighty feet wide. Only the spar boom remained in place. The Union sentries had apparently taken shelter, as Billups and Matherson were not spotted.

The freshet, Savez realized, had opened the river for the James River Squadron to steam down and go on the attack. With most of the fleet off Wilmington, the defenses at City Point would be weak. Destruction of the supplies at City Point would slow Grant's spring offensive.

Savez informed Maj. Gen. George E. Pickett, who gave Savez a horse and told him to go see Lee at Petersburg. Lee then ordered Savez to ride to Richmond and ask Mallory to send the ironclads downriver.

Savez rode the twenty-five miles to Richmond. Reining up at the Mechanics' Institute, Savez explained everything to the secretary of the navy. Without any hesitation, Mallory wrote an order to Flag Officer Mitchell to move as soon as possible, if he deemed it practical. By 3:00 P.M. the next day a tired Savez went aboard the *Virginia II* and delivered the message to Mitchell.[17]

Mitchell received the message with cautious optimism and wrote back that the freshet had temporarily rendered the river impractical to check Savez's information. Mitchell added that he would gladly incur all hazards if passage through the obstructions was practicable. He concluded by asking for more men.

Days slipped by and still the James River Squadron lay at anchor. If Mitchell waited too long, the water would fall. To Savez this was reminiscent of Mitchell's delay in granting his request to take command of the *Resolute* after the battle of New Orleans.

Mallory was also exasperated with Mitchell. On January 21 he sent Mitchell an unofficial letter trying to prod him into action by reminding him he had an opportunity rarely presented to a naval officer. Fearing that Savez might not be used, Mallory added as a postscript a suggestion that Savez be put in command of the three small steam launches.[18]

Even with Mallory's urging, another day was lost because of heavy fog. Finally, on January 23 at 6:00 P.M., the squadron raised anchor. Mitchell had two and one half hours to meet the high tide at Trent's Reach. That meant the ironclads would not have enough water under their hulls to clear the obstructions.

To try to make up for lost time the slower vessels were lashed to the faster ironclads. The ironclad *Fredericksburg* took the lead with the *Hampton* and *Hornet* secured alongside. Next came Mitchell's flagship, the *Vir-*

ginia II, with *Nansemond* and *Torpedo*. Towed behind the *Torpedo* was the *Scorpion*. Bringing up the rear was the ironclad *Richmond* with the *Drewry* and *Beaufort* plus *Wasp*. Savez had gotten command of the steam launches and equipped them with spar torpedoes. Billups and Matherson had obtained transfers to serve as boat coxswains for the *Hornet* and *Wasp*. Savez made Lt. Edward Lakin coxswain for the *Scorpion*. For the trip downriver, Savez went aboard the *Scorpion*.

Night had fallen when the squadron reached a line of moored torpedoes and carefully maneuvered through them. These weapons would later be known as mines. They were set just upriver from the ominous sounding Graveyard Reach to stop any Union ships that could get by the obstructions.

The squadron crept on past Battery Brooke. The cannons were kept inside the ironclad behind closed gun port shutters. Mitchell did not want any lights to give them away. Just ahead on the north bank was Fort Brady —Union-held territory.

The guns of the Yankee fort opened fire. Savez watched as the *Virginia II*'s helmsman steered toward the Confederate side of the river. The squadron hugged the river bank and did not return fire.

The squadron cleared Fort Brady without being damaged; however, near Cox's Landing, the *Virginia II* swung too close to the south bank of the river and drove the *Torpedo* aground. The flagship rocked under the impact and the lashings holding the tug parted. Luckily for Savez, the *Scorpion* did not also run aground. Mitchell ordered the *Nansemond* cut loose to pull the *Torpedo* off the bank. The *Nansemond* was unsuccessful and the *Drewry* would later return to free her stuck sister ship.

At 9:00 P.M., Mitchell brought the squadron to anchor off Battery Dantzler.[19] Ahead lay Trent's Reach and the obstructions. The river level was starting to fall. Even at the height of the freshet, the squadron would have to pass through sunken wrecks one at a time. Still uncertain of the water depth, Mitchell ordered Savez to take the *Virginia II*'s pilot and make soundings. Savez had Lakin light the boiler fires on the *Scorpion*.

While waiting for the *Scorpion*'s boiler pressure to rise, Savez put part of his crew into a small boat. He had them muffle the oarlocks and row toward the Confederate shore. He was near Battery Semmes and needed to alert the Southern pickets.

The launch slid noiselessly ashore. The lone sentry on the shore had not noticed his approach. The surprised sentry was Jimmy Morgan. Savez told Morgan of the planned attack and added, "Now remember, youngster, you fellows make those guns of yours hum when the Yanks open, and mind you don't shoot too low, for I will be down there in the middle of the river." Savez then put his hand on his friend's shoulder, saying he wished Jimmy could go with him because a "sailor has no business on shore anyway."[20]

When Savez returned to the *Virginia II*, steam pressure was up in the *Scorpion*'s boiler. After casting off the lashings, Savez had Lakin head the launch to Trent's Reach. The cold night might keep the Federal pickets huddled around their campfires.

As they approached the obstructions, Savez ordered the launch slowed. The pilot cast out the sounding lead. Just then a Union rifle fired. More rifles started firing. The dull thud of a coehorn mortar added to the rattle of small arms fire.

The pilot panicked, stopped sounding, and yelled that the channel was not open. Bullets whizzed by the *Scorpion*. On the south side of the river the Confederates returned the fire.[21] The pilot then demanded to be taken back to the *Virginia II*; Savez ordered the launch to return.

Instead of returning to the *Virginia II*, Savez pulled up to the *Fredericksburg* and got her pilot. He then borrowed a boat from the *Fredericksburg*. With both pilots in the boat, the *Scorpion* towed them back to the obstructions.

The *Virginia II*'s pilot finally stopped complaining. Both pilots started taking soundings as the shots flew overhead. The channel proved to be eighteen feet deep. With the *Virginia II* and the *Richmond* drawing fourteen feet and the *Fredericksburg* nine and a half, the squadron could make it through. The channel, however, had a long wooden spar boom chained between two of the remaining wrecks. Savez felt that a few strong blows with a cold chisel would break the chains.[22]

Returning to the *Virginia II*, Savez reported the pilots' soundings to Mitchell. Satisfied, Mitchell told Savez to take a couple of armed cutters and cut the chains, after informing the captain of the *Fredericksburg* to get underway. Savez obeyed the orders, sending both of the *Virginia II*'s cutters.

Back at the obstructions, Savez found that the gunfire had not slackened. Cutting the chains took longer than he had anticipated. Mitchell approached in the *Virginia II*'s launch to assure himself that the channel was deep enough. Savez had soundings taken again. Satisfied, Mitchell returned upriver.

At 1:00 A.M., the *Fredericksburg* approached. All the chains were not broken, but the ironclad rode over the boom. The *Fredericksburg* did, however, graze a wreck.

The sailors finally broke through the chains. Savez again saw Mitchell approach. He had taken the *Fredericksburg* through the obstructions. Now he told Savez to take the *Scorpion* upriver and get the *Hampton*. Since the gunboat was bigger than the *Scorpion*, the *Hampton* could push the boom aside. Mitchell also wanted a lantern placed on the wreck nearest to shore.

Savez had Lakin get the launch underway. Since the *Hampton* had been with the *Fredericksburg*, Savez assumed the gunboat was back where the ironclad had been. Not finding the gunboat, Savez concluded that the *Hampton* had gone past him in the darkness and proceeded downriver.

Giving up the search Savez decided to get the lantern. He ordered Lakin to head back toward the *Virginia II*, which had anchored too close to shore. By then, the tide was ebbing and the flagship had grounded. The *Beaufort* and *Nansemond* were struggling, trying to pull the ironclad free.[23]

The Confederate gunners ashore had increased their tempo. To Savez the bombardment sounded like a great battle.[24]

When the *Scorpion* came alongside the flagship, Mitchell yelled above the roar of the cannons to Savez. The *Fredericksburg* was being recalled. The squadron would not go through the obstructions. Savez witnessed one of the axioms of war: no battle plan survives the first contact with the enemy intact. Mitchell told Savez to take the launches upriver before daylight.

As Savez brought his launch in close enough to hear his commanding officer, he did not see the towing hawser stretched between the *Beaufort* and *Virginia II*. The *Scorpion* caught on the hawser. As the line slid along the launch it caught the torpedo spar and broke it. The torpedo dangled alongside the launch.

Savez had the torpedo secured to the launch and ordered Lakin to take the *Scorpion* to the shore. There he delivered the ordnance to the *Torpedo*. She had come downriver after being pulled off the riverbank.

Heading back into the river Savez saw the *Hornet*. Hailing Billups, Savez had the *Scorpion* brought alongside. Since the *Hornet* had a torpedo, Savez went aboard. He then told Lakin to take the *Scorpion* upriver, saying he would follow. Before Billups got the *Hornet* underway, the *Scorpion* had vanished into the darkness ahead.

Savez soon found the *Scorpion* hard aground. Near the launch was the *Drewry*, also grounded by the falling tide. Savez went to the *Richmond* to get the *Wasp* to help him pull the *Scorpion* off the bank. Savez found the *Richmond* also aground.

Grounded ironclads were not Savez's problem; the grounded *Scorpion* was. Leaving the *Richmond*, Savez took both launches back. Towing hawsers were rigged. Despite the combined pulling, the *Scorpion* remained hard aground. Once the *Wasp* grounded, but Matherson managed to get the launch off the mudbank. To obey his orders, Savez would have to move the *Hornet* and *Wasp* even if he had to abandon the *Scorpion*. He told Lakin to keep the *Scorpion's* crew working, but go ashore before they became targets for the Federal gunners. Savez got his two launches upriver out of range just as dawn broke on January 24.[25]

The *Fredericksburg* by then had returned. She had taken up position near the *Virginia II* to provide gunfire support for both grounded ironclads as they waited for the rising tide. After the dawn, Savez thought the Federal fire rained down like a shower of lead. The *Onondaga* came upriver and started shelling the Southerners. Later, the *Hunchback*, *Massassoit*, and *Spuyten Duyvil* joined the ironclad.[26]

At 7:10 A.M. the *Drewry* took a direct hit and exploded. The debris from the blast damaged the *Scorpion*.

Two of the crew were killed and two more wounded. Lakin was seriously wounded, but in time he recovered. The rising tide finally floated the ironclads clear and they moved upriver to safety at Battery Dantzler.

That afternoon Mitchell called a council of war in the wardroom of the *Virginia II*. Shot from the *Onondaga's* two 15-inch Dahlgrens had broken through the *Virginia II's* four-inch iron armor and the two feet of wood behind the iron.[27] Savez, being the junior officer, by tradition spoke first. Savez argued for pressing the attack during daylight when the obstructions could be seen and avoided. The ironclads could be rigged with spar torpedoes. The *Onondaga*, the only serious threat, could be rammed with a torpedo and a hole blown in her hull. Confederate guns could finish off the Union ironclad. The other officers were divided in their opinions with some preferring to wait until dark. In the end Mitchell decided to wait until 9:00 P.M.[28]

On the evening of January 24, the squadron again started toward the obstructions. Ashore a Union soldier lit a Drummond searchlight. As the calcium light probed the darkness, Federal shots whizzed through the air. The *Virginia II's* pilot again panicked. He had been atop the ironclad's casemate and declared he could not see because of the light. Mitchell ordered the squadron to withdraw.[29]

This was the last chance for the James River Squadron. When the Union navy returned from taking Fort Fisher, two more monitors were added to guard the river. In February, Mitchell was removed from command. Ten weeks after the attack the Confederates would destroy the squadron as they retreated from Richmond.

Savez decided to try one more raid. He had started his plan before the battle at Trent's Reach. Savez wanted enough men, boats, and torpedoes for a major raid. His plan was to again go behind Grant's army and then double back to Burwell's Bay. Once there he would launch the boats, which would move upriver to attack and sink the monitors at City Point. The James River Squadron could then fight their way past the obstructions and destroy the Union supplies at City Point. Without supplies Grant might be forced to retreat to Norfolk.[30]

Savez's plan had a minimal chance of success, but both General Lee and President Davis approved it.

On the morning of February 3, 1865, Savez inspected his men. Besides the sailors from his gun batteries, he had gotten volunteers from the army and marines. All totaled, he had 120 men. The sailors and soldiers were armed with cutlasses and old flintlock pistols, making them look like buccaneers. The marines had rifles.

During the inspection, four mule-drawn wagons arrived. Each wagon carried a boat armed with a spar torpedo. The sailors and soldiers took the lead followed by the wagons. The marines brought up the rear.

Savez had sent Lt. John Lewis ahead to reconnoiter the route, because the roads needed to be solid enough to support the wagons' weight. Savez knew, from his previous raids, the good roads only as far as Blackwater River. From there to the James River, Lewis seemed like a good scout, because at the start of the war, he had been stationed at Norfolk. Northern born, Lewis resigned, joined the Confederate Army, and was wounded at Bull Run. In 1864 Lewis left the army and joined the navy.[31] Savez had told Lewis the expedition would meet up with him at a ford on the Blackwater River.

The first day's march went through Confederate-held territory. By evening the expedition stopped two miles east of Petersburg. They camped at Lt. Gen. Richard Anderson's headquarters on the right wing of the Confederate army. There Savez met two young English gentlemen who were guests of Anderson. When they asked to accompany Savez, he agreed.

The next day the raiders passed through the Confederate picket lines and started down the Boydton Plank Road. Suddenly, horses were heard approaching fast. Savez ordered everyone off the road and into hiding. A Federal cavalry patrol galloped past, assuming that the Confederates were only a picket post.

When they resumed their march, Savez looked for his English guests, but they were no longer riding with him. They had ridden back to the Southern lines.[32]

The Boydton Plank Road, while relatively good, headed away from the James River. Near Burgess's Mill, Savez turned to the left onto a muddy road. By nightfall his expedition had covered only fourteen miles. The Confederates would have to travel more than fifty miles to reach Burwell's Bay.

On February 5, Savez started early but had only gone a short way when Confederate cavalrymen warned him that the enemy was advancing toward him. Savez took the first road he found and headed south to avoid the Federals. By nightfall the raiders were well behind Union lines, having marched some thirty miles that day.

Even in the middle of winter, Grant was trying to extend his lines westward to encircle Petersburg. The II and V Corps, a Union cavalry division, and part of the VI Corps were advancing toward the Boydton Plank Road. In the battle of Hatcher Run (February 5–7) the Confederates checked the advance with a cost to Lee of 1,200 men. For Grant it was almost 1,500, but he could replace his losses. The Union army managed to extend their lines to within three miles of Burgess's Mill.[33]

On February 6 the weather turned extremely cold. After covering only fifteen miles, Savez camped near the Wakefield Station of the Norfolk and Petersburg Railroad.[34] He still had twenty-five miles to travel to get to Burwell's Bay.

Around midnight, a sailor sleeping too close to the fire set afire one of his coattails. His screaming awakened the whole camp. Later he cut off the other coattail to make both tails equal.

By morning a mixture of cold rain, snow, sleet, and hail fell. After struggling for hours, Savez halted at an abandoned farmhouse a few miles from the Blackwater River. Savez knew Lewis would wait for them at the ford to guide them to Burwell's Bay.

The Confederates started a fire in the fireplace to dry their clothes. A lone rider galloped down the road, drawn by the smoke from the fireplace. As he drew nearer, his Confederate uniform could be seen.

The rider had been a prisoner of war at Fort Monroe. From his cell window, he overheard a conversation between Lewis, the scout whom

Savez had sent ahead to reconnoiter the route to the James River, and a Federal officer. Lewis told how Savez's expedition could be ambushed at the Blackwater River ford. Afterward, the rider managed to escape and had hurried to warn Read.[35]

The Confederates put out the fire. Savez moved the expedition back about a mile, then brushed their tracks away and hid his men in the woods. Savez told everyone that he would ride ahead to check the story. If he was not back by sunset on the following day, they were to return without him.

That evening Savez set out for the ford. The enemy would be looking for 120 men and not a single horseman. Drawing near the river, he could see that the Union cavalry was looking for the expedition. If he had not been delayed by the bad weather, he would have walked into a trap.

Savez reconnoitered the area, avoiding the roads guarded by soldiers. It was impossible to maneuver troops around them. Even retreat would be difficult. On the afternoon of the next day, February 6, he returned to his hidden Confederates.

As soon as it was dark, Savez led the expedition southward. They marched by night and camped by day. The Southerners swung wide in their detour going by way of Sussex Court House, Stony Creek, and Dinwiddie Court House. Near the Appomattox River, an old man in a stovepipe hat showed them a ford across the river.

Breaking through a thin coat of ice, the Confederates waded across, their thin clothes freezing. At last, they were safe behind southern lines. Eleven days had passed since Savez left on his expedition.

Because of Lewis's treachery, Savez had failed to reach the James River. Savez, however, had come back during bad weather without the loss of a single man, save Lewis, or any mules or wagons. Lee called February 7 the most inclement day of the winter. After Savez's return, seventy-five of his men were confined to the Naval Hospital in Richmond suffering from exposure.[36]

On February 15, the *Richmond Whig* reprinted an article from a northern paper:

We learn that a naval party consisting of 12 officers and 100 men under the command of Lieutenant (Tacony) Savez were recently captured by the Yankees near Smithfield, Isle of Wright County. Among the party was Assistant Engineer Tomlinson, of the James

River Fleet, who was married the night before his departure. We do not deem it prudent to give any information as to the object of their expedition, and think we are sufficiently explicit when we say that they started for a purpose, failed in accomplishing it, and are now no doubt in a Yankee prison doing anything else than blessing their luck.[37]

CHAPTER TEN

CSS <u>WEBB</u>

For Savez, the war in and around Richmond and Petersburg was tiresome. The war in the Trans-Mississippi Department promised more action. He had heard of the CSS *Webb*, a side-wheel steamer on the Red River in Louisiana. Savez thought he could load the *Webb* with cotton bales and sell the cotton in Cuba. He would then use the *Webb* as a blockade runner and steam to Galveston, Texas, avoiding the Mississippi River, which was patrolled by the Union navy. He would escape the Red River by way of the Atchafalaya River, and down the Atchafalaya into the Gulf of Mexico.[1]

On February 17, Savez went to Mallory with his plan. To Savez's delight Mallory approved. The secretary of the navy sent a message to the Confederate naval agent in England, authorizing him to give Savez up to £10,000 for his cruise.

Savez was not alone as he set out for Louisiana. Because the James River Squadron had been bottled up, others wanted to join him. Savez got five officers for the *Webb*, including John E. Billups.[2]

The fastest way for Savez's party to go westward should have been by rail. At the start of the war the South had two main railroad lines to the Mississippi River. One went through Wilmington, Augusta, Atlanta, Montgomery, and Vicksburg. Lee had used that railroad to send Longstreet's troops to north Georgia to reinforce General Bragg in the battle of Chickamauga. The other ran from Petersburg through eastern Tennessee, northern Alabama, and back into Tennessee ending at Memphis, but that was in 1863.

On the day of Savez's meeting with Mallory, the Confederate troops evacuated Charleston, because they were in danger of being trapped in the city by Sherman's advancing troops. Behind Sherman lay miles of destroyed railroads. Rails were heated in a fire made of railroad ties, then bent and twisted. Bent rails could be straightened out, but twisted ones required a mill to straighten. The rail line had been cut at Knoxville when Union troops took the city in September 1863.

Savez and his party took the Southside Railroad out of Petersburg as far as they could. They continued down into North Carolina. When they reached Lincolnton, Savez learned that Lt. J. W. Alexander was in town on furlough. Savez asked his friend for a wagon.[3] The Confederate army had taken most of the horses; getting mounts for six men was impossible.

The wagon helped make a good cover story in case Federal cavalry stopped them. Lee's forces were being depleted by desertions. Savez could maintain that his men had deserted the Confederacy.

Savez stopped in Mobile. Units of Gen. John B. Hood's army had been redeployed to Mobile after the Federals had crushed his force at Franklin and Nashville. Since the Union navy had entered Mobile Bay the previous August, the Confederate ships were bottled up. Savez attempted to recruit engineers to help him with the *Webb*. A despondent Capt. Ebenezer Farrand, commander of the naval forces, showed no interest in Savez's request.[4]

Savez and his party moved westward. Taking care to avoid the Federal gunboats, they crossed the Mississippi River. Savez was wise in exercising caution, because a spy had learned that Savez was bound for Louisiana and warned the captain of the ironclad USS *Lafayette*. Finally, on March 31, eighty miles below Shreveport, Savez reached the CSS *William H. Webb*.[5]

The *Webb* was a 206-foot-long side-wheel steamer. Built as a tug in New York before the war, the vessel was eventually sold to the Southern Steamship Company. When the war started the owners wanted to use the *Webb* as a commerce raider for profit. They obtained a privateers' commission to prevent everyone on board from being hanged as pirates if captured. The *Webb* had snared three ships before the blockade of the Mississippi River ended the privateering. Taken by the Confederate Government, the *Webb* was converted into a ram. Having been in New Orleans and missing the battle at the forts, the *Webb* was sent up the Red River to avoid being captured by Farragut's fleet. On February 24, 1863, the *Webb* took part in the sinking of the Union's ironclad, *Indianola*. After that the *Webb* remained up the Red River and fell into disrepair.[6]

Savez was shocked at the *Webb*'s condition. There was not a single cannon on board. The steamer had hardly enough of a crew to get underway, which would have been impossible in any event since there was no fuel on board. Lacking small arms, the crew had only a few cutlasses.

Savez had the crew bring aboard wood for the boiler's firebox, then got the *Webb* underway upriver.

At Shreveport, Savez got all the help he needed from the head of the Trans-Mississippi Department, Gen. Edmund Kirby Smith. A 30-pound Parrott cannon was mounted on pivot on the bow. A pair of 12-pounder boat howitzers was also brought aboard. Savez completed arming his ship by taking aboard five 100-pound spar torpedoes.

Carpenters built a rough bulwark around the bow to protect the Parrott from being washed away in a storm. One month's worth of food and water was loaded. Since the blockade had cut off the supply of coal, Savez was forced to use pine knots for fuel. Packed around the machinery were 190 bales of cotton to stop Union cannon balls. Remembering Maffitt's camouflage of the *Florida,* Savez had the steamer whitewashed. Volunteers from the army rounded out the crew. All totaled, Savez had sixteen officers and fifty-one men.[7]

Savez had instructed his officers not to tell the crew of his intentions. Savez knew that Yankee spies could be in Shreveport.[8]

By April 16 the steamer was ready. The additions had increased the draft to nine and a half feet, two feet deeper than when the *Webb* had come upriver. The added two feet meant that the *Webb* drew too much water to navigate the Atchafalaya River; Savez would have to go down the Mississippi.

The Federal navy was waiting for the *Webb* to come out. From the mouth of the Red River to the Gulf of Mexico was over 300 miles; all of it controlled by the Federals. Gunboats were stationed at regular intervals. Savez would have to pass Union-occupied Port Hudson, Baton Rouge, and New Orleans. The twin walking-beam engines would propel the *Webb,* but the ship's deep draft would require the engines to work harder.

Savez planned to stop frequently and send the crew ashore to cut telegraph lines. He needed to keep the Federals from sending word of his approach downriver.

As the *Webb* started to leave the wharf, the rats scampered off the steamer. That told the superstitious seamen that the ship was doomed.[9]

As Read was getting the *Webb* ready for sea, the Confederacy in the east was collapsing. Sunday, April 2, Lee telegraphed Davis that he was forced to abandon Petersburg and Richmond. The Army of Northern Virginia retreated westward. Davis fled to Danville. Grant cut off Lee's escape route. On Palm Sunday, April 9, Lee surrendered his army at Appomattox Court House.

Five days later, President Lincoln, wanting to relax, attended Ford's Theater. Shortly after 10:00 P.M., John Wilkes Booth squeezed the trigger of his derringer. At 7:22 A.M. on April 15, Lincoln died.

When the *Webb* approached Alexandria, Savez told the helmsman to bring the ship up to the wharf. He needed to take on fuel and send a report back to Secretary Mallory. Savez ordered his officers to keep the crew on board. As the *Webb* neared the bank, a soldier shouted the news of what had happened in the east.[10]

The surrender presented questions for Savez and all the other Confederates to answer. Why go on? What would the Yankees do to armed Rebels now that a southern sympathizer had killed Lincoln? Why not just quietly go home?

Kirby Smith issued a general order declaring that the war was still being fought in Trans-Mississippi. The Army of Northern Virginia had surrendered, not the Confederacy. He was sure the European countries would still come to the aid of the South. After all, President Davis and his cabinet had not been caught.

Savez would fight on for the same reason he resigned from the United States Navy. His sense of honor demanded that he fight for the South, as if there were still forces in the field. Only when he was overwhelmed without chance of retreat, could he surrender with honor.

Savez made up his mind to press on toward Cuba. He wrote a final message to Mallory. In it he said he would "have to stake everything on speed and time."

Savez had 200 cords of wood taken aboard for the boilers. At 4:30 A.M. on April 23 the *Webb* left Alexandria. Savez planned to reach the Mississippi River about 8:00 P.M. that evening. Savez needed the cover of darkness because, while ashore, he had learned that the Union navy had stationed four ships on the Mississippi to prevent the *Webb* from coming out.[11]

The side-wheel ironclad USS *Lafayette* was armed with a pair of 100-pounders in the bow, and side batteries of one 11-inch and two 9-inch smoothbores. The ironclad USS *Tennessee* had been brought to the river after being captured from the Confederates during the battle of Mobile Bay. The *Tennessee's* battery was two 7-inch and four 6.4-inch Brooke rifles. The lightly built side-wheel steamer USS *Gazelle* carried only six 12-pounders.

With the *Webb's* 190 bales of cotton, she could possibly survive a hit from any of these guns. The monitor USS *Manhattan,* however, had twin

15-inch Dahlgrens that each fired 330-pound shells.[12] These were bigger than the guns Savez had faced at the battle of New Orleans. If one of those shells hit, the explosion would smash the *Webb.*

Where would the Union navy station their ships? If they laid off the Red River's entrance to the Mississippi, as the blockaders did at Mobile when the *Florida* ran out, he could not wait for bad weather as Maffitt had.

To Savez's advantage, the Yankees used steamers to transport the cotton they bought from the South, despite the war. It had been more than two years since the *Webb* went up the Red River. The awaiting Federals might mistake the *Webb* for one of their own steamers.

If they blocked his entrance, Savez hoped he could get close to the Federals without being recognized. He could then ram one with a spar torpedo and use the ensuing confusion to escape. He might even get close enough to attack the *Manhattan.*

Shortly after leaving Alexandria, Savez saw a man hailing from the shore. He had the *Webb* swung into the bank to pick up the stranger. The man turned out to be a pilot who had intended to take the *Webb* down the Atchafalaya. Even though Savez had decided to use the Mississippi, he let the pilot stay on board.

Farther downriver, Savez stopped the *Webb* and took on more wood. While the crew was loading wood, Savez ordered the torpedo rigged on the bow.[13]

Not wanting to get to the Mississippi before dark, Savez ordered the *Webb* to slow down. As the Confederates steamed downriver, he finally told the crew of his plans.

As darkness approached, the *Webb* was ten miles from the Mississippi. First, however, Savez had to pass Turnbull's Island, which lay just ahead. The island was big enough that Savez could not see around it. The right branch of the Red River formed the Atchafalaya before it reached the Mississippi. Three and a half miles down the Atchafalaya was Federal-held Simmesport. The left branch was safer, but shallower. Savez knew he could not afford to take a chance on grounding the *Webb* on a sand bar. He ordered the pilot to take the right branch.[14]

A flatboat loaded with cotton appeared. On the flatboat were men in blue uniforms. Savez brought the *Webb* alongside and seized the flatboat, whose Union soldiers had been trading for cotton. Not all the Federals were caught. Some who were in a small boat managed to escape into a bayou.

Savez held the Federals until dark before freeing them. If the Federals who had earlier escaped had made it back to the Union ships, the *Webb* would steam into an ambush.

At eight o'clock Savez ordered the *Webb* to get underway again. Forty-five minutes later the *Webb* steamed into the Mississippi. No ships were at the entrance. The Union ships were anchored on the far side of the river. The Mississippi curved, making the far side the inside bend. Since the current was slower there, the ships had less of a chance of dragging their anchors.

Two new gunboats, the USS *Vindicator* and the USS *Lexington*, had joined the *Tennessee* and the *Lafayette*. The steamers USS *Samson* and USS *Champion* had reinforced the *Gazelle*. The *Manhattan* was anchored a quarter mile downriver on Savez's side of the river. The monitor's crew had set out two anchors to hold their ship against the current.

Savez realized he would not have to ram his way through with a torpedo, because the Federals were far enough apart for him to get through. Savez ordered the helmsman to steer clear of the monitor and head out into the river between the blockaders.

The engineer called Savez through the speaking tube. The boiler pressure was getting close to exploding. Just then the *Manhattan* fired a boat howitzer, a signal to heave to and stop.[15] On the far shore a rocket soared upward.

The *Webb*'s bells rang out for full speed ahead; she bolted forward. Savez urged the crew to head for the biggest opening between the ships.[16]

If the gun crews of the monitor were already at general quarters, they could load and fire the Dahlgrens in a minute and forty-five seconds.[17] That was not enough time for the *Webb* to pass without being fired upon. The Union guns, however, were in a circular turret, which would have to be turned to bring the guns to bear. As the *Webb* sped diagonally across the river, the Federals misjudged the *Webb*'s speed.

As the *Webb* passed within 500 yards of the *Manhattan*, the monitor fired a single Dahlgren and missed. One cannon meant only one gun was working!

The *Manhattan*'s officer of the deck had noticed the *Webb*'s smoke and sounded the alarm. After the howitzer was fired, the commanding officer ordered the Dahlgren fired. The only thing that could be seen as the *Webb* sped by was her smoke.

The other Federals continued shooting, but they too missed. The *Lafayette*, *Vindicator*, and *Lexington* got underway in pursuit.[18] They were too late. The *Webb* had disappeared into the darkness.

Savez had the pilot steer toward the outer loop of the river bends where the current was faster. Five miles downriver Savez passed his first gunboat, the USS *Fort Hindman*. The four gun side-wheel steamer showed no sign of life. Even so, Savez had the pilot give the gunboat a wide berth.[19]

When Savez felt confident that he had left his pursuers behind, he stopped the *Webb* and sent a party of men ashore to cut the telegraph line. A party of black Federal soldiers appeared before the wire could be cut. The Confederates returned to the *Webb* and the steamer got underway. Farther downriver, below the town of Morganza, the crew successfully cut the telegraph line.[20]

Eighteen miles past the mouth of the Red River the *Webb* approached Bayou Sara and St. Francisville. It was 10:15 P.M. Anchored about a mile away were the ironclad USS *Choctaw* and the tug USS *Hyacinth*. Savez ordered the *Webb* over to the far side of the river.

Other traffic on the river showed signal lights. Savez had the quartermaster flash signals. With luck, by the time the *Choctaw* figured out the signals were wrong, the *Webb* would be safely past.

Leaving the ironclad astern, the Confederates came upon the anchored gunboat USS *Nymph*. Since the river was about a mile wide, Savez ordered the *Webb* to stay on course. The night's silence was broken by two loud blasts from a ship's whistle. A steamer, coming upriver, had signaled that she would stay to port. Savez had the bell rung once to acknowledge that he would stay to starboard. The *Nymph* watched in silence.

Once past St. Francisville, Savez again had the telegraph line cut. Either the *Choctaw* or *Nymph* may have suspected something was wrong. He still had 160 miles to go before he reached New Orleans, which was, by now, a major base for the Union navy.

The *Lafayette* had outrun the other pursuers and persuaded the *Fort Hindman* to join the chase. The captain of the *Lafayette* tried to telegraph New Orleans from Morganza, only to find the line was cut. The *Fort Hindman* arrived at Bayou Sara fifty minutes after Savez passed. The *Choctaw*'s captain sent the *Hyacinth* down to Baton Rouge.[21]

Farther downriver at Port Hudson, Savez ordered the fireman to reduce speed. A low haze hung over the river. Ahead, a transport, coming out from shore, turned and headed downriver. Once he was sure the vessel was not approaching the *Webb*, Savez ordered the fireman to resume speed. At the shoreline, an officer aboard the USS *Naiad* wondered why the fort's commander had not ordered the stranger to land as he customarily did.

As the *Webb* approached Baton Rouge, Savez passed the sight where he had had to abandon the *Arkansas*. Baton Rouge was the site of an army barracks and the USS *General Price*. Like the *Tennessee*, the *General Price* had been captured from the Confederates.

Savez had enough of the ship lighted to make her look like a Union transport. At 1:30 A.M. the *General Price* was passed without incident. Below Baton Rouge, Savez had the telegraph line cut. One hour later the *Hyacinth* arrived to find the line dead.

Just before sunrise, the *Webb* cautiously approached Donaldsonville. Trying to look like a cotton transport, the *Webb* came abeam of the gunboat USS *Ouachita*. Just then, the Federal raised signal flags and ran out her guns. Savez ordered his flags raised in response. He was greatly relieved as he watched the Federal pull in her guns. The *Ouachita* had been conducting a morning drill.[22]

At Orange Grove below Donaldsonville, Savez sent men ashore to cut the telegraph line. The *Webb* was less than seventy-five miles from New Orleans.

Thirteen miles above Bonnet Carre Bend, Savez decided to again cut the telegraph line. Before he sent his men ashore, he made sure they were wearing their captured blue uniforms. A passerby spotted the party this time. The quick-thinking Confederates told the stranger that the rebels from Mobile had taken New Orleans.

A passing Union soldier also saw uniformed men chopping down telegraph poles and cutting the line. The soldier informed a lieutenant who rode to Bonnet Carre Bend to alert the colonel. There he discovered that his only telegraph operator had left his post, contrary to orders. The operator was found drunk in a local coffeehouse. By then Savez had cut the line below the bend. The colonel loaded the telegraph key in an ambulance with the intoxicated operator and sent him and the soldiers to repair the line and send the alert. The line was repaired, but the operator did not send the message until he returned to Bonnet Carre Bend, where the furious colonel kept him under guard in the telegraph office.[23]

Back in Donaldsonville, news of the *Webb*'s flight finally reached the captain of the *Ouachita,* who realized the steamer that had passed them earlier was not the army towboat, but rather the *Webb*. He then sent the news to the army asking that a telegram be sent to New Orleans. Finding the direct line cut, the operator used a second line that ran inland.

At the Headquarters Southern Division of Louisiana, New Orleans, the telegraph clicked out the warning that the *Webb* was coming downriver. The news was passed to Navy Headquarters on Canal Street. Every available gun in the fleet was ordered to bear on the point where the *Webb* would pass. The fleet, however, was waiting for a ram, because the telegram from the *Ouachita* failed to provide a good description of the Confederate steamer.[24]

As the *Webb* approached the bend at Twelve Mile Point, Savez had the American flag raised to half staff to seemingly honor Lincoln. The Crescent City lay ten miles ahead. Savez told part of the crew to put on their Union army coats, go out on deck, and smoke their pipes. The firemen were ordered to keep the boiler pressure up, but slow the steamer's speed.

As the *Webb* moved through New Orleans, crews of passing ships yelled out, asking if he had heard anything about an approaching Confederate blockade runner. Savez was relieved; they thought the *Webb* was a Union transport.[25]

The Federal ships were moored off the French Quarter. It was noon and the wharf was busy. The *Webb* steamed past ship after ship.

Suddenly, an orange flame spit out from a cannon on the USS *Lackawana*. The ship's pilot had seen the *Webb* earlier in the war, and convinced the captain to open fire. The shot crashed into the *Webb*'s bow four feet above the waterline. Plowing through the bow, the shot flew across the river into the town of Algiers.[26]

Savez yelled down the speaking tube for the engineer to give him full speed ahead. Turning, Savez then ordered the American flag lowered and the Confederate flag raised.

The quartermaster jumped to Savez's command. The cotton bale protecting the pilothouse disintegrated under the impact of a cannon ball. Shots parted the smokestack guy wires. The quartermaster had to lie flat on the deck as he changed flags.[27]

Savez then discovered that he could not see the spar torpedo. The *Lackawana*'s shot had broken it loose from the bow. The torpedo's lanyards trailed over the bow and down under the *Webb*. Hanging by a few ropes and banging against the hull were a hundred pounds of explosive. If the detonator hit, the steamer would be blown to pieces. The torpedo could not be pulled back aboard. Yet if Savez had cut it loose, the *Webb*'s wake could wash it into the churning paddlewheels and explode it.

Savez ordered the torpedo cut free. He had to take the chance that it would sink clear of the *Webb*.[28]

Then the *Webb* was passing a French warship. Savez ordered the Confederate flag dipped as a salute. Even under fire courtesy prevailed.[29]

As the *Webb* rounded the bend in the river across from Algiers, Savez saw what he thought was the sloop USS *Portsmouth*, anchored away from the riverbank. Savez ordered another spar torpedo rigged; he wanted to ram the sloop. The crew discovered that the *Lackawana*'s shot though the bow had smashed all the rigging. The *Webb*'s speed luckily closed the distance between the two ships before there was time to repair the rigging.

In his haste, Savez had forgotten that there was only one type of ship that was anchored away from all others. The sloop was the ammunition ship USS *Fearnot*. In her holds were over 3,000 barrels of black powder. An explosion would have destroyed a good portion of New Orleans and Algiers.[30]

As the *Webb* passed the *Fearnot*, Savez saw one of his pilots pick up a rifle. Standing on the sloop's deck was a Federal officer and a lady. Savez ordered the pilot to lower the rifle. The pilot muttered that it was the first time he had ever been ordered not to shoot a Yankee.

Rounding English Bend, Savez looked back upriver. Only the side-wheel steamer USS *Hollyhock* was starting out in pursuit. Savez knew the *Hollyhock* could not catch him. By the time the steamer had gotten up full steam pressure, the *Webb* would be well downriver.[31]

Behind him, Savez left a city in confusion. The *Webb* was said to be carrying Jefferson Davis and Kirby Smith. John Wilkes Booth was supposed to be at the helm. The gold and silver of the Confederate Treasury were aboard. Fort Morgan at Mobile Bay was alerted in case the *Webb* should try to enter the bay. Allan Pinkerton, the famous detective, later wrote a long letter detailing the escapade. With all the shots fired at the *Webb*, there was not much serious damage done. The roofs of two houses in Algiers were hit by cannon balls; the only fatalities were a couple of cows.

As the *Webb* continued downriver, Savez decided against stopping to cut the telegraph line. There had been enough time to notify Forts Jackson and St. Philip, but still maybe there was a chance of getting past them. Knowing that the *Hollyhock* was in pursuit, Savez thought that he would capture the steamer and transfer his crew to the *Hollyhock*.[32]

By three o'clock the *Webb* came to the *Richmond*. Fifty miles beyond the steam sloop lay the forts.

After ordering the spar torpedo rigging repaired, Savez told the pilot to make for the *Richmond*'s bow to clear the *Webb* of the Federal's broadside cannons. Maybe he could ram the *Richmond* and make it past the ship. The pilot replied that there was a shoal just ahead of the *Richmond*. He would have to swing wide and come in alongside. Just then the *Richmond* ran out her guns. Savez announced that he had been under the *Richmond*'s broadsides before and he did not wish to do it again.[33]

Ordering the *Webb* slowed, Savez then called together his officers in front of the pilot house.

Admitting that the mission had failed, he said:

> The *Richmond* will drown us all, and if she does not, the forts below will, as they have a range of three miles each way up and down the river, and they know by this time that we are coming. Had we passed New Orleans without being discovered I would have cut the wires below the city and we could have reached the Gulf with little trouble. As it is, I think the only thing for us to do is to set the *Webb* on fire and blow her up![34]

The *Webb* turned toward the left bank where the steamer grounded fifty yards from the shore. Lines were thrown over the bow and the word was passed to abandon ship. Savez helped light the bonfires to destroy her. When he saw the *Hollyhock* approaching, he jumped over the side and waded toward the bank.

Once ashore, the Confederates made for a nearby sugar plantation. There they hid behind some buildings and watched the crew of the *Hollyhock* try to put out the fire. At 4:30 P.M., April 24, 1865, the flames reached the magazine and blew up the *Webb*.[35]

Savez split up the crew into three groups to improve their chances of getting back to the Confederate lines in small groups, but he soon realized that all hope of escape was futile. The Union cavalry combed the roads, and the swamps were impassable. Not wanting to surrender to the army, Savez led his party back to the river. There he signaled a passing Union ship. Once aboard, he recognized the captain as his Annapolis classmate, Winfield S. Schley. Savez offered him his sword.

"Hell, Read. Put your sword away and have some coffee," replied his friend.[36]

That was the end of the war for Charles William Read. It had lasted four years, and finished close to where he started. During the war he had served on commerce raiders, ironclads, shore batteries, torpedo launches, and a side-wheel steamer.

Savez was taken back to New Orleans and placed aboard the USS *Florida,* which took him to New York. From there he was sent back to Fort Warren. The Confederacy was over. On May 26, 1865, Kirby Smith surrendered the Army of Trans-Mississippi. His was the last major Confederate army.

On June 28, Savez wrote the governor of Mississippi explaining that he had applied for the oath of allegiance and written to President Andrew Johnson requesting permission to take the amnesty oath. He also mentioned he was an Annapolis graduate. Savez wanted the governor to ask the president to grant him amnesty so he could go home. Savez took the oath of amnesty and was released from Fort Warren on July 24, 1865.[37]

CHAPTER ELEVEN

AN OLD PIRATE

Starting anew was difficult for Savez. The Radical Republicans in Congress were determined to make the southern "traitors" pay for what they had done. The Fourteenth Amendment forbade Confederate officers from holding civilian or military office if they had previously taken an oath to support the Constitution. It would take a two-thirds vote by each house to remove this disability.

It was impossible for a former "pirate" to serve on a United States' warship. Also, the fires Savez had lit in the Atlantic were still fresh in the memories of the New England merchant shipowners.

Old men, such as Maffitt and Semmes, could write their memoirs after the war. Some younger men joined other navies. Jimmy Morgan would eventually serve in Egypt. Savez, though, was undecided.

Returning to New Orleans Savez found that even in the Crescent City there were no jobs for an "ex-pirate." He knew of a small island in the West Indies that was not frequented by ships. On the island were plantations growing fruit. He could buy the fruit there and bring it back to New Orleans to sell. Savez did not have the money to buy the small brig he needed.

Savez told Morgan that other southern officers were serving as common sailors. His friend begged him not to do that. Morgan, having some wealth, offered to give Savez the money to buy the brig. Savez accepted and in less than a week he had outfitted the brig for sea.[1]

The fruit business venture failed. Savez even tried growing oranges in Florida, but he was not cut out to be a farmer.[2] Savez became embroiled in arguments with customhouse officials, who he believed, held a grudge against him. Savez finally had to abandon the brig.

Months later Savez explained to Morgan that no one could make a living in the fruit trade without being in what Savez called "the side lines." Morgan assumed Savez meant smuggling. Savez said that he was living in the French Quarter and that revenue officials needed time to cool down before he could be friendly with them. Morgan was not concerned about his money and agreed to keep quiet.

A few days later, Morgan came to see Savez with an old Annapolis classmate of Savez's, Edmund Gaines Read (no relative). Edmund, who had also fought for the South, knew about a civil war being fought in Colombia. The Colombian government was willing to pay cash for a gunboat.

Edmund had heard that the Federal Government was getting rid of most of the ships it used during the war. He knew of one in New York that was for sale cheap because it had dry rot and was not especially seaworthy. Edmund figured they could buy the boat, outfit it, and slip it out of the harbor without telling the authorities. With Savez's seamanship they could sail to Colombia.

That night the two Reads left for New York. Once there, the ship was purchased. After slapping on some paint, they bought and loaded a couple of small cannons and ammunition into the ship's hold. A small crew was hired. Savez sailed the ship out of the harbor without telling the custom officials.

Once in Puerto Colombia, the Reads sold the ship to the Colombian government. The money was split, and Edmund and the crew returned to the United States. Savez stayed behind to hunt up the leader of the Colombian rebels. He told the leader that their condition was hopeless because he had sold the government a "fine man-of-war." But, for a price, Savez offered to deliver the ship to the rebels. They accepted his offer.

Savez gathered up a baker's dozen of wharf bums and with their help seized the "fine man-of-war." He turned the ship over to the rebels and collected his money. Savez then left Colombia for the island of Trinidad.

From the safety of British soil, Savez wrote the president of Colombia, expressing his regret about being compelled to give the ship to the rebels. For a price, Savez offered to deliver the ship back to the government. The president wrote back saying if Savez ever set foot on Colombian soil again, he would hang him.[3]

The money Savez made off the "man-of-war" did not last long. Broke in Havana, Savez signed on as a sailor aboard a Spanish bark bound for Liverpool, England. The bark ran into a hurricane during the crossing. The ship was dismasted and passed through the eye of the storm. Afterward, Savez said that nothing had ever tried his courage like that storm.

After he arrived in England, Savez signed on a British merchantman, sailing for two years under the British flag. He eventually returned to New Orleans.

There Savez got a job as a captain for the United Fruit Company. He became master of the steamer *City of Dallas.* The vessel hauled fruit and passengers between Belize and New Orleans.

On December 3, 1867, having a job with a steady income, Savez married Rosa Hall in his mother's home in Raymond. The Reads had six children, although three died in childhood. The oldest, Roby, became the first officer on a merchant ship that sailed in both the Atlantic and the Pacific. He later was inspector of ships in Yokohama, Japan. Roby met Admiral Dewey, who told him that he remembered his father. Their second son, Mallory, also went to sea as a first officer on a ship running between New York and New Orleans. He later worked on a dredge boat on the Mississippi. Their third child was a daughter named Louise.

In 1878, Rosa died of yellow fever. On February 23, 1884, Savez married Nebraska May, the daughter of a judge in Meridian, Mississippi. Savez and Nebraska had a daughter whom they named May.

The long years at sea eventually affected Savez's health. He was no longer up to the rigors of long voyages. Still, Savez could not totally give up the sea; so he got a job as a pilot on the Southwest Pass.[4]

As the years passed, Savez decided to write his memoirs. He sent in an article for the *Southern Historical Society Papers.* Unlike Semmes, Savez was not bitter. He did, however, have strong opinions that offended some veterans. The Society wrote that they did not want to get embroiled in controversy.[5]

Some of Savez's old shipmates would write him asking if anything had been written about their wartime episodes. Occasionally in the evenings he would sit on the porch and make notes, but the old drive was gone. One old man in Meridian, Mississippi, referring to Savez later, said that one of his aunts had married "an old river pilot who never amounted to anything."[6]

Savez was not completely anonymous. Once, as he was piloting an inbound ship, he met Morgan. They talked about the old times. Savez looked the ship over and laughed, "Jimmie, wouldn't she make a bully blaze?"

The ship's captain instantly said, "I don't feel safe with you two pirates aboard!"[7]

The governor of Louisiana appointed Savez to the presidency of the Board of Harbor Masters at New Orleans, a position he held until the late 1880s. Savez then became ill with Bright's disease, a painful kidney infection.

He went to Meridian to get help from a friend who was a doctor. Convalescing at his father-in-law's home, he contracted influenza. In his weakened condition, the influenza developed into pneumonia. Charles William Read died at 2:00 A.M. on January 25, 1890. Savez is buried in Meridian's Rose Hill Cemetery. A tombstone with a simple fouled anchor marks the grave of a Southern hero.[8]

EPILOGUE

Charles William Read's greatest role was as a commerce raider. By relentlessly hunting Yankee merchant ships, the Confederate raiders crippled Northern maritime trade. At the start of the war, American ships carried more than twice the dollar value in foreign trade than the rest of the world's ships combined. By the end of the war, with the loss in ships through sinking and the transfer of American ships to foreign ownership, Great Britain ruled the seas. The American merchant marine did not recover until World War I.[1]

There is a subtle, but distinctive, difference between battle at sea and battle on land. Military historian John Keegan commented in his *The Face of Battle* that "the common sailor cannot, as the common soldier can by running away or sitting tight easily confound his commander's wishes. All being in the same boat, a ship's company generally does as its captain directs. . . ."[2] The effectiveness of a ship in battle is a measure of the commanding officer's leadership, skill, and aggressive spirit. Twentieth-century writers call it bushido—the way of the samurai. It is a blend of justice, courage, benevolence, politeness, honor, loyalty, and self-control. Read like Horatio Nelson displayed bushido. Both had an aggressive spirit, dared to do the unorthodox, and had a realistic sense of the uncertainty of battle.[3]

Read inspired and impressed not only his fellow Confederates, but also the Federals. The Confederate Congress issued a joint resolution thanking him for the part he played in the battle of New Orleans. Fellow officer J. Thomas Sharf in his *History of the Confederate States Navy* stated that Read's actions showed "magnificent courage and seamanship." Noting his reputation for coolness and determination at the battle of New Orleans, Maffitt personally applied for Read by stating that "as military officer of the deck he is not equal to many." In fifty-one days A. Drayton, one of the crew on the *Clarence*, the *Tacony*, and the *Archer*, changed his view of Read from disgust to admiration. Writers have compared Read with John Paul Jones. The *Dictionary of American Biography* says Read's "brilliant record was unsurpassed by any of his rank in the Union or Confederate Navies." Admiral Dewey wrote that Read's raiding off the East Coast was "worthy of the days of Drake" and "America never produced a navy officer more worthy of a place in history."[4]

The courageous are remembered for the inspirational examples they set. In recognition of his valor Lt. Charles William Read was awarded the Medal of Honor by the Sons of Confederate Veterans on August 9, 1979.[5]

SHIPS CAPTURED BY READ

DATE	NAME	TYPE	DISPOSITION
June 6	*Whistling Wind*	Bark	Burned
June 7	*Alfred H. Partridge*	Schooner	Bonded
June 9	*Mary Alvina*	Bark	Burned
June 12	*Tacony*★	Bark	Burned
June 12	*M. A. Shindler*	Schooner	Burned
June 12	*Kate Steward*	Schooner	Bonded
June 12	*Arabella*	Brig	Bonded
June 15	*Umpire*	Brig	Burned
June 20	*Isaac Webb*	Packet	Bonded
June 20	*Micawber*	Fishing Schooner	Burned
June 21	*Byzantium*	Clipper	Burned
June 21	*Goodspeed*	Bark	Burned
June 22	*Marengo*	Fishing Schooner	Burned
June 22	*Elizabeth Ann*	Fishing Schooner	Burned
June 22	*Rufus Choate*	Fishing Schooner	Burned
June 22	*Ripple*	Fishing Schooner	Burned
June 22	*Florence*	Fishing Schooner	Bonded
June 23	*Ada*	Fishing Schooner	Burned
June 23	*Wanderer*	Fishing Schooner	Burned
June 24	*Shatemuc*	Packet	Bonded

DATE	NAME	TYPE	DISPOSITION
June 24	*Archer*★	Fishing Schooner	Recaptured
June 26	*Caleb Cushing*	Revenue Cutter	Burned

★used as raider

SAIL PLAN (USS CONSTITUTION TAKEN FROM DICTIONARY OF AMERICAN NAVAL FIGHTING SHIPS)

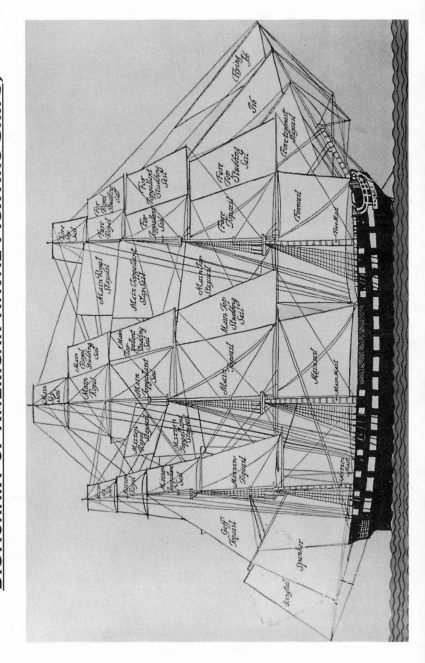

NAVAL GLOSSARY

abaft. In back of, farther aft.

abeam. At a right angle to the ship.

aft. Near the stern or back of the ship.

aloft. In the upper rigging; above the deck.

ashore. To leave the ship and go to the beach.

astern. Signifying position, in the rear of the stern.

athwartship. Perpendicular to the keel.

bar. A build up of sand or mud on the bottom of the entrance to a harbor or in a river.

bark. A sailing vessel with three masts with the forward two square-rigged and the mizzen, fore-and-aft.

beam. The width of the ship.

beat to windward. A ship sailing upwind in a zigzag fashion.

berth deck. The deck where hammocks are stowed for sleeping.

bilge. Curved section between the bottom and side of the ship.

bitts. A vertical post used in making fast lines.

boat howitzer. A brass cannon small enough to be used in a ship's boat.

boatswain. A petty officer (non-commissioned) with a broad knowledge and experience in rigging, boat handling, tackle, and general seamanship.

bobstays. A chain or wire rope running diagonally from the end of the bowsprit to the hull.

bow. The forward part of the ship.

bowsprit. A spar projecting forward over the bow for the purpose of holding the lower ends of the head sails.

braces. Ropes attached to the yard, used to alter its position in the horizontal plane.

breechings. The sheet metal connecting the boilers to the smokestacks.

brig. A two-masted sailing vessel, mostly square-rigged, but with a fore-and-aft mainsail.

bulkhead. A vertical partition corresponding to a wall of a room.

bulwarks. The ship's sides above the weather deck.

bunkers. A compartment used for stowage of coal.

buttock. The round part of a ship's stern.

capstan. A revolving drum, with usually a vertical axis, used for heaving in lines.

casemate. A sloping armor plated exterior bulkhead on an ironclad designed to protect the gun crews.

cathead. Two short beams of oak, projecting almost horizontally over each side of the ship's bow.

clew (to). To haul up a square sail to a yard.

clewlines. Lines running from the corner of the sail, know as the clew, to the yardarm and down to the deck.

clipper. A long three-masted sailing vessel with a narrow beam designed for long, fast passages.

close-hauled. Sailing as close to the wind as possible.

cutter. A single-masted sailing vessel with a fore-and-aft mainsail, foresail, and jibs.

deck. A part of a ship corresponding to the floor in a building.

dory. A flat-bottom boat with flaring hull and a narrow stern.

Downeaster. A person from Maine.

draft. The depth of the ship below the waterline.

ensign. A country's flag.

fathom. Six feet.

footrope. A rope under the yard for walking on while handling sails.

fore-and-aft. In line with the length of the ship.

foremast. The forward most mast on a sailing vessel having more than one mast.

forward. In the direction of the bow.

fouled anchor. An anchor with its anchor line twisted around it; small replicas used as jewelry.

freeboard. The vertical distance from the waterline to the weather deck.

gangplank. A term applied to boards used in transferring passengers or cargo from the ship to the dock.

grog. Rum diluted with water.

gunports. Openings in the hull for cannon to fire through.

halyards. Ropes used in hoisting sails, yards, or signal flags.

hatch. A opening in the deck for passage of cargo.

hawser. A large rope used in towing or mooring.

hermaphrodite. A two-masted sailing vessel square rigged on the fore mast and fore-and-aft on the mainmast.

holystones. Large porous flat stone used to scrub the decks.

hull. The outer body of a ship.

jibsheet. The rope used to haul in the jib.

ketch. A two masted sailing vessel without a fore mast.

knots. A nautical mile (approximately $1^1/_7$ statute miles); ship's speed is given in knots meaning knots per hour.

land breeze. A night breeze from land to sea.

lanyard. A piece of rope having one end free and the attached to any object for the purpose of control.

lapstrake. A term applied to boats having the strakes or other planks overlapping.

lashings. Rope used to secure or tied something down.

latitude. The distance north or south of the equator measured in degrees.

leeward. In the opposite direction from which the wind is blowing.

longitude. The distance east or west of Greenwich, England, measured in degrees.

main deck. The principal deck of the ship, usually the highest extending from bow to stern.

mainmast. The tallest mast on a sailing vessel.

man-of-war. An armed naval vessel.

marlinespike. A pointed tapering tool used in separating strands of rope in splicing.

masthead. Top of the mast.

mizzen. The aft most mast on a sailing vessel.

mooring lines. The ropes used to tied up a ship to a dock or pier.

oilskins. Waterproof clothing.

packet. A full-bodied, three-masted sailing vessel.

pendant. A length of rope or wire often fitted with an eye at each end.

petty officer. An enlisted man temporarily raised to rank as an officer.

poop deck. The raised deck on the aft end of a sailing vessel.

port. The left-hand side of a ship when looking forward; an opening in the side of a ship.

pounder. A rating of a cannon roughly corresponding to the weight of the projectile fired.

powder monkeys. Young boys used to carry powder from the magazine and the guns.

quarter. The upper part of a ship near the stern.

quarterdeck. A term applied to the aft part of the upper deck reserved for officers.

race. Water disturbed by conflicting currents.

ratlines. Short lines secured to the shrouds serving as the rungs of a ladder.

reef. Shorten sail.

reef points. Short lines used to reef sails.

rigging. A term used collectively for all the ropes and chains employed to support the masts, yards, and booms of a ship.

roll. The rocking side-to-side motion of a ship.

sailing master. An officer in charge of the sailing of the ship.

schooner. A two or more masted fore-and-aft sailing vessel.

scuttle. The act of deliberately sinking a ship; a very small hatch.

sea breeze. A breeze blowing from the ocean to land.

sea chanties. Songs sung by sailors.

sextant. A navigation instrument for determining the altitude of the sun or stars.

shackle. A U-shaped fitting with a pin or bolt.

sheer. The curvature of a deck in a fore and aft direction.

sheet. A line used for trimming a sail.

shipmates. A term used for sailors aboard the same ship.

shrouds. The rope or wire extending from the masthead to the sides of a ship providing lateral support to the mast.

sloop. A loosely applied term to small sailing vessel carrying less than twenty-four cannons.

sou'wester. Oilskin rain gear; A rain hat with a broad brim in the back.

spars. A term applied to a pole serving as a mast, yard, or boom.

square-rigger. A general term used for sailing vessel with sails running athwarthship.

starboard. The right-hand side of a ship when looking forward.

stays. Ropes supporting the mast.

stern. The after or back of the ship.

tack. Moving to windward on a zigzag course.

tackle. Any combination of ropes and blocks (pulleys) that multiplies power.

tompion. A plug that fits into the bore of a cannon.

tholepin. Oarlocks made from pins.

tiller. An arm attached to the rudder head for operating the rudder.

trail boards. Decorative boards on the bow sometimes with the ship's name.

wardroom. A room or space set aside for use of the officers for social purposes. Also used as the officers' mess or dining room.

warrant officer. A non-commissioned officer.

watch. One of the four-hour periods into which the twenty-four-hour day is divided.

waterline. The intersection of the water and the hull of the ship.

weatherdeck. The uppermost deck exposed to the weather.

whip. A term used for hoisting light loads.

windlass. A machine used to hoist anchors.

windward. Toward the wind.

yard. A term applied to a spar attached at its middle to a mast and running across a ship for the supporting of sails.

NOTES

ABBREVIATIONS

BL *Battles and Leaders of the Civil War* (New York: Thomas Yoseloff, 1887–1888: reprinted 1956).

CWNC *Civil War Naval Chronology,* Naval History Division, Navy Department.

DANFS *Dictionary of American Naval Fighting Ships,* Naval History Division.

MDAH Mississippi Department of the Archives and History, Jackson, Miss.

MHSL Maine Historical Society Library, Portland, Maine.

NARG National Archives and Record Administration, Record Group, Washington, D.C.

NHC/ZB U.S. Naval Historical Center, ZB File Operation Division, Washington Navy Yard, Washington, D.C.

OICN *Ordnance Instructions for the Confederate Navy Relating to the Preparation of Vessels of War for Battle,* Confederate Navy Department.

OR *War of the Rebellion: A Compilation of the Official Records of the Union and Confederate Armies,* 128 volumes and index, Washington, D.C.

ORN *Official Records of the Union and Confederate Navies in the War of The Rebellion,* 30 volumes and index, Washington, D.C.

ORUSNA   *Official Register of the Officers and Acting Midshipmen of*
          the United States Naval Academy, Annapolis, Md.
ROCSN   *Register of Officers of the Confederate States Navy,*
          1861–1865.
SHC/CHNC Southern Historical Collection Manuscripts Depart-
          ment, Wilson Library, the University of North Car-
          olina, Chapel Hill, N.C.
SHC/TSHS Southern Historical Collection, *Transactions of the*
          Southern Historical Society.
SHSP   *Southern Historical Society Papers.*
USDCA   *United States District Court for the District of Columbia*
          Sitting in Admiralty.

CHAPTER 1: A WOLF IN FISHERMAN'S CLOTHING

1. Gideon Welles, *Diary of Gideon Welles* (Boston and New York: Houghton Mifflin, 1911), 1:345–346.
2. Unsigned news story, *New York Daily Tribune,* 23, no. 6935 (June 26, 1863): 1.
3. Southern Historical Collection, *Transactions of the Southern Historical Society* (Baltimore, Md.: Turnbull Brothers, 1874), 1 (January to December 1874): 83 (hereafter cited as SHC/*TSHS*); *Portland Press,* June 27, 1923, *Southern Historical Society Papers* (hereafter cited as *SHSP*). Newspaper courtesy Maine Historical Society Library (hereafter cited as MHSL).
4. National Archives and Record Administration, Washington, D.C., Coast Guard Division, Record Group 26, *Register of Revenue Cutter Service Officers, 1790–1914,* Dudley Davenport service record (hereafter cited as NARG).
5. A. A. Hoehling, "When the Confederates Invaded Portland," Features section, *Portland Sunday Telegram,* May 18, 1958.
6. Louise D. Rich, *The Coast of Maine* (New York: Thomas Y. Crowell, 1970), 169–170.
7. Florence Kern, *The United States Revenue Cutters, in the Civil War* (Bethesda, Md.: Alised Enterprises, 1976), 12–13.
8. James M. Morgan and John Marquand, *Prince and Boatswain: Sea Tales from the Recollection of Rear Admiral Charles E. Clark* (Greenfield, Mass.: E. A. Hall & Company, 1915), 33.
9. Carl von Clausewitz, *On War,* ed. Anatol Rapoport (New York: Penguin Books, 1968), 172.
10. Edward H. Elwell, *Portland and Vicinity* (1876: reprint, Portland, Maine: Greater Portland Landmarks, 1975), 38–85; Winfield M. Thompson, "A Confederate Raid (concluded)," *The Rudder* 16, no. 4 (April 1905): 243.
11. Howard I. Chapelle, *The History of American Sailing Ships* (New York: Bonanza Books, 1935), 215.
12. United States Department of the Navy, *Official Records of the Union and Confederate Navies in the War of The Rebellion,* statistical data, 30 volumes and index. 1st ser., vol. 2 (Washington, D.C.: Government Printing Office, 1894–1927), 330 (hereafter cited as *ORN*); Eugene B. Canfield, *Notes on Naval Ordnance of the American Civil War, 1861–1865* (Washington, D.C.: The American Ordnance Association, 1960), 8. Although this *ORN* citation refers to the howitzer as brass, Canfield states that the howitzers were bronze.
13. Mallory J. Read, data concerning Charles W. Read from Read's grandson, Mallory J. Read (Arlington, Va.: n.d., hereafter cited as Read, Mallory J.); Frank Moore, *The*

Rebellion Record: A Diary of American Events with Documents, Narratives, Illustrative Incidents, Poetry, Etc. (New York: D. Van Nostrand, 1864), 7: 134.

14. Thompson, "A Confederate Raid, (concluded)," 243. The various sources used by the author differ somewhat in their accounts of the Portland raid. The cited reference is the principal work used.
15. *ORN,* 1st. ser., vol. 2, 657.
16. Thompson, "A Confederate Raid, (concluded)," 243.
17. Moore, *The Rebellion Record,* 7: 133.
18. Robert Hunt, "The Johnny's Story," a paper read before the Confederates' Veteran Association of Savannah, Ga., on October 27, 1894, MHSL.
19. Thompson, "A Confederate Raid (concluded)," 244. Some accounts of the capture of the *Caleb Cushing* state that Davenport was an Annapolis classmate of Read. Francis O. Davenport (MI Class of 1861) was a classmate. Dudley Davenport's service record shows that he was older than Read and the ships on which he was stationed never came to Annapolis.
20. Moore, *The Rebellion Record,* 7: 130; Clarence Hale, "The Capture of the *Caleb Cushing,*" *Collections of the Maine Historical Society,* 3rd ser., vol. 1 (Portland, Maine, 1901), 195; James D. Hill, "Charles W. Read: Confederate Von Luckner," *The South Atlantic Quarterly* (Durham, N.C.) 28 (January to October, 1929): 403.
21. William B. Kenniston, "The Capture of the *Caleb Cushing,*" Illustrated Magazine Section, *Lewiston Journal,* May 30, 1908, newspaper courtesy MHSL; Hunt, "The Johnny's Story."
22. Thompson, "A Confederate Raid (concluded)," 224.
23. Hunt, "The Johnny's Story."
24. Moonset data calculated by author using computer program "Moon Phase."
25. Moore, *The Rebellion Record,* 133.
26. Hoehling, "When the Confederates Invaded Portland"; Read, Mallory J.
27. Moore, *The Rebellion Record,* 133. Data on the course used to escape from Portland harbor derived by the author using "Portland Harbor and Vicinity," chart C&GS 325 (U.S. Department of Commerce, Washington, D.C.).
28. Thompson, "A Confederate Raid (concluded)," 244; Moore, *The Rebellion Record,* 133.
29. Kenniston, "The Capture of the *Caleb Cushing.*"
30. Thompson, "A Confederate Raid (concluded)," 245.
31. Mason Smith, *Confederates Downeast: Confederate Operations in and around Maine* (Portland, Maine: Provincial Press, 1985), 96. The author discussed the location of the shot lockers and magazine with Howard I. Chapelle on February 4, 1971.
32. Thompson, "A Confederate Raid (concluded)," 245.
33. Notes taken by the author from the files of the MHSL (hereafter cited as Notes, MHSL).
34. Hoehling, "When the Confederates Invaded Portland."
35. Hale, "The Capture of the *Caleb Cushing,*" 198; *Portland Press*; Notes, MHSL.
36. Hale, "The Capture of the *Caleb Cushing,*" 198.
37. Hunt, "The Johnny's Story."
38. Ibid.
39. Moore, *The Rebellion Record,* 133.
40. Canfield, *Notes on Naval Ordnance of the American Civil War, 1861–1865,* 8.
41. Hunt, "The Johnny's Story."
42. Hale, "The Capture of the *Caleb Cushing,*" 199.
43. *ORN,* 1st. ser., vol. 2, 327–328.
44. Moore, *The Rebellion Record,* 131.
45. Hale, "The Capture of the *Caleb Cushing,*" 200.
46. Unsigned news story, *Evening Courier,* June 29, 1863, MHSL.
47. Thompson, "A Confederate Raid (concluded)," 246.
48. *ORN,* 1st ser., vol. 2, 326.

49. Thompson, "A Confederate Raid (concluded)," 248.
50. Hoehling, "When the Confederates Invaded Portland."
51. Hunt, "The Johnny's Story."
52. Notes, MHSL.
53. George W. Rice, *The Shipping Days of Old Boothbay From the Revolution to the World War,* (Portland, Maine: Southworth-Anthoensen Press, 1938), 327.
54. *ORN,* 1st ser. vol. 2, 323.
55. Edward H. Elwell, *Portland and Vicinity,* 140; Dennis Noble, *Historical Register: U.S. Revenue Cutter Service Officers, 1790–1914* (Washington, D.C.: Printed by the Coast Guard Historian's Office, A Bicentennial Publication, 1990), 48; NARG 29; *Portland Press;* Department of Transportation, United States Coast Guard, *Record of Movements: Vessels of the United States Coast Guard, 1790–December 31, 1933* (Washington, D.C.: Reprinted by the Coast Guard Historian's Office, A Bicentennial Publication, 1989), 202; Notes, MHSL; Moore, *The Rebellion Record,* 131.

CHAPTER 2: A YOUNG MISSISSIPPIAN

1. Read, Mallory J.; Mr. and Mrs. John Maynard, data concerning Charles W. Read from Read's great-grandson, John Maynard (Woodland Hills, Calif.: n.d., hereafter cited as Maynard, John R. and Betty).
2. Maynard, John R. and Betty; Mrs. William T. Read, data concerning Charles W. Read from the wife of Read's nephew, Mrs. William T. Read (Pasadena, Tex.: n.d., hereafter cited as Read, Mrs. William T).
3. NARG 29, 1850 Census, Mississippi, Hinds County.
4. Maynard, John R. and Betty; Mississippi Department of the Archives and History, data concerning Charles W. Read (hereafter cited as MDAH), 1.
5. Maynard, John R. and Betty.
6. MDAH, 2.
7. Douglas W. Jerrold, "Black-Eyed Susan; or, All in the Downs, A Nautical and Domestic Drama in Two Acts" (Boston: Spencer's Boston Theater, 1856; Library of Congress, Washington, D.C.).
8. MDAH, 2.
9. Read, Mallory J.
10. Maynard, John R. and Betty; U.S. Naval Historical Center, ZB file Travel Records Operation Division, Washington Navy Yard, Washington, D.C. (hereafter cited as NHC/ZB).
11. NARG 45, *Letters and Reports Received by the Superintendent Relating to Individual Midshipman, 1846–88.*
12. Edwards C. Marshall, *The History of the United States Naval Academy* (New York: D. Van Nostrand, 1862), 50–53; Jack Sweetman, *The U.S. Naval Academy* (Annapolis, Md.: Naval Institute Press, 1979), 25–26.
13. Marshall, *The History of the United States Naval Academy,* 132–134; James R. Soley, *Historical Sketch of the United States Naval Academy* (Washington, D.C.: Government Printing Office, 1872), 129; United States Naval Academy, *Minutes of the Academic Board: United States Navy,* vol. 2 (Annapolis, Md., 1856).
14. The United States Naval Academy Alumni Association, Inc., *Register of Alumni, Graduates, and former Naval Cadets and Midshipmen* (Annapolis, Md.: The Association, Publishers, 1983), 138.
15. United States Naval Academy, *Regulations of the U.S. Naval Academy at Annapolis, Maryland* (Washington, D.C.: A. O. Nicholson, 1855), 11.
16. Sweetman, *The U.S. Naval Academy,* 49.
17. NARG 45, *Naval Records Collection of the Office of Naval Records and Library: Correspondence between the Superintendent of the Naval Academy and the Secretary of the Navy,* Letter dated March 24, 1856.

18. Ibid.
19. Marshall, *The History of the United States Naval Academy,* 68.
20. United States Naval Academy, *Regulations of the United States Naval Academy, as approved by the Secretary of the Navy* (Washington, D.C.: Government Printing Office, 1867), 120–123, 161. The description of a typical day combines this source with Marshall, *The History of the United States Naval Academy.*
21. NARG 45.
22. United States Naval Academy, *Conduct Roll: U.S. Naval Academy Registers of Delinquencies* (Annapolis, Md., 1857, 1858–1859, 1859–1860).
23. Ibid.
24. Morgan and Marquand, *Prince and Boatswain,* 31–32.
25. Sweetman, *The U.S. Naval Academy,* 37, 48–49.
26. Ralph J. Roske and Charles Van Doren, *Lincoln's Commando: The Biography of Commander W. B. Cushing, U.S.N.* (New York: Harper Brothers, 1957), 62.
27. George Dewey, *Autobiography of George Dewey* (New York: Charles Scribner's Sons, 1913), 17.
28. Leland Lovette, *School of the Sea* (New York: Frederick A. Stokes, 1941), 73; William H. Parker, *Recollections of a Naval Officer, 1841–1865* (New York: Charles Scribner's Sons, 1883), 119.
29. NARG 45.
30. Read, Mallory J.
31. United States Naval Academy, *Official Register of the Officers and Acting Midshipmen of the United States Naval Academy,* June 1856 (Washington, D.C.: William A. Harris, Public Printer, 1858), 7 (hereafter cited as *ORUSNA*).
32. Marshall, *The History of the United States Naval Academy,* 53–55; H. Magruder, "A Walk Through Annapolis in Bygone Days," *U.S. Naval Institute Proceedings,* June 1929, 516.
33. Robert Seager II, *Alfred Thayer Mahan: The Man and His Letters* (Annapolis, Md.: Naval Institute Press, 1977), 15–16.
34. Sweetman, *The U.S. Naval Academy,* 52.
35. *ORUSNA,* June 1859, 4, 8.
36. Howard I. Chapelle, *The History of the American Sailing Navy* (New York: Bonanza Books, 1949), 440.
37. NARG 45, *Logbook Journal of a Summer's Cruise Aboard USS* Plymouth, *June–Aug. 1859.* Except as noted the summer cruise is taken from the ship's logbook.
38. Nathaniel Bowditch, *American Practical Navigator: An Epitome of Navigation,* pub. no. 9, vol. 1 (Washington, D.C.: Defense Mapping Agency Hydrographic Center, 1977), 781. The description of the Gulf Stream from this source was added to the *Plymouth's* logbook record of the voyage. Data used on the *Plymouth's* voyage were derived by the author using the "Pilot Chart of the North Atlantic Ocean," Chart no. 16 (U.S. Naval Oceanographic Office, Washington, D.C.).
39. Christopher Martin, *Damn the Torpedoes! The Story of America's First Admiral, David Glasgow Farragut* (New York: Abelard-Schuman, 1970), 21. Although Farragut's day on the USS *Essex* occurs before the sailing of the *Plymouth,* it is typical of a day at sea at this time.
40. Bowditch, *American Practical Navigator,* 781. The description of the fog from this source was added to the *Plymouth's* logbook record of the voyage.
41. Ibid., 1267. The description of the storm from this source was added to the *Plymouth's* logbook record of the voyage.
42. Darcy Lever, *The Young Sea Officer's Sheet Anchor; or, A Key to the Leading of Rigging, and to Practical Seamanship* (1808; reprint, Providence, R.I.: The Ship Model Society of Rhode Island, 1930), 83. The description of reefing the topsail from this source was added to the *Plymouth's* logbook record of the voyage.
43. NARG 45.
44. Ibid.

45. Bowditch, *American Practical Navigator,* 782. The description of the Canary and North Equatorial currents from this source were added to the *Plymouth's* logbook record of the voyage.

46. Winfield S. Schley, *Forty-five Years under the Flag* (New York: D. Appleton, 1904), 7.

47. NARG 45.

48. William S. Dudley, *Going South: U.S. Navy Officer Resignations and Dismissals on the Eve of the Civil War* (Washington, D.C.: Naval Historical Foundation, 1981), 45.

49. NARG 45.

50. Schley, *Forty-five Years under the Flag,* 8.

51. *ORUSNA,* June 1860, 7.

52. NARG 45, *Journal of the Naval Academy,* 1854–1857.

53. Schley, *Forty-five Years under the Flag,* 9.

54. *ORUSNA,* June 1860, 7.

55. Morgan and Marquand, *Prince and Boatswain,* 31.

56. NHC/ZB; NARG 45, Log of the USS *Powhatan,* 1860–1861.

57. Naval History Division, *Dictionary of American Naval Fighting Ships,* vol. 5 (Washington, D.C.: Government Printing Office, 1970), 365 (hereafter cited as *DANFS*).

58. NARG 45.

59. Charles W. Read, "Reminiscences of the Confederate States Navy," *Southern Historical Society Papers 1,* no. 5 (Richmond: 1876), 331 (hereafter cited as *SHSP*).

60. MDAH, 2.

61. Read, "Reminiscences of the Confederate States Navy," 331.

62. NARG 45.

63. Lovette, *School of the Sea,* 82–83.

64. MDAH

65. NHC/ZB.

66. Read, "Reminiscences of the Confederate States Navy," 331.

67. T. C. Leon, *Four Years in Rebel Capitals* (Mobile, Ala.: The Gossip Printing Company, 1890), 23–26. The description of Montgomery from this source was added to Read's "Reminiscences of the Confederate States Navy."

68. NARG 29, 1860 Census, Mississippi, Hinds County.

69. MDAH, 4.

70. Office of Naval Records and Library United States Navy Department, *Register of Officers of the Confederate States Navy, 1861–1865* (Washington, D.C.: Government Printing Office, 1931), 161 (hereafter cited as *ROCSN*).

71. NHC/ZB.

72. Read, Mrs. William T. During the war, Maria and Elizabeth stayed with Maria's brother. Union troops held Confederate prisoners in the house. Upon learning that two of the soldiers were sleeping atop the piano, seventeen-year-old Elizabeth ordered them to get off.

As they got down one said, "We will if you will play for us."

"I will not play for you, but I will play for the two Confederate prisoners you have over there."

As she played, one of the Federals started to turn the music. Noticing a diamond ring on his finger, Elizabeth told him she knew he had stolen it from some southern girl.

"You can have it, if you can get if off my finger."

Elizabeth asked for his knife and the soldier, thinking she was joking, handed it to her. In a flash, she opened it and whacked at the soldier's finger. Blood flew as he draw back a cut hand.

"I believe you want to kill me!" he yelped.

"No, not you, but I would like to kill Capt. Chambers."

The soldier, thinking his commanding officer would be amused by the teenager, handed her his pistol, saying, "He is out on the porch; go kill him."

Just at that moment, Maria walked past the parlor door. Seeing Elizabeth with the pistol, she screamed and hustled her daughter upstairs to her room.

73. Maynard, John R. and Betty. After the war, John Read had little for Savez to inherit. His farm had been cleaned out by both the Confederate and Union armies, forcing him to live off a pension he had gotten because of his War of 1812 service. In 1872, John Read filed a claim for property damage by the Union army. When asked if he or any of his family served in the Confederacy, John failed to mention Savez. Perhaps this was more in fear of being denied the pension than disowning Savez. The claim was followed by a series of hearings, denials of the claim, and appeals that continued even after John Read died in 1878. The court finally concluded that his pension proved his loyalty and a settlement of $2,160.00 was made in 1916. Only two of his grandchildren were alive to collect the money.

74. Charles L. Dufour, *The Night the War Was Lost* (Garden City, N.Y.: Doubleday, 1960), 34.

CHAPTER 3: CSS *McRAE*

1. Alfred T. Mahan, *The Influence of Sea Power upon History* (1890; reprint, New York: Hill and Wang, 1957), 25.

2. William Still, "The Common Sailor," *Civil War Times Illustrated* 24, no. 1 (March 1985): 12.

3. E. B. Potter and Chester W. Nimitz, *Sea Power: A Naval History* (Englewood Cliffs, N.J.: Prentice-Hall, 1960), 248–251; J. Thomas Scharf, *History of the Confederate States Navy from Its Organization to the Surrender of Its Last Vessel* (New York: Fairfax Press, 1887; reprint, 1977), 24–25, 32–33.

4. NHC/ZB.

5. Stephen R. Wise, *Lifeline of the Confederacy: Blockade Running during the Civil War* (Columbia: University of South Carolina Press, 1988), 21–22.

6. Read, "Reminiscences of the Confederate States Navy," 332.

7. *DANFS,* Vol. II, 521.

8. Ibid., 548; Raimondo Luraghi, *A History of the Confederate Navy* (Naval Institute Press: Annapolis, Md., 1996), 3, 33.

9. Shelby Foote, *The Civil War: A Narrative: Fredericksburg to Meridian* (New York: Random House, reprint, New York: 1963; Vintage Books, 1986), 154.

10. James R. Soley, *The Blockade and the Cruisers* (New York: Charles Scribner's Sons, 1883), 241; Francis T. Miller, *The Photographic History of the Civil War: The Navies* (New York: Thomas Yoseloff, 1912; reprint, New York: Castle Books, 1957), 118.

11. Dufour, *The Night the War Was Lost,* 108; H. Allen Gosnell, *Rebel Raider: Being an Account of Raphael Semmes's Cruise in the C.S.S.* Sumter (Chapel Hill: University of North Carolina Press, 1948), 12. Huger's problems getting the *McRae* ready for sea were similar to Semmes's problems outfitting the *Sumter.* Luraghi, *A History of the Confederate Navy,* 28.

12. Luraghi, *A History of the Confederate Navy,* 82.

13. NHC/ZB. When the author started working for the Navy Department, the mileage allowance was sixteen cents a mile.

14. Dufour, *The Night the War Was Lost,* 41–42; *ORN,* 1st. ser., vol. 16, 535–536.

15. Read, "Reminiscences of the Confederate States Navy," 333.

16. *ORN,* 1st. ser. vol. 16, 582–583.

17. Read, "Reminiscences of the Confederate States Navy," 333; Benjamin F. Butler, *Butler's Book* (Boston: A. M. Thayer, 1892), 351–352.

18. NARG 45, *Logbook of USS* Massachusetts.

19. Zeb H. Burns, *Ship Island and the Confederacy* (Hattiesburg: University and College Press of Mississippi, 1971), 11.

20. Read, "Reminiscences of the Confederate States Navy," 333–334.

21. Burns, *Ship Island and the Confederacy,* 14.

22. Read, "Reminiscences of the Confederate States Navy," 334.

23. Confederate Navy Department, *Ordnance Instructions for the Confederate Navy Relating to the Preparation of Vessels of War for Battle* (London: Saunders, Otley, 1864), 140 (hereafter cited as *OICN*).

24. James M. Morgan, *Recollections of a Rebel Reefer* (Boston and New York: Houghton Mifflin, 1917), 53.

25. Read, "Reminiscences of the Confederate States Navy," 334.

26. Wise, *Lifeline of the Confederacy: Blockade Running during the Civil War,* 22.

27. Gosnell, *Rebel Raider: Being an Account of Raphael Semmes's Cruise in the C.S.S.* Sumter, 25–28.

28. Read, "Reminiscences of the Confederate States Navy," 334. Read identifies the steamer as the *Joy.* The DANFS, vol. 2, 536 and other sources state that the steamer was the *Ivy.* The *Joy* could possibly have been an earlier name for the vessel.

29. Morgan and Marquand, *Prince and Boatswain,* 34.

30. Maynard, John R. and Betty.

31. Naval History Division, Navy Department, *Civil War Naval Chronology,* part 1 (Washington, D.C.: Government Printing Office, 1965), 18 (hereafter cited as *CWNC*).

32. Allen H. Gosnell, *Guns on the Western Waters* (Baton Rouge: Louisiana State University Press, 1949), 35; Frederic S. Hill, *Twenty Years at Sea* (Boston and New York: Houghton Mifflin, 1893), 150.

33. *DANFS,* vol. 2, 536, 577.

34. Ibid., 546. The *Manassas's* 64-pound Dahlgren was later replaced with a 32-pounder cannonade.

35. Morgan, *Recollections of a Rebel Reefer,* 55.

36. William N. Still Jr., *Iron Afloat: The Story of the Confederate Armorclads* (Columbia: University of South Carolina Press, 1985), 50–51.

37. George N. Hollins, "Autobiography of Commodore George Nicholas Hollins, C.S.A.," *Maryland Historical Magazine* 34 (1939): 240.

38. Read, "Reminiscences of the Confederate States Navy," 335.

39. Hill, *Twenty Years at Sea,* 153–157.

40. Gosnell, *Guns on the Western Waters,* 40; *ORN,* 1st ser. vol. 16, 712–716.

41. Read, "Reminiscences of the Confederate States Navy," 335.

42. Morgan and Marquand, *Prince and Boatswain,* 36.

43. Hill, *Twenty Years at Sea,* 158–161.

44. Dufour, *The Night the War Was Lost,* 85.

45. Read, "Reminiscences of the Confederate States Navy," 336.

46. Morgan and Marquand, *Prince and Boatswain,* 36–37.

47. Ibid., 37–39.

48. *ORN,* 1st ser., vol. 22, 842.

49. Read, "Reminiscences of the Confederate States Navy," 336.

50. Luraghi, *A History of the Confederate Navy,* 82; Morgan, *Recollections of a Rebel Reefer,* 61. Although Morgan says that the *Tuscarora* accompanied the *McRae, DANFS,* vol. 2, 524, states that the *Tuscarora* was destroyed by a fire on November 23, 1861, at Helena, Arkansas.

51. Morgan and Marquand, *Prince and Boatswain,* 40.

52. Morgan, *Recollections of a Rebel Reefer,* 61.

53. *ORN,* 1st ser., vol. 22, 804–805; *DANFS,* vol. 2, 577.

54. Morgan and Marquand, *Prince and Boatswain,* 40.

55. *DANFS,* vol. 2, 524, 537.

56. Read, "Reminiscences of the Confederate States Navy," 336; Luraghi, *A History of the Confederate Navy,* 389 n. 117, states "By this date, several Union gunboats did arrive and were ready for action and capable of inflicting on the Confederates a rough retreat." John D. Milligan, *Gunboats down the Mississippi* (Annapolis, Md.: United States Naval

Institute, 1965), 22–23, states that the gunboats were not finished. The author feels that if the Confederates had attacked they could have inflicted enough damage to set back the construction and thus delay the attack on Fort Henry.

57. *ROCSN,* 161.
58. Read, "Reminiscences of the Confederate States Navy," 337.
59. Morgan, *Recollections of a Rebel Reefer,* 62.
60. Ibid., 62–63.
61. Larry J. Daniel and Lynn N. Bock, *Island No. 10: Struggle for the Mississippi Valley* (Tuscaloosa: The University of Alabama Press), 45–46, 50.
62. United States War Department, *War of the Rebellion: A Compilation of the official Records of the Union and Confederate Armies,* 128 volumes and index, 1st ser., vol. 8 (Washington, D.C.: Government Printing Office, 1880–1902), 81 (hereafter cited as *OR*).
63. *OICN,* 137.
64. Joseph C. Bruzek, *The IX" Dahlgren Broadside Gun* (Annapolis, Md.: United States Naval Academy Museum, n.d.), 6.
65. Morgan, *Recollections of a Rebel Reefer,* 67–68.
66. *OR,* 1st. ser., vol. 8, 81.
67. Morgan and Marquand, *Prince and Boatswain,* 41.
68. Morgan, *Recollections of a Rebel Reefer,* 64.
69. *OICN,* 137.
70. Morgan, *Recollections of a Rebel Reefer,* 65; Daniel and Bock, *Island No. 10: Struggle for the Mississippi Valley,* 57.
71. *ORN,* 1st ser., vol. 8, 81.
72. Morgan and Marquand, *Prince and Boatswain,* 41.
73. *ORN,* 1st ser., vol. 8, 82; Daniel and Bock, *Island No. 10: Struggle for the Mississippi Valley,* 61.
74. *DANFS,* vol. 2, 547, 558.
75. Daniel and Bock, *Island No. 10; Struggle for the Mississippi Valley,* 63.
76. *OR,* 1st ser., vol. 8, 82.
77. Morgan, *Recollections of a Rebel Reefer,* 68–69.
78. *CWNC,* part 2, 36.
79. Read, "Reminiscences of the Confederate States Navy," 337–338.
80. Morgan and Marquand, *Prince and Boatswain,* 41–42.
81. Ibid., 42.
82. Read, "Reminiscences of the Confederate States Navy," 338.
83. Morgan and Marquand, *Prince and Boatswain,* 42.
84. *CWNC,* part 2, 45–46.
85. Read, "Reminiscences of the Confederate States Navy," 339.
86. Virgil C. Jones, *The Civil War at Sea,* vol. 2 (New York: Holt, Rinehart and Winston, 1961), 66.
87. Read, "Reminiscences of the Confederate States Navy," 339; Morgan, *Recollections of a Rebel Reefer,* 70.
88. Morgan, *Recollections of a Rebel Reefer,* 74.
89. Read, "Reminiscences of the Confederate States Navy," 339–340.
90. Ibid.

CHAPTER 4: GÖTTERDÄMMERUNG

1. Read, "Reminiscences of the Confederate States Navy," 339–340.
2. Dufour, *The Night the War Was Lost,* 209–211.
3. George W. Cable, "New Orleans before the Capture," *Battles and Leaders of the Civil War* (New York: Thomas Yoseloff, 1887–1888: reprint, New York: Appleton-Century-Crofts 1956), vol. 2, 19 (hereafter cited as *BL*).
4. Luraghi, *A History of the Confederate Navy,* 160.

5. *DANFS*, vol. 2, 544, 548–549. The *Virginia* was built on the hull of the USS *Merrimack* whereas the *Mississippi* and the *Louisiana* were built from the keel up.

6. Read, "Reminiscences of the Confederate States Navy," 340–341.

7. Jack Coggins, *Arms and Equipment of the Civil War* (Garden City, N.Y.: Doubleday, 1962), 143.

8. Ibid., 88; Luraghi, *A History of the Confederate Navy* 159–160; Editors, "The Opposing Forces in the Operations at New Orleans," *BL,* vol. 2, 75.

9. David D. Porter, "The Opening of the Lower Mississippi," *BL,* vol. 2, 33. Current velocity verified from data received by the author from the United States Army Corps of Engineers, New Orleans District, New Orleans, La.

10. Editors, "The Opposing Forces in the Operations at New Orleans, LA," *BL,* vol. 2, 75.

11. Commander John R. Bartlett, "The *Brooklyn* at the Passage of the Forts," *BL,* vol. 2, 68. The author realizes that in the strictest sense there were batteries at Chalmette, but given Bartlett's description of how easily they were dealt with, the batteries can hardly be counted as a creditable force.

12. Jones, *The Civil War at Sea,* vol. 2, 93.

13. Confederate Congress, "Report of Brigadier General J. K. Duncan, Commanding Coast Defenses," *Proceedings of the Court of Inquiry Relative to the Fall of New Orleans* (Richmond, Va.: R. M. Smith, Public Printer, 1864), 169.

14. Jones, *The Civil War at Sea,* vol. 2, 86.

15. Confederate Congress, "Report of Brigadier General J. K. Duncan, Commanding Coast Defenses," 169.

16. Read, "Reminiscences of the Confederate States Navy," 341.

17. Maurice Melton, *The Confederate Ironclads* (New York: Thomas Yoseloff, 1968), 88.

18. Jones, *The Civil War at Sea,* vol. 2, 91.

19. Confederate Congress, "Report of Brigadier General J. K. Duncan, Commanding Coast Defenses," 13.

20. Ibid., 171; Shelby Foote, *The Civil War: A Narrative: Fort Sumter to Perryville* (New York: Random House, 1963; reprint, New York: Vintage Books, 1986), 365.

21. Morgan, *Recollections of a Rebel Reefer,* 71.

22. Read, "Reminiscences of the Confederate States Navy," 342.

23. Moonrise data calculated by author using computer program "Moon Phase"; *ORN,* 1st ser., vol. 18, 295; Dufour, *The Night the War Was Lost,* 265.

24. Read, "Reminiscences of the Confederate States Navy," 342.

25. Porter, "The Opening of the Lower Mississippi," *BL,* vol. 2, 41.

26. Melton, *The Confederate Ironclads,* 94–95; *ORN,* 1st ser., vol. 18, 294.

27. Samuel Brock, "Admiral Farragut and others vs. The United States for Bounty Money and Prize," *United States District Court for the District of Columbia Sitting in Admiralty,* Nos. 191–210, 99 (hereafter cited as *USDCA*).

28. Read, "Reminiscences of the Confederate States Navy," 342.

29. Melton, *The Confederate Ironclads,* 98.

30. Read, "Reminiscences of the Confederate States Navy," 342.

31. *ORN,* 1st ser., vol. 18, 754. The battle below New Orleans was a night action. The reports filed are somewhat contradictory. The battle description contained in this work is a composite of several sources.

32. Ibid., 322, 345.

33. Brock, *USDCA,* 99.

34. Porter, "The Opening of the Lower Mississippi," *BL,* vol. 2, 42; Read, "Reminiscences of the Confederate States Navy," 342.

35. Bartlett, "The Opening of the Lower Mississippi," *BL,* vol. 2, 67.

36. *ORN,* 1st ser., vol. 18, 332.

37. Brock, *USDCA,* 100.

38. *ORN,* 1st ser., vol. 18, 332, 345.

39. Read, "Reminiscences of the Confederate States Navy," 343.

40. George W. Gift, "The Story of the Arkansas," *SHSP* (Richmond, Va., 1884), 12:116. Although Gift states that number 6 was the USS *Kineo, ORN,* 1st ser., vol. 18, 132, states that the *Kineo* was number 3 and the USS *Pinola* was number 6; Read, "Reminiscences of the Confederate States Navy," 343.

41. Morgan and Marquand, *Prince and Boatswain,* 43–44.

42. *ORN,* 1st ser., vol. 18, 333.

43. Read, "Reminiscences of the Confederate States Navy," 343–344.

44. David D. Porter, *USDCA,* 58.

45. *ORN,* 1st ser., vol. 18, 186; Bartlett, "The Opening of the Lower Mississippi," *BL,* vol. 2, 65.

46. Read, "Reminiscences of the Confederate States Navy," 343; George Philips, *USDCA,* 95–97; *ORN,* 1st ser., vol. 18, 297; Confederate Congress, "Report of Brigadier General J. K. Duncan, Commanding Coast Defenses," 173.

47. Dufour, *The Night the War Was Lost,* 337.

48. *ORN,* 1st ser., vol. 18, 333.

49. Read, "Reminiscences of the Confederate States Navy," 343–344.

50. *ORN,* 1st ser., vol. 18, 333.

51. George Dewey, *Autobiography of George Dewey* (New York: Frederick A. Stokes, 1941), 75.

52. *ORN,* 1st ser., vol. 18, 331, 334.

53. Brock, *USDCA,* 101–102.

54. *ORN,* 1st ser., vol. 18, 334.

55. Morgan and Marquand, *Prince and Boatswain,* 45.

56. *ORN,* 1st ser., vol. 18, 334.

57. Ibid., 311.

58. Ibid., 287.

59. United States Senate, Fifty-eighth Congress, Second Session, *Journal of the Congress of the Confederate States of America, 1861–1865,* vol. 2, Sept. 23, 1862 (Washington, D.C.: Government Printing Office, 1904), 318.

60. Read, "Reminiscences of the Confederate States Navy," 346–349.

CHAPTER 5: IRON WARRIOR

1. Isaac N. Brown, "The Confederate Gun-boat *Arkansas,*" *BL,* vol. 3, 572; Tom Z. Parrish, *The Saga of the Confederate Ram* Arkansas: *The Mississippi Valley Campaign, 1862* (Hillsboro, Tex.: Hill College Press, 1987), 145.

2. Still, *Iron Afloat: The Story of the Confederate Armorclads,* 63.

3. Jones, *The Civil War at Sea,* vol. 2, 165.

4. Brown, "The Confederate Gun-boat *Arkansas,*" *BL,* vol. 3, 572.

5. Gift, "The Story of the *Arkansas,*" 49.

6. Brown, "The Confederate Gun-boat *Arkansas,*" *BL,* vol. 3, 572.

7. Read, "Reminiscences of the Confederate States Navy," 349.

8. Melton, *The Confederate Ironclads,* 116.

9. W. E. Geoghegan, "Drawings of the Confederate Ironclad Ram *Arkansas,*" Order No. 295, sheet 1 of 2: Line drawings including outboard profile details and deck plans; sheet 2 of 2: inboard profile, gun and berth deck plans, midships section, and "T" rail armor details (Washington, D.C.: Smithsonian Institution, 1964). The different accounts of the *Arkansas* vary in their description of the ship's guns. The author has chosen this one.

10. Parrish, *The Saga of the Confederate Ram* Arkansas: *The Mississippi Valley Campaign, 1862,* 151.

11. Read, "Reminiscences of the Confederate States Navy," 349–350.

12. Ibid., 350.

13. Still, *Iron Afloat: The Story of the Confederate Armorclads,* 66.

14. Melton, *The Confederate Ironclads,* 115–116; Read, "Reminiscences of the Confederate States Navy," 351.
15. Parrish, *The Saga of the Confederate Ram* Arkansas: *The Mississippi Valley Campaign, 1862,* 152.
16. Read, "Reminiscences of the Confederate States Navy," 351.
17. Snead, "The Conquest of Arkansas," *BL,* vol. 3, 446.
18. Read, "Reminiscences of the Confederate States Navy," 352.
19. Parrish, *The Saga of the Confederate Ram* Arkansas: *The Mississippi Valley Campaign, 1862,* 172.
20. Melton, *The Confederate Ironclads,* 120; Edwin C. Bearss, *Rebel Victory at Vicksburg* (Vicksburg, Miss,: Vicksburg Centennial Commemoration Commission, 1963), 213.
21. Read, "Reminiscences of the Confederate States Navy," 352.
22. *ORN,* 1st ser., vol. 19, 132.
23. Brown, "The Confederate Gun-boat *Arkansas,*" *BL,* vol. 3, 572; Bearss, *Rebel Victory at Vicksburg,* 207.
24. Gift, "The Story of the Arkansas," 51.
25. Read, "Reminiscences of the Confederate States Navy," 353.
26. Foote, *The Civil War: A Narrative: Fort Sumter to Perryville,* 550.
27. Brown, "The Confederate Gun-boat *Arkansas,*" *BL,* vol. 3, 573.
28. Scharf, *History of the Confederate States Navy,* 310; Foote, *The Civil War: A Narrative: Fort Sumter to Perryville,* 548.
29. Brown, "The Confederate Gun-boat *Arkansas,*" *BL,* vol. 3, 573; Foote, *The Civil War: A Narrative: Fort Sumter to Perryville,* 551.
30. Gift, "The Story of the *Arkansas,*" 50.
31. Read, "Reminiscences of the Confederate States Navy," 353.
32. Gift, "The Story of the *Arkansas,*" 50.
33. Scharf, *History of the Confederate States Navy,* 310–311.
34. Bearss, *Rebel Victory at Vicksburg,* 210.
35. Gift, "The Story of the *Arkansas,*" 52.
36. Gosnell, *Guns on the Western Waters,* 114.
37. Brown, "The Confederate Gun-boat *Arkansas,*" *BL,* vol. 3, 574.
38. Read, "Reminiscences of the Confederate States Navy," 354.
39. Gift, "The Story of the *Arkansas,*" 52; Bearss, *Rebel Victory at Vicksburg,* 213.
40. Melton, *The Confederate Ironclads,* 124–125.
41. Brown, "The Confederate Gun-boat *Arkansas,*" *BL,* vol. 3, 575.
42. Scott, John White, *John White Scott Correspondence,* Manuscript Division, Library of Congress, Washington, D.C.
43. Jones, *The Civil War at Sea,* vol. 2, 195–196.
44. Bearss, *Rebel Victory at Vicksburg,* 212.
45. Read, "Reminiscences of the Confederate States Navy," 339.
46. Brown, "The Confederate Gun-boat *Arkansas,*" *BL,* vol. 3, 575.
47. Bearss, *Rebel Victory at Vicksburg,* 218.
48. Gift, "The Story of the *Arkansas,*" 115.
49. Still, *Iron Afloat: The Story of the Confederate Armorclads,* 69.
50. Brown, "The Confederate Gun-boat *Arkansas,*" *BL,* vol. 3, 576.
51. Gift, "The Story of the *Arkansas,*" 116. Note: Although Gift states that number 6 was the USS *Kineo, ORN,* 1st ser., vol. 18, 132, states that the *Kineo* was number 3 and the USS *Pinola* was number 6. The log of the *Pinola* on 805–806 places the gunboat at Vicksburg whereas 517 states that Farragut left the *Kineo* at Baton Rouge.
52. Gift, "The Story of the *Arkansas,*" 117.
53. Bearss, *Rebel Victory at Vicksburg,* 222.
54. Brown, "The Confederate Gun-boat *Arkansas,*" *BL,* vol. 3, 576.
55. Gift, "The Story of the *Arkansas,*" 118.

56. Parrish, *The Saga of the Confederate Ram* Arkansas, *The Mississippi Valley Campaign, 1862,* 175.
57. Melton, *The Confederate Ironclads,* 129.
58. Gift, "The Story of the *Arkansas,*" 117.
59. Bearss, *Rebel Victory at Vicksburg,* 224–225.
60. *ORN,* 1st ser., vol. 19, 133.
61. Brown, "The Confederate Gun-boat *Arkansas,*" *BL,* vol. 3, 576.
62. Melton, *The Confederate Ironclads,* 130.
63. *ORN,* 1st ser., vol. 19, 133.
64. Brown, "The Confederate Gun-boat *Arkansas,*" *BL,* vol. 3, 577.
65. Read, "Reminiscences of the Confederate States Navy," 355; Gift, "The Story of the *Arkansas,*" 163.
66. Charles L. Lewis, *David Glasgow Farragut: Our First Admiral* (Annapolis, Md.: United States Naval Institute, 1943), 113; Foote, *The Civil War: A Narrative: Fort Sumter to Perryville,* 553.
67. Parrish, *The Saga of the Confederate Ram* Arkansas: *The Mississippi Valley Campaign, 1862,* 183.
68. Read, "Reminiscences of the Confederate States Navy," 355.
69. Jones, *The Civil War at Sea,* vol. 2, 205.
70. Read, "Reminiscences of the Confederate States Navy," 355–356.
71. Gift, "The Story of the *Arkansas,*" 165; Melton, *The Confederate Ironclads,* 132–133.
72. Brown, "The Confederate Gun-boat *Arkansas,*" *BL,* vol. 3, 577.
73. Read, "Reminiscences of the Confederate States Navy," 357.
74. Ibid.
75. Brown, "The Confederate Gun-boat *Arkansas,*" *BL,* vol. 3, 577.
76. Lewis, *David Glasgow Farragut: Our First Admiral,* 116–117.
77. Ibid., 122.
78. Read, "Reminiscences of the Confederate States Navy," 357.
79. Brown, "The Confederate Gun-boat *Arkansas,*" *BL,* vol. 3, 577. The different accounts written after the war vary as to the number of men on the *Arkansas;* Read ("Reminiscences of the Confederate States Navy," 358) said forty-eight, although Gift ("The Story of the *Arkansas,*" 168) said thirty.
80. Brown, "The Confederate Gun-boat *Arkansas,*" *BL,* vol. 3, 578.
81. Bearss, *Rebel Victory at Vicksburg,* 262.
82. Gift, "The Story of the *Arkansas,*" 170.
83. Brown, "The Confederate Gun-boat *Arkansas,*" *BL,* vol. 3, 579.
84. Read, "Reminiscences of the Confederate States Navy," 359; Brown, "The Confederate Gun-boat *Arkansas,*" *BL,* vol. 3, 579.
85. Read, "Reminiscences of the Confederate States Navy," 359.
86. Gift, "The Story of the *Arkansas,*" 206–207.
87. *ORN,* 1st ser., vol. 19, 135.
88. Gift, "The Story of the *Arkansas,*" 207.
89. Read, "Reminiscences of the Confederate States Navy," 359.
90. Gift, "The Story of the *Arkansas,*" 207; Still, *Iron Afloat: The Story of the Confederate Armorclads,* 76.
91. *DANFS,* vol. 2, 39, 366.
92. Gift, "The Story of the *Arkansas,*" 209.
93. Read, "Reminiscences of the Confederate States Navy," 360.
94. Gift, "The Story of the *Arkansas,*" 209.
95. Read, "Reminiscences of the Confederate States Navy," 360.
96. Melton, *The Confederate Ironclads,* 140–141.
97. Foote, *The Civil War: A Narrative: Fort Sumter to Perryville,* 580.
98. Morgan and Marquand, *Prince and Boatswain,* 47.

99. Sarah M. Dawson, *A Confederate Girl's Diary* (Boston: Houghton Mifflin, 1913), 152.
100. Still, *Iron Afloat: The Story of the Confederate Armorclads,* 78.
101. *ROCSN,* 23, 70, 187.
102 Royce Shingleton, *High Seas Confederate: The Life and Times of John Newland Maffitt* (Columbia: University of South Carolina Press, 1994), 50–53.
103. Read, "Reminiscences of the Confederate States Navy," 362.

CHAPTER 6: ABOARD THE CSS *FLORIDA*

1. Emma M. Maffitt, *The Life and Services of John Newland Maffitt* (New York: Neale Publishing, 1906), 259; John Newland Maffitt Papers, Southern Historical Collection Manuscripts Department, Wilson Library, the University of North Carolina at Chapel Hill, N.C. (hereafter cited as Maffitt Papers, SHC/CHNC).
2. *DANFS,* vol. 2, 520–521.
3. James D. Bulloch, *The Secret Service of the Confederate States in Europe,* vol. 1 (New York: Thomas Yoseloff, 1884: reprint, New York: Thomas Yoseoff, 1959), 57–58; Shingleton, *High Seas Confederate: The Life and Times of John Newland Maffitt,* 43.
4. Read, Mallory J.
5. Maffitt, *The Life and Services of John Newland Maffitt,* 265; Maffitt Papers, SHC/CHNC.
6. Frank L. Owsley Jr., *The C.S.S. Florida: Her Building and Operations* (Philadelphia: University of Pennsylvania Press, 1956), 43; Read, Mallory J.
7. Chester G. Hearn, *Gray Raiders of the Sea* (Camden, Maine: International Marine Publishing, 1992), 67.
8. Hamilton Cochran, *Blockade Runners of the Confederacy* (Indianapolis: Bobbs–Merrill, 1958), 245.
9. Maynard, John R. and Betty.
10. Scharf, *History of the Confederate States Navy,* 537.
11. Maffitt, *The Life and Services of John Newland Maffitt,* 266; Shingleton, *High Seas Confederate: The Life and Times of John Newland Maffitt,* 57–58.
12. Read, Mallory J.
13. A. L. Drayton, *A. L. Drayton Diary,* Jan. 16 to June 26, 1863, Ac. 2110, Manuscript Division, Library of Congress, Washington, D.C. (hereafter cited as Drayton Diary); Maffitt, *The Life and Services of John Newland Maffitt,* 267.
14. Read, Mallory J.
15. Maffitt, *The Life and Services of John Newland Maffitt,* 267.
16. Ibid., 268.
17. Maffitt Papers, SHC/CHNC.
18. *ORN,* 2nd ser., vol. 1, 252; William S. Hoole, *Four Years in the Confederate Navy: The Career of Capt. John Low on CSS Fingal, Florida, Alabama, Tuscaloosa, and Ajax* (Athens: University of Georgia Press, 1964).
19. Shingleton, *High Seas Confederate: The Life and Times of John Newland Maffitt,* 60.
20. *ORN,* 1st ser., vol. 2, 534.
21. Read, Mallory J.
22. Ibid.
23. Jones, *The Civil War at Sea,* vol. 2, 347.
24. Maffitt, *The Life and Services of John Newland Maffitt,* 268.
25. *ORN,* 1st ser., vol. 2, 673.
26. Maffitt, *The Life and Services of John Newland Maffitt,* 268–269.
27. *ORN,* 1st ser., vol. 2, 345.
28. Jones, *The Civil War at Sea,* vol. 2, 348.
29. Maffitt, *The Life and Services of John Newland Maffitt,* 263, 269–270.
30. *ORN,* 1st ser., vol. 2, 674; John M. Taylor, *Confederate Raider: Raphael Semmes of the*

Alabama (Washington D.C.: Brassey's, 1994), 243. The right to the use of another country's flag to capture merchant ships is recognized by international law.

31. Maffitt, *The Life and Services of John Newland Maffitt*, 271; data used for the *Florida's* January 19, 1863, position derived by the author using "Pilot Chart of the North Atlantic Ocean."

32. Edward Boykin, *Sea Devil of the Confederacy: The Story of the* Florida *and Her Captain, John Newland Maffitt* (New York: Funk & Wagnalls, 1959), 144–145. John M. Taylor, *Confederate Raider*, 243. Precedent for burning captured ships was established by the U.S. Navy during the American Revolution and War of 1812.

33. *ORN*, 1st ser., vol. 2, 674.

34. Read, Mallory J.

35. *ORN*, 1st ser., vol. 2, 674; Maffitt, *The Life and Services of John Newland Maffitt*, 271–272.

36. Read, Mallory J.

37. Shingleton, *High Seas Confederate: The Life and Times of John Newland Maffitt*, 62.

38. *ORN*, 1st ser., vol. 2, 674.

39. Boykin, *Sea Devil of the Confederacy*, 153–154.

40. Hearn, *Gray Raiders of the Sea*, 74.

41. *ORN*, 1st ser., vol. 2, 674.

42. Boykin, *Sea Devil of the Confederacy*, 152; Owsley, *The C.S.S.* Florida: *Her Building and Operations*, 52.

43. Data used to describe coast and at sea features derived by the author using *ORN*, 1st ser., vol. 2, 674; Maffitt, *The Life and Services of John Newland Maffitt*, 272; Read, Mallory J.; "Straights of Florida and Approaches," chart C&GS 1002 (U.S. Department of Commerce, Washington, D.C.).

44. *ORN*, 1st ser., vol. 2, 674; Read, Mallory J.

45. *ORN*, 1st ser., vol. 2, 640.

46. Boykin, *Sea Devil of the Confederacy*, 155; Hearn, *Gray Raiders of the Sea*, 74–75.

47. Maffitt Papers, SHC/CHNC.

48. *ORN*, 1st ser., vol. 2, 674; Read, Mallory J.; "Straights of Florida and Approaches," C&GS 1002. Note: The position of the *Florida* for the January 23 and 24, 1863, entries in the *ORN* is in error because it places the ship in the middle of Cuba. Shingleton, *High Seas Confederate: The Life and Times of John Newland Maffitt*, 63; Maffitt Papers, SHC/CHNC.

49. Boykin, *Sea Devil of the Confederacy*, 154–155.

50. *ORN*, 1st ser., vol. 2, 675.

51. Read, Mallory J.

52. Ibid.

53. Maffitt, *The Life and Services of John Newland Maffitt*, 273; Read, Mallory J.

54. Read, Mallory J.

55. Maffitt, *The Life and Services of John Newland Maffitt*, 273.

56. *DANFS*, vol. 2, 520; *ORN*, 1st ser., vol. 2, 70.

57. Maffitt, *The Life and Services of John Newland Maffitt*, 273.

58. Maffitt, *The Life and Services of John Newland Maffitt*, 273–274.

59. Andrew Lambert, *Battleships in Transition: The Creation of the Steam Battlefleet, 1815–1860* (London: Conway Maritime Press, n.d., reprint, Annapolis, Md.: Naval Institute Press, 1984), 59. Author's note: the HMS *Warrior's* design was typical of hoistable propellers.

60. Maffitt, *The Life and Services of John Newland Maffitt*, 274; *DANFS*, vol. 7, 463.

61. Boykin, *Sea Devil of the Confederacy*, 155–156.

62. Maffitt, *The Life and Services of John Newland Maffitt*, 274; Shingleton, *High Seas Confederate: The Life and Times of John Newland Maffitt*, 65; *ORN*, 1st ser., vol. 2, 675.

63. Read, Mallory J.

64. Mrs. H. Dwight Williams, *A Year in China and a Narrative of Capture and Imprisonment When Homeward Bound, on Board the Rebel Pirate* Florida (New York: Hurd and Houghton, 1864), 303–306.

65. Shingleton, *High Seas Confederate: The Life and Times of John Newland Maffitt*, 66.

66. Howard I. Chapelle, *The Search for Speed under Sail, 1700–1855* (New York: Bonanza Books, 1967), 369.

67. Maffitt, *The Life and Services of John Newland Maffitt*, 274–275; ORN, 1st ser., vol. 2, 675; Williams, *A Year in China*, 310–311.

68. Williams, *A Year in China*, 315–316. Read continued to keep the sheets with him. ORN, 1st ser., vol. 2, 331, lists items from the *Archer* including three sheets marked "Jacob Bell."

69. Read, Mallory J.; Boykin, *Sea Devil of the Confederacy*, 167–168.

70. Shingleton, *High Seas Confederate: The Life and Times of John Newland Maffitt*, 69.

71. ORN, 1st ser., vol. 2, 675–676.

72. Boykin, *Sea Devil of the Confederacy*, 176.

73. Owsley, *The C.S.S. Florida: Her Building and Operations*, 57–58; ORN, 1st ser., vol. 2, 676; Boykin, *Sea Devil of the Confederacy*, 176.

74. ORN, 1st ser., vol. 2, 676; Maffitt Papers, SHC/CHNC.

75. ORN, 1st ser., vol. 2, 676.

76. Maffitt Papers, SHC/CHNC.

77. Maffitt, *The Life and Services of John Newland Maffitt*, 280; Boykin, *Sea Devil of the Confederacy*, 178–179.

78. Shingleton, *High Seas Confederate: The Life and Times of John Newland Maffitt*, 71.

79. ORN, 1st ser., vol. 2, 677; Hearn, *Gray Raiders of the Sea*, 79.

80. ORN, 1st ser., vol. 2, 677–678; Maffitt, *The Life and Services of John Newland Maffitt*, 281; ORN, 1st ser., vol. 2, 678.

81. Read, Mallory J. Note: Although Read's writing places this conversation before the capture of the *Lapwing*, he identifies the ship as a bark. Since no bark was captured and burned before the *Lapwing*, the author believes that the ship was the *M. J. Colcord*.

82. Maffitt, *The Life and Services of John Newland Maffitt*, 283–284; Charles Darwin, the *Voyage of the Beagle* (1845; reprint, New York: Bantam Books, 1958), 6. Darwin's description of St. Paul's Rocks was used to supplement Maffitt's description; Maffitt Papers, SHC/CHNC.

83. Maffitt, *The Life and Services of John Newland Maffitt*, 284.

84. Read, Mallory J.; Maffitt, *The Life and Services of John Newland Maffitt*, 285.

85. Hearn, *Gray Raiders of the Sea*, 80.

86. Maffitt, *The Life and Services of John Newland Maffitt*, 285.

87. Boykin, *Sea Devil of the Confederacy*, 185–186; Bulloch, *The Secret Service of the Confederate States in Europe*, vol. 2, 275; Maffitt, *The Life and Services of John Newland Maffitt*, 285; Hearn, *Gray Raiders of the Sea*, 81.

88. ORN, 1st ser., vol. 2, 649; Raphael Semmes, *The Confederate Raider* Alabama (1869; reprint, Greenwich, Conn.: Fawcett Publications, 1962), 232.

89. Read, Mallory J.

90. Maffitt, *The Life and Services of John Newland Maffitt*, 287.

91. Winfield M. Thompson, "A Confederate Raid," *The Rudder* 16, no. 3 (March 1905): 132; Maffitt Papers, SHC/CHNC.

92. Maffitt, *The Life and Services of John Newland Maffitt*, 288; Maffitt Papers, SHC/CHNC.

93. Read, Mallory J.; Thompson, "A Confederate Raid," 133.

94. Maffitt, *The Life and Services of John Newland Maffitt*, 288.

95. Thompson, "A Confederate Raid," 133.

CHAPTER 7: RAISING CAIN AND THE PRICE OF FISH

1. Morgan and Marquand, *Prince and Boatswain,* 49. Wind data used for the *Clarence* derived by the author using "Pilot Chart of the North Atlantic Ocean."
2. Drayton, *Drayton Diary.*
3. Read, Mallory J.
4. Drayton, *Drayton Diary.*
5. Ibid.
6. Robert H. Woods, "The Cruise of the *Clarence–Tacony–Archer:* A True Tale of the Sea during the Civil War," *Richmond Dispatch,* November 24, 1895. Also printed with minor variations in the *SHSP,* vol. 23 (Richmond, Va.), 1895; *Maryland Historical Magazine,* 1914, 42–44; and *U.S. Naval Institute Proceedings,* vol. 35, no. 131 (September 1909).
7. Walter S. Meriwether, "The Paul Jones of Mississippi," Charleston, Miss., *Mississippi Sun,* June 3, 1921.
8. Drayton, *Drayton Diary.*
9. Read, Mallory J.
10. Meriwether, "The Paul Jones of Mississippi," June 3, 1921; Read, Mallory J.; Thompson, "A Confederate Raid," 133; *ORN,* 1st ser., vol. 2, 655.
11. *ORN,* 1st ser., vol. 2, 655.
12. Meriwether, "The Paul Jones of Mississippi," June 10, 1921.
13. Morgan and Marquand, *Prince and Boatswain,* 49–50; *ORN,* 1st ser., vol. 2, 656; Thompson, "A Confederate Raid," 133.
14. Moore, *The Rebellion Record,* 7.
15. NARG 45, *Logbook: Voyages of the American Bark* "Tacony," *Oct. 1, 1862, to June 25, 1863;* Thompson, "A Confederate Raid," 134; *ORN,* 1st ser., vol. 2, 656.
16. Woods, "The Cruise of the *Clarence–Tacony–Archer,* 45.
17. Thompson, "A Confederate Raid," 134; *ORN,* 1st ser., vol. 2, 656.
18. Drayton, *Drayton Diary; Daily Press,* Portland, Maine, July 1, 1863; MHSL.
19. Read, Mallory J.
20. *ORN,* 1st ser., vol. 2, 656; NARG 45, *Logbook: Voyages of the American Bark* "Tacony." The author noted the difference in penmanship, which was also noted in an unsigned news story, *New York Daily Tribune,* 23, no. 6937 (June 29, 1863), 8.
21. Welles, *Diary of Gideon Welles,* 327.
22. *ORN,* 1st ser., vol. 2, 247–291, 656.
23. NARG 45, *Logbook: Voyages of the American Bark* "Tacony."
24. John Cranwell, *Spoilers of the Sea: Wartime Raiders in the Age of Steam* (New York: W. W. Norton, 1941), 72; Drayton, *Drayton Diary; Daily Press,* Portland, Maine, July 1, 1863.
25. *ORN,* 1st ser., vol. 2, 656; Charles G. Davis, *American Sailing Ships: Their Plans and History* (New York: Dover Publications, 1984), 62–65.
26. Read, Mallory J.; *ORN,* 1st ser., vol. 2, 656; unsigned news story, *New York Daily Tribune,* 23, no. 6936 (June 27, 1863), 1.
27. *ORN,* 1st ser., vol. 2, 656; Read, Mallory J.; unsigned news story, *New York Daily Tribune,* 23, no. 6936 (June 27, 1863), 1.
28. *ORN,* 2nd ser., vol. 1, 296–313, 653.
29. Unsigned news story, *New York Daily Tribune,* 23, no. 6925 (June 26, 1863), 1; Boykin, *Sea Devil of the Confederacy,* 207.
30. *ORN,* 2nd ser., vol. 1, 300, 304; Boykin, *Sea Devil of the Confederacy,* 207–208.
31. *ORN,* 2nd ser., vol. 1, 340, 345–346.
32. Unsigned new story, *New York Daily Tribune,* 23, no. 6925 (June 26, 1863), 1; Owsley, *The C.S.S. Florida: Her Building and Operations,* 86.
33. Boykin, *Sea Devil of the Confederacy,* 207.
34. Welles, *Diary of Gideon Welles,* 342–343.

35. Thompson, "A Confederate Raid," 135; *ORN,* 1st ser., vol. 2, 656. Read was not the first to capture and burn fishing schooners. During the Revolutionary War John Paul Jones while in command of the *Providence* captured and burned British fishing schooners off Nova Scotia.

36. Read, Mallory J.

37. *ORN,* 1st ser., vol. 2, 656; Drayton, *Drayton Diary*; *Daily Press,* Portland, Maine, July 1, 1863; Thompson, "A Confederate Raid," 135; Read, Mallory J.; *ORN,* 1st ser., vol. 2, 656.

38. Thompson, "A Confederate Raid," 135–136; Smith, *Confederates Downeast: Confederate Operations in and Around Maine,* 110.

39. *ORN,* 1st ser., vol. 2, 329.

40. Thompson, "A Confederate Raid," 136; Rich, *The Coast of Maine,* 244.

41. Thompson, "A Confederate Raid," 136; John Gardner, "The Elusive Hampton Boats," *The Small Boat Journal,* 1, no. 4 (November 1979), 14. The various accounts of the capture of Bibber and Titcomb disagree on the type of boat they were using, calling it a dory, a fishing sloop's dory, a rowboat, or just a boat. The author believes a dory would have been too small. The boat was most likely a Hampton, a type of craft used by fishermen, which could be rowed or sailed. Hamptons were widely used in Casco Bay in the midpoint of the 1800s. Moore, *The Rebellion Record,* 132.

42. Read, Mallory J.; Moore, *The Rebellion Record,* 132.

43. Ibid.

44. Drayton, *Drayton Diary.*

45. Thompson, "A Confederate Raid," 136.

46. George W. Dalzell, *The Flight from the Flag* (Chapel Hill: University of North Carolina Press, 1940), 112, 244; Paul F. Johnston, "Maritime Archaeology and Civil War Shipwrecks," *Underwater Archaeology: Shipwrecks of the Civil War* (notes taken by the author from a lecture given at the Smithsonian Institution, Washington, D.C., April 15, 1992). After the war, the United States Government demanded compensation from Great Britain since most of the raiders were British-built. These claims were known as the *Alabama* Claims and included the ships Read sank. Her Majesty's Government denied liability and the diplomatic arguing started. At one time Sen. Charles Sumner, still bitter over the caning Congressman Preston Brooks gave him before the war, demanded Canada, Newfoundland, Bermuda, and the British West Indies as compensation. On September 14, 1872, the claims were finally settled with the United States accepting $15,500,000 and both countries agreeing not to build commerce raiders. Hearn, *Gray Raiders of the Sea,* 302–306, 311–317.

CHAPTER 8: IN OLD ABE'S DOMAIN

1. *Evening Courier,* Portland, Maine, June 29, 1863. Newspaper courtesy MHSL.

2. Read, Mallory J.

3. *Evening Courier,* Portland, Maine, June 29, 1863.

4. Ibid., John M. Adams, "Incidents Anecdotes, and Facts, Relative to the Cutter," *Eastern Argus,* Portland, Maine, June 30, 1863. Newspaper courtesy MHSL.

5. Read, Mallory J.

6. *Eastern Argus,* Portland, Maine, June 30, 1863; Dalzell, *The Flight from the Flag,* 115; Smith, *Confederates Downeast: Confederate Operations in and around Maine,* 111–113; *ORN,* 2nd ser., vol. 2, 336.

7. *ORN,* 2nd ser., vol. 2, 339–340; Morgan and Marquand, *Prince and Boatswain,* 56.

8. David D. Porter, *The Naval History of the Civil War* (New York: Sherman Publishing, 1886), 814.

9. Moore, *The Rebellion Record,* 134.

10. *ORN*, 2nd ser., vol. 2, 327; unsigned news story, *Boston Evening Journal*, July 29, 1863; NARG 109, "War Department Collection of Confederate Records."

11. *The Romance of Fort Warren*, pamphlet distributed by Robert Industries (Hull, Mass., n.d.), 5–7; Edward R. Snow, *An Island Citadel* (Braintree, Mass.: Glenrose Press, n.d.). By the time Read got to Georges Island, Fort Warren had already played a part in the Civil War. The 2nd Massachusetts Infantry had been stationed at the fort at the start of the war. One of the soldiers, named John Brown, was teased by his friends who said he could not be John Brown since John Brown's body was moldering in the grave. The verses were set to the tune of a popular religious song and "John Brown's Body" was the result. There is even a story about the "Ghost of the Lady in Black." The wife of a Confederate prisoner, disguised in male clothing, managed to get into the prison to help her husband escape. The guards foiled the escape and the woman fired her pistol at a guard, but missed and killed her husband. She was condemned to hang as a spy. Her last request was to wear woman's clothing and black robes were found. Years later, guards were court-martialed for shooting at a ghost in black.

12. *The Romance of Fort Warren*, 15; William B. Hesseltine, *Civil War Prisons* (Kent, Ohio: Kent State University Press, 1962), 44. Notes taken by the author during a visit to Fort Warren (hereafter cited as Notes Fort Warren).

13. *ORN*, 1st ser., vol. 2, 654–655; Joseph W. Alexander, "An Escape from Fort Warren," *Histories of the Several Regiments and Battalions from North Carolina in the Great War, 1861–65*, vol. 4 (Goldsboro, N.C.: Nash Brothers, 1901), 735.

14. Notes Fort Warren; "Escape from Fort Warren," *Harper's New Monthly Magazine*, 28, no. 167 (April 1864): 699.

15. Alexander, "An Escape from Fort Warren," 735–736; Notes Fort Warren.

16. "Escape from Fort Warren," *Harper's New Monthly Magazine*, 697.

17. Alexander, "An Escape from Fort Warren," 735; "Escape from Fort Warren," *Harper's New Monthly Magazine*, 699.

18. Tide times and currents calculated by the Oceanography Division of the Coast and Geodetic Survey, U.S. Department of Commerce.

19. "Escape From Fort Warren," *Harper's New Monthly Magazine*, 699–700; Alexander, "An Escape from Fort Warren," 736.

20. "Escape from Fort Warren," *Harper's New Monthly Magazine*, 700.

21. Alexander, "An Escape from Fort Warren," 738–739.

22. Read, Mallory J.

23. "Escape from Fort Warren," *Harper's New Monthly Magazine*, 698, 701.

24. Alexander, "An Escape from Fort Warren," 738–739.

25. Smith, *Confederates Downeast: Confederate Operations in and around Maine*, 125–129; Snow, *An Island Citadel*.

26. Edward R. Snow, *Historic Fort Warren* (Braintree, Mass.: Glenrose Press, n.d.).

27. Maynard, John R. and Betty; Notes Fort Warren.

28. Bruce Catton, *Grant Takes Command* (Boston: Little, Brown, 1968), 371; NHC/ZB.

29. William Alexander Hoke Papers, no. 345, Southern Historical Collection at the North Carolina Library, Chapel Hill, N.C.

30. Hesseltine, *Civil War Prisons*, 45; Snow, *An Island Citadel*.

31. Hoke Papers, no. 345.

32. *The Romance of Fort Warren*.

33. *ROCSN*, 161; *CWNC*, part 3, 74, part 5, 36.

34. Snow, *An Island Citadel*.

35 Alexander, "An Escape from Fort Warren," 742; Morgan and Marquand, *Prince and Boatswain*, 57–60; Notes Fort Warren. Alexander's account of the escape states that the presence of a sentry near the top of the chimney prevented the escape. Morgan and Marquand provide a detailed account stating that Read, still limping from the wound, told Alexander about it in the autumn of 1864. The author believes that

since a mistake made by Alexander resulted in their capture, he did not include the escape.

36. Ralph W. Donnelly, *The History of the Confederate Marine Corps* (New Bern, N.C.: Owen G. Dunn, 1976), 163; NARG, 109; Donnelly, *The History of the Confederate Marine Corps,* 163; Notes Fort Warren.

CHAPTER 9: ON THE JAMES RIVER

1. John B. Jones, *A Rebel War Clerk's Diary* (New York: A. S. Barnes, 1866; reprint, ed. Earl S. Miers, Perpetua, 1961), 429.
2. Benjamin F. Butler, *Private and Official Correspondence of Gen. Benjamin F. Butler* (privately issued, 1917), vol. 1, 490.
3. Miller, *The Photographic History of the Civil War: Prisons and Hospitals,* 101; Butler, *Butler's Book,* 605–606.
4. Welles, *Diary of Gideon Welles,* vol. 1, 169–171.
5. Butler, *Butler's Book,* 390–391.
6. Butler, *Private and Official Correspondence of Gen. Benjamin F. Butler,* 267; Miller, *The Photographic History of the Civil War: Prisons and Hospitals,* 106, 345; Jones, *A Rebel War Clerk's Diary,* 432.
7. Morgan and Marquand, *Prince and Boatswain,* 60.
8. *ROCSN,* 136.
9. *DANFS,* vol. 2, 503, 516, 521, 532, 535, 551, 561, 565, 576, 580.
10. *ORN,* 1st ser., vol. 10, 748, 802, 804.
11. Read, Mallory J.; Miller, *The Photographic History of the Civil War: Forts and Artillery,* 133. Although Read said Battery Wood shelled the canal, he should have said Battery Semmes because Semmes was across from Dutch Gap. Ultimately the canal had no effect on the outcome of the war because by the time it was widened for ironclads, the war was over. The main channel of James River today occupies the former canal.
12. Read, Mallory J.
13. *OR,* 1st ser., vol. 35, part 2, 648–649.
14. Morgan and Marquand, *Prince and Boatswain,* 61–63.
15. Read, Mallory J.
16. *ORN,* 1st ser., vol. 11, 797.
17. Read, Mallory J.; Joseph T. Durkin, *Stephen R. Mallory: Confederate Navy Chief* (Chapel Hill: University of North Carolina Press, 1954), 136.
18. *ORN,* 1st ser., vol. 11, 798–799, 803.
19. John M. Coski, *Capital Navy: The Men, Ships, and Operations of the James River Squadron* (Campbell, Calif.: Savas Woodbury Publishers, 1996), 194, 198–199, map "Battle of Trent's Reach, January 23–25, 1865"; *ORN,* 1st ser., vol. 11, 669.
20. Morgan, *Recollections of a Rebel Reefer,* 218–219; Morgan and Marquand, *Prince and Boatswain,* 64; *ORN,* 1st ser., vol. 11, 683.
21. *ORN,* 1st ser., vol. 11, 683–684; Morgan, *Recollections of a Rebel Reefer,* 219.
22. *ORN,* 1st ser., vol. 11, 684, 668, 681; *DANFS,* vol. 2, 521, 561, 579; Read, Mallory J.
23. *ORN,* 1st ser., vol. 11, 684. The author assumes that the *Virginia II* like the *Virginia* carried two cutters.
24. Read, Mallory J.
25. *ORN,* 1st ser., vol. 11, 673, 684.
26. Read, Mallory J.; Coski, *Capital Navy: The Men, Ships, and Operations of the James River Squadron,* 206.
27. Still, *Iron Afloat: The Story of the Confederate Armorclads,* 83–184; *ORN,* 1st ser., vol. 11, 684; Coski, *Capital Navy: The Men, Ships, and Operations of the James River Squadron,* 206.
28. Read, Mallory J.

29. Scharf, *History of the Confederate States Navy*, 742; Coski, *Capital Navy: The Men, Ships, and Operations of the James River Squadron*, 207.

30. Coski, *Capital Navy: The Men, Ships, and Operations of the James River Squadron*, 216; W. Frank Shippey, "A Leaf from My Log Book," *SHSP*, vol. 12, 416–417.

31. Freeman W. Jones, "A Daring Expedition," *War Talks of Confederate Veterans* (Petersburg, Va.: Fenn & Owen, Publishers, 1892), 232; Ralph W. Donnelly, "A Confederate Navy Forlorn Hope," *Military Affairs*, vol. 28, no. 2 (Washington, D.C.: American Military Institute, 1964), 74, 77.

32. Shippey, "A Leaf from My Log Book," 418; Donnelly, "A Confederate Navy Forlorn Hope," 76. The author agrees with Donnelly that Shippey was mistaken when he stated that the road was the Jerusalem Plank Road.

33. Jones, "A Daring Expedition," 232–233; Richard W. Lykes, *Campaign for Petersburg* (Washington D.C.: Government Printing Office, 1970), 46; William H. Price, *The Civil War Handbook* (Fairfax, Va.: L. B. Prince Co. Inc., 1961), 69.

34. Jones, "A Daring Expedition," 233.

35. Shippey, "A Leaf from My Log Book," 419; Jones, "A Daring Expedition," 233; Ralph W. Donnelly, "A Confederate Navy Forlorn Hope," 77.

36. Shippey, "A Leaf from My Log Book," 420–421; Jones, "A Daring Expedition," 233.

37. *OR*, 1st ser., vol. 46, part 2, 566.

CHAPTER 10: CSS *WEBB*

1. John D. Winters, *The Civil War in Louisiana* (Baton Rouge: Louisiana State University Press, 1963), 420; SHC/*TSHS*, vol. 1, January to December 1874 (Baltimore: Turnbull Brothers, 1874), 88.

2. *ORN*, 2nd ser., vol. 2, 748; SHC/*TSHS*, 83.

3. Hoke Papers, no. 345.

4. SHC/*TSHS*, 82–83; *ROCSN*, 58.

5. *OR*, 1st ser., vol. 49, part 2, 142; vol. 22, 168.

6. *DANFS*, vol. 2, 581; excerpts from the *New York Herald* from April 23, May 1, and May 3, 1865, published in the SHC/*TSHS*, 85.

7. *ORN*, 1st ser., vol. 22, 168–170; Francis B. C. Bradlee, *Blockade Running during the Civil War* (Salem, Mass.: The Essex Institute, 1925), 150–151.

8. Michael L. Gillespie, "The Great Gunboat Chase," *Civil War Times Illustrated*, 33, no. 3 (July–August 1994): 32.

9. *ORN*, 1st ser., vol. 22, 168–169; Bradlee, *Blockade Running during the Civil War*, 151–152.

10. *ORN*, 1st ser., vol. 22, 152; Gillespie, "The Great Gunboat Chase," 32.

11. Edward A. Pollard, *The Lost Cause: A New Southern History of the War of the Confederates* (New York: E. B. Treat, 1867), 725; *ORN*, 1st ser., vol. 22, 152, 169.

12. *DANFS*, vol. 4, 13, vol. 3, 30, vol. 7, 86; Coggins, *Arms and Equipment of the Civil War*, 145.

13. *ORN*, 1st ser., vol. 22, 153; Bradlee, *Blockade Running during the Civil War*, 152.

14. Gillespie, "The Great Gunboat Chase," 34; George B. Davis, Leslie J. Perry, and Joseph W. Kirkley, *The Official Military Atlas of the Civil War*, comp. Calvin D. Cowles (New York: Gramercy Books, 1983), originally published as *Atlas to Accompany the Official Records of the Union and Confederate Armies* (Washington, D.C.: Government Printing Office, 1891–1895), plate LII.

15. *ORN*, 1st ser., vol. 22, 150, 153, 161, 162, 163.

16. Bradlee, *Blockade Running during the Civil War*, 152–153.

17. Coggins, *Arms and Equipment of the Civil War*, 143.

18. *ORN*, 1st ser., vol. 22, 151, 161, 163.

19. Gillespie, "The Great Gunboat Chase," 34; *DANFS,* vol. 2, 433.

20. Bradlee, *Blockade Running during the Civil War,* 153; *ORN,* 1st ser., vol. 22, 153.

21. *ORN,* 1st ser., vol. 27, 156–157; Gillespie, "The Great Gunboat Chase," 34; *ORN,* 1st ser., vol. 22, 163; *ORN,* 1st ser., vol. 27, 156.

22. *ORN,* 1st ser., vol. 27, 156–157; Gillespie, "The Great Gunboat Chase," 35; Bradlee, *Blockade Running during the Civil War,* 154; *ORN,* 1st ser., vol. 22, 143.

23. *ORN,* 1st ser., vol. 22, 144, 147–148.

24. Gillespie, "The Great Gunboat Chase," 36; *ORN,* 1st ser., vol. 22, 142, 144–145; William F. Keeler, *Aboard the U.S.S.* Florida*: 1863–65,* ed. Robert W. Daily (Annapolis, Md.: United States Naval Institute, 1968), 216.

25. *ORN,* 1st ser., vol. 22, 153; Meriwether, "The Paul Jones of Mississippi," June 24, 1921.

26. Bradlee, *Blockade Running during the Civil War,* 154–155; *ORN,* 1st ser., vol. 22, 166. Gillespie, "The Great Gunboat Chase," 36–37.

27. Keeler, *Aboard the U.S.S.* Florida*: 1863–65,* 217.

28. *ORN,* 1st ser., vol. 22, 153. Pinkerton's account states that Read stopped the *Webb* for two or three minutes to cut the torpedo loose, then got under way again. The author believes that with the *Webb's* speed and the river's current, Read could not have stopped the steamer, but rather had the torpedo cut away as they continued steaming.

29. SHC/*TSHS,* 86.

30. Keeler, *Aboard the U.S.S.* Florida*: 1863–65,* 218; Bradlee, *Blockade Running during the Civil War,* 155. Bradlee's account states that Read thought the ship was the USS *Hartford.* The *Hartford* was a steam sloop. Read would not have mistaken a steamship for a sailing ship.

31. Bradlee, *Blockade Running during the Civil War,* 155.

32. *SHSP,* 86–87; *ORN,* 1st ser., vol. 22, 147, 152–154, 165; Keeler, *Aboard the U.S.S.* Florida*: 1863–65,* 219.

33. Woods, "The Cruise of the *Clarence–Tacony–Archer,*" 684.

34. Bradlee, *Blockade Running during the Civil War,* 156.

35. *OR,* 1st ser., vol. 48, part 1, 206, vol. 22, 147.

36. Bradlee, *Blockade Running during the Civil War,* 156; Read, Mallory J.

37. Keeler, *Aboard the U.S.S.* Florida*: 1863–65,* 219; Maynard, John R. and Betty; *ROCSN,* 161; NARG 109.

CHAPTER 11: AN OLD PIRATE

1. Morgan and Marquand, *Prince and Boatswain,* 68–69.

2. Read, Mallory J.

3. Morgan and Marquand, *Prince and Boatswain,* 69–71.

4. Read, Mallory J.; Maynard, John R. and Betty; MDAH.

5. Read, "Reminiscences of the Confederate States Navy," 331–362; Editors of the Southern Historical Society, "Operations of Confederate States Navy in Defense of New Orleans," *SHSP,* vol. 2 (Richmond, 1876), 240–241.

6. Read, Mallory J.; Maynard, John R. and Betty.

7. Morgan and Marquand, *Prince and Boatswain,* 71–72.

8. Maynard, John R. and Betty; MDAH.

EPILOGUE

1. Johnston, Paul F., "Maritime Archaeology and Civil War Shipwrecks."

2. John Keegan, *The Face of Battle* (New York: Penguin Books, 1976), 26–27.

3. Ruth Benedict, *The Chrysanthemum and the Sword: Patterns of Japanese Culture* (New York: Meridian Books, 1974), 317; John Horsfield, *The Art of Leadership in War* (Westport, Conn.: Greenwood Press, 1980), 69, 70, 72.

4. Dumas Malone, *Dictionary of American Biography*, vol. 8 (New York: Charles Scribner's Sons, 1935), 420; Dewey, *Autobiography of George Dewey*, 75; Meriwether, "The Paul Jones of Mississippi."

5. Gregg S. Clemmer, *Valor in Gray: The Recipients of the Confederate Medal of Honor* (Staunton, Va.: Hearthside Publishing, 1996), 104–105. The Congress of the Confederate States of America authorized medals for courage and good conduct on the field of battle. Read was awarded the Medal of Honor by the Sons of Confederate Veterans at Beauvoir, the last home of Jefferson Davis, in Biloxi, Miss.

BIBLIOGRAPHY

UNPUBLISHED MATERIAL

Chapelle, Howard I. Data concerning the *Caleb Cushing*.

Department of the Archives and History of the state of Mississippi. Data concerning Charles W. Read.

Hoke, William Alexander, Papers. no. 345, in the Southern Historical Collection Manuscripts Department, Wilson Library, the University of North Carolina at Chapel Hill.

Johnston, Paul F. "Maritime Archaeology and Civil War Shipwrecks," *Underwater Archaeology: Shipwrecks of the Civil War* (notes taken by the author from a lecture given at the Smithsonian Institution, Washington, D.C., April 15, 1992).

Maffitt, John Newland, Papers in the Southern Historical Collection Manuscripts Department, Wilson Library, the University of North Carolina at Chapel Hill.

Maynard, Mr. and Mrs. John. Data concerning Charles W. Read from Read's great-grandson, John Maynard, Woodland Hills, Calif.

Read, Mallory J. Data concerning Charles W. Read from Read's grandson, Mallory J. Read, Arlington, Va.

Read, Mrs. William T. Data concerning Charles W. Read from the wife of Read's nephew, Mrs. William T. Read, Pasadena, Tex.

United States Army Corps of Engineers, New Orleans District, Data concerning current velocity in the Mississippi River.

GOVERNMENT DOCUMENTS

Department of Commerce. "Portland Harbor and Vicinity." Chart C&GS 325.

Department of the Navy. *Official Records of the Union and Confederate Navies in the War of The Rebellion.* 30 volumes and index. Washington, D.C.: Government Printing Office, 1894–1927.

————. Naval History Division. *Civil War Naval Chronology.* 6 volumes. Washington, D.C.: Government Printing Office, 1965.

————. Naval History Division. *Dictionary of American Naval Fighting Ships.* 8 volumes. Washington, D.C.: Government Printing Office, 1970.

————. Naval Historical Center. ZB file, Travel Records Operation Division.

————. Naval Oceanographic Office. "Pilot Chart of the North Atlantic Ocean." Chart no. 16, Washington, D.C.

————. Naval Oceanographic Office. "Straights of Florida and Approaches." Chart C&GS 1002, U.S. Department of Commerce, Washington, D.C.

————. Office of Naval Records and Library of United States Navy Department. *Register of Officers of the Confederate States Navy, 1861–1865.* Washington, D.C.: Government Printing Office, 1931.

Department of Transportation. United States Coast Guard. *Record of Movements: Vessels of the United States Coast Guard, 1790–December 31, 1933.* Washington, D.C.

National Archives and Record Administration. Washington, D.C., Coast Guard Division. Record Group 26, *Register of Revenue Cutter Service Officers 1790–1914.*

————. Record Group 29, 1850 Census, Mississippi, Hinds County.

————. Record Group 29, 1860 Census, Mississippi, Hinds County.

————. Record Group 45, *Journal of the Naval Academy, 1854–1857.*

————. Record Group 45, *Letters and Reports Received by the Superintendent Relating to Individual Midshipmen, 1846–88.*

————. Record Group 45, *Log of the USS* Powhatan, *1860–1861.*

————. Record Group 45, *Logbook Journal of a Summer's Cruise Aboard USS* Plymouth, *June–Aug. 1859.*

————. Record Group 109, "War Department Collection of Confederate Records."

Noble, Dennis. *Historical Register: U.S. Revenue Cutter Service Officers, 1790–1914.* Washington, D.C.: Printed by the Coast Guard Historian's Office, A Bicentennial Publication, 1990.

United States Naval Academy. *Conduct Roll: U.S. Naval Academy Registers of Delinquencies.* Annapolis, Md., 1857, 1858–1859, 1859–1860.

———. *Minutes of the Academic Board United States Navy.* Annapolis, Md., 1856.

———. *Official Register of the Officers and Acting Midshipmen of the United States Naval Academy.* Washington, D.C.: William A. Harris, Public Printer, 1858.

———. *Regulations of the U.S. Naval Academy at Annapolis, Maryland, 1855.*

———. *Regulations of the United States Naval Academy, as approved by the Secretary of the Navy, 1867.*

United States Naval Academy Alumni Association, Inc. *Register of Alumni: Graduates and Former Naval Cadets and Midshipmen.*

United States Senate, Fifty-eighth Congress, Second Session. *Journal of the Congress of the Confederate States of America*, Vol. II. Washington, D.C.: Government Printing Office, 1904.

United States War Department. *War of the Rebellion: A Compilation of the Official Records of the Union and Confederate Armies.* 128 volumes and index. Washington, D.C.: Government Printing Office, 1880–1902.

MISCELLANEOUS

Brock, Samuel. *United States District Court for the District of Columbia Sitting in Admiralty.* No. 191–210. "Admiral Farragut and Others vs. the United States for Bounty Money and Prize."

Computer program "Moon Phase."

Confederate Congress. "Report of Brigadier General J. K. Duncan, Commanding Coast Defenses." *Proceedings of the Court of Inquiry Relative to the Fall of New Orleans.* Richmond: R. M. Smith, Public Printer, 1864.

Confederate Navy Department. *Ordnance Instructions for the Confederate Navy Relating to the Preparation of Vessels of War for Battle.* London: Saunders, Otley, 1864.

Drayton, A. L. *A. L. Drayton Diary, Jan. 16–June 26, 1863,* Ac. 2110, Manuscript Division, Library of Congress, Washington, D.C.

Geoghegan, W. E. "Drawings of the Confederate Ironclad Ram *Arkansas,*" Order No. 295, sheets 1 and 2. Washington, D.C.: Smithsonian Institution, 1964.

Hunt, Robert. "The Johnny's Story." A paper read before the Confederates' Veteran Association of Savannah, Ga., on October 27, 1894.

Jerrold, Douglas W. "Black-eyed Susan; or, All in the Downs: A Nautical and Domestic Drama In Two Acts." Boston: Spencer's Boston Theater. 1856, Library of Congress, Washington, D.C.

Romance of Fort Warren, The. Pamphlet distributed by Robert Industries Inc., Hull, Mass.

Scott, John White. *John White Scott Correspondence.* Manuscript Division, Library of Congress, Washington, D.C.

NEWSPAPERS

Boston Evening Journal
Daily Press
Evening Courier
Lewiston Journal
Mississippi Sun
New York Daily Tribune
New York Herald
Portland Press
Portland Sunday Telegram

ARTICLES

Adams, John M. "Incidents Anecdotes, and Facts, Relative to the Cutter." *Eastern Argus,* June 30, 1863.

Donnelly, Ralph W. "A Confederate Navy Forlorn Hope." *Military Affairs.* Vol. 28, no. 2. Washington, D.C.: American Military Institute, 1964.

Gardner, John. "The Elusive Hampton Boats." *The Small Boat Journal,* Vol. 1, no. 4, November 1979.

Gift, George W. "The Story of the *Arkansas.*" *The Southern Historical Society Papers,* Vol. 12. Richmond, Va., 1884.

Gillespie, Michael L. "The Great Gunboat Chase," *Civil War Times Illustrated* 33, no. 3 (July–August 1994).

Hale, Clarence. "The Capture of the *Caleb Cushing.*" *Collections of the Maine Historical Society.* Portland, 1901.

"Escape from Fort Warren, An." *Harper's New Monthly Magazine* 28, no. 167 (April 1864).

Hill, James D. "Charles W. Read: Confederate Von Luckner." *The South Atlantic Quarterly* 28 (January to October 1929).

Hollins, George N. "Autobiography of Commodore George Nicholas Hollins." *Maryland Historical Magazine* 34 (1939).

Kenniston, William B. "The Capture of the *Caleb Cushing.*" *Lewiston Journal,* Illustrated Magazine Section, May 30, 1908.

Magruder, P. H. "A Walk Through Annapolis in Bygone Days." *U.S. Naval Institute Proceeding,* June 1929.

Read, Charles W. "Reminiscences of the Confederate States Navy." *Southern Historical Society Papers,* Vol. 1, no. 5, 1876.

Shippey, W. Frank. "A Leaf from My Log Book." *Southern Historical Society Papers,* Vol. 12.

Still, William. "The Common Sailor," *Civil War Times Illustrated* 24, no. 1 (March 1985).

Southern Historical Society editors. "Operations of Confederate States Navy in Defense of New Orleans." *Southern Historical Society Papers,* Vol. 2. Richmond, Va., 1876.

Southern Historical Society Papers. Vol. 1, January–December 1874. Baltimore: Turnbull Brothers, 1874.

Thompson, Winfield M. "A Confederate Raid." *The Rudder* 16, no. III (March 1905).

———. "A Confederate Raid (concluded)." *The Rudder* 16, no. 4 (April 1905).

Woods, Robert H. "The Cruise of the *Clarence–Tacony–Archer*: A True Tale of the Sea during the Civil War." *Richmond Dispatch,* November 24, 1895. Also printed with minor variations in the *Southern Historical Society Papers.* Vol. 23. Richmond, Va., 1895; *Maryland Historical Magazine,* 1914; and *U.S. Naval Institute Proceedings* 35, no. 131 (September 1909).

BOOKS

Alexander, Joseph W. "An Escape from Fort Warren." *Histories of the Several Regiments and Battalions from North Carolina in the Great War, 1861–65.* Vol. 4, Goldsboro, N.C.: Nash Brothers, 1901.

Bartlett, John R. "The *Brooklyn* at the Passage of the Forts." *Battles and Leaders,* Vol. 2, New York: Thomas Yoseloff, 1887–1888. Reprint, New York: Thomas Yoseloff, 1956.

Bearss, Edwin C. *Rebel Victory at Vicksburg.* Vicksburg, Miss.: Vicksburg Centennial Commemoration Commission, 1963.

Benedict, Ruth. *The Chrysanthemum and the Sword: Patterns of Japanese Culture.* New York: Meridian Books, 1974.

Bowditch, Nathaniel. *American Practical Navigator: An Epitome of Navigation.* Pub. no. 9, Vol. 1, Washington, D.C.: Defense Mapping Agency Hydrographic Center, 1977.

Boykin, Edward. *Sea Devil of the Confederacy: The Story of the* Florida *and Her Captain, John Newland Maffitt.* New York: Funk & Wagnalls, 1959.

Bradlee, Francis B. C. *Blockade Running during the Civil War*. Salem, Mass.: The Essex Institute, 1925.

Brown, Isaac N. "The Confederate Gun-boat *Arkansas.*" *Battles and Leaders*, Vol. 2, New York: Thomas Yoseloff, 1887–1888. Reprint, New York, Thoms Yoseloff, 1956.

Bruzek, Joseph C. *The IX" Dahlgren Broadside Gun*. Annapolis, Md.: United States Naval Academy Museum, n.d.

Bulloch, James D. *The Secret Service of the Confederate States in Europe*. New York: Thomas Yoseloff, 1884. Reprint, New York: Thomas Yoseloff, 1959.

Burns, Zeb H. *Ship Island and the Confederacy*. Hattiesburg: University and College Press of Mississippi, 1971.

Butler, Benjamin F. *Butler's Book*. Boston: A. M. Thayer & Company, 1892.

———. *Private and Official Correspondence of Gen. Benjamin F. Butler*. Vol. 1. Privately issued, 1917.

Cable, George W. "New Orleans before the Capture." *Battles and Leaders of the Civil War*, Vol. 2, New York: Thomas Yoseloff, 1887–1888. Reprint, New York: Thomas Yoseloff, 1956.

Canfield, Eugene B. *Notes on Naval Ordnance of the American Civil War, 1861–1865*. Washington, D.C.: The American Ordnance Association, 1960.

Catton, Bruce. *Grant Takes Command*. Boston: Little, Brown, 1968.

Chapelle, Howard I. *The History of the American Sailing Navy*. New York: Bonanza Books, 1949.

———. *The History of American Sailing Ships*. New York: Bonanza Books, 1935.

———. *The Search for Speed Under Sail, 1700–1855*. New York: Bonanza Books, 1967.

Cochran, Hamilton. *Blockade Runners of the Confederacy*. Indianapolis: Bobbs-Merrill, 1958.

Coggins, Jack. *Arms and Equipment of the Civil War*. Garden City, N.Y.: Doubleday, 1962.

Coski, John M. *Capital Navy: The Men, Ships, and Operations of the James River Squadron*. Campbell, Calif.: Savas Woodbury Publishers, 1996.

Cranwell, John P. *Spoilers of the Sea: Wartime Raiders in the Age of Steam*. New York: W. W. Norton, 1941.

Dalzell, George W. *The Flight from the Flag*. Chapel Hill: University of North Carolina Press, 1940.

Daniel, Larry J., and Lynn N. Bock. *Island No. 10: Struggle for the Mississippi Valley.* Tuscaloosa: University of Alabama Press, 1996.

Darwin, Charles. *The Voyage of the Beagle.* 1845. Reprint, New York: Bantam Books, 1958.

Davis, Charles G. *American Sailing Ships: Their Plans and History.* New York: Dover Publications, 1984.

Davis, George B., Leslie J. Perry, and Joseph W. Kirkley. *The Official Military Atlas of the Civil War.* Compiled by Calvin D. Cowles. New York: Gramercy Books, 1983. Originally published as *Atlas to Accompany the Official Records of the Union and Confederate Armies.* Washington, D.C.: Government Printing Office, 1891–1895.

Dawson, Sarah M. *A Confederate Girl's Diary.* Boston: Houghton Mifflin, 1913.

Dewey, George. *Autobiography of George Dewey.* New York: Charles Scribner's Sons, 1913.

Donnelly, Ralph W. *The History of the Confederate Marine Corps.* New Bern, N.C.: Owen G. Dunn, 1976.

Dudley, William S. *Going South: U.S. Navy Officer Resignations and Dismissals on the Eve of the Civil War.* Washington, D.C.: Naval Historical Foundation, 1981.

Dufour, Charles L. *Nine Men Gray.* Garden City, N.Y.: Doubleday, 1963.

———. *The Night the War Was Lost.* Garden City, N.Y.: Doubleday, 1960.

Elwell, Edward H. *Portland and Vicinity.* 1876. Reprint, Portland, Maine: Greater Portland Landmarks, 1975.

Foote, Shelby. *The Civil War: A Narrative: Fort Sumter to Perryville.* New York: Random House, 1963. Reprint, New York: Vintage Books, 1986.

———. *The Civil War: A Narrative: Fredericksburg to Meridian.* New York: Random House, 1963. Reprint, New York: Vintage Books, 1986.

Gosnell, H. Allen. *Guns on the Western Waters.* Baton Rouge: Louisiana State University Press, 1949.

———. *Rebel Raider: Being an Account of Raphael Semmes' Cruise in the C.S.S. Sumter.* Chapel Hill: University of North Carolina Press, 1948.

Hearn, Chester G. *Gray Raiders of the Sea.* Camden, Maine: International Marine Publishing, 1992.

Hesseltine, William B. *Civil War Prisons.* Kent, Ohio: Kent State University Press, 1962.

Hill, Frederic S. *Twenty Years at Sea.* Boston and New York: Houghton, Mifflin, 1893.

Hoole, William S. *Four Years in the Confederate Navy: The Career of Capt. John Low on the C.S.S. Finial, Florida, Tuscaloosa, and* Ajax. Athens: University of Georgia Press, 1964.

Horsfield, John. *The Art of Leadership in War.* Westport, Conn.: Greenwood Press, 1980.

Jones, Freeman W. "A Daring Expedition." *War Talks of Confederate Veterans,* Petersburg, Va.: Fenn & Owen, Publishers, 1892.

Jones, John B. *A Rebel War Clerk's Diary.* New York: A. S. Barnes, 1866. Reprint, edited by Earl S. Miers, New York: Perpetua, 1961.

Jones, Virgil C. *The Civil War at Sea.* Vol. 2. New York: Holt, Rinehart and Winston, 1961.

Keegan, John. *The Face of Battle.* New York: Penguin Books, 1976.

Keeler, William F. *Aboard the U.S.S. Florida: 1863–65.* Edited by Robert W. Daily. Annapolis, Md.: United States Naval Institute, 1968.

Kern, Florence. *The United States Revenue Cutters, in the Civil War.* Bethesda, Md.: Alised Enterprises, 1976.

Lambert, Andrew. *Battleships in Transition: The Creation of the Steam Battlefleet, 1815–1860.* London: Conway Maritime Press, n.d. Reprint, Annapolis, Md.: Naval Institute Press, 1984.

Leon, T. C. *Four Years in Rebel Capitals.* Mobile, Ala.: Gossip Printing Company, 1890.

Lever, Darcy. *The Young Sea Officer's Sheet Anchor; or, A Key to the Leading of Rigging, and to Practical Seamanship.* 1808. Reprint, Providence: Ship Model Society of Rhode Island, 1930.

Lewis, Charles L. *David Glasgow Farragut: Our First Admiral.* Annapolis, Md.: United States Naval Institute, 1943.

Lovette, Leland P. *School of the Sea.* New York: Frederick A. Stokes, 1941.

Luraghi, Raimondo. *A History of the Confederate Navy.* Annapolis, Md.: Naval Institute Press, 1996.

Lykes, Richard W. *Campaign for Petersburg.* Washington, D.C.: Government Printing Office, 1970.

Maffitt, Emma M. *The Life and Services of John Newland Maffitt.* New York: Neale Publishing, 1906.

Mahan, Alfred T. *The Influence of Sea Power upon History.* New York: Hill and Wang, 1890. Reprint, New York: Hill and Wang, 1957.

Malone, Dumas. *Dictionary of American Biography.* Vol. 8. New York: Charles Scribner's Sons, 1935.

Marshall, Edwards C. *The History of the United States Naval Academy.* New York: D. Van Nostrand, 1862.

Martin, Christopher. *Damn the Torpedoes! The Story of America's First Admiral, David Glasgow Farragut.* New York: Abelard-Schuman, 1970.

Melton, Maurice. *The Confederate Ironclads.* New York: Thomas Yoseloff, 1968.

Milligan, John D. *Gunboats down the Mississippi.* Annapolis, Md.: United States Naval Institute, 1965

Miller, Francis T. *The Photographic History of the Civil War: Prisons and Hospitals.* New York: Thomas Yoseloff, 1912. Reprint, Castle Books, 1957.

————. *The Photographic History of the Civil War: The Navies.* New York: Thomas Yoseloff, 1912. Reprint, New York: Castle Books, 1957.

Moore, Frank. *The Rebellion Record: A Diary of American Events with Documents, Narratives, Illustrative incidents, Poetry, Etc.* New York: D. Van Nostrand, 1864.

Morgan, James M., and John P. Marquand. *Prince and Boatswain: Sea Tales from the Recollection of Rear Admiral Charles E. Clark.* Greenfield, Mass.: E. A. Hall, 1915.

————. *Recollections of a Rebel Reefer.* Boston and New York: Houghton, Mifflin, 1917.

"Opposing Forces in the Operations At New Orleans, LA, The." *Battles and Leaders.* Vol. 2. New York: Thomas Yoseloff, 1887–1888. Reprint, New York: Thomas Yoseloff, 1956.

Owsley, Frank L., Jr. *The C.S.S. Florida: Her Building and Operations.* Philadelphia: University of Pennsylvania Press, 1956.

Parker, William H. *Recollections of a Naval Officer, 1841–1865.* New York: Charles Scribner's Sons, 1883.

Parrish, Tom Z. *The Saga of the Confederate Ram Arkansas: The Mississippi Valley Campaign, 1862.* Hillsboro, Tex: Hill College Press, 1987.

Pollard, Edward A. *The Lost Cause.* New York: E. B. Treat, 1867.

Porter, David D. *The Naval History of the Civil War.* New York: Sherman Publishing, 1886.

————. "The Opening of the Lower Mississippi." *Battles and Leaders.* Vol. 2. New York: Thomas Yoseloff, 1887–1888. Reprint, New York: Thomas Yoseloff, 1956.

Potter, E. B., and Chester W. Nimitz. *Sea Power: A Naval History.* Englewood Cliffs, N.J.: Prentice-Hall, Inc., 1960.

Price, William H. *The Civil War Handbook.* Fairfax, Va.: L. B. Prince, 1961.

Rice, George W. *The Shipping Days of Old Boothbay From the Revolution to the World War.* Portland, Maine: Southworth-Anthoensen Press, 1938.

Rich, Louise D. *The Coast of Maine.* New York: Thomas Y. Crowell Company, 1970.

Roske, Ralph J., and Charles Van Doren. *Lincoln's Commando: The Biography of Commander W. B. Cushing, U.S.N.* New York: Harper Brothers, 1957.

Scharf, J. Thomas. *History of the Confederate States Navy from Its Organization to the Surrender of Its Last Vessel.* New York: Fairfax Press, 1875. Reprint, New York: Fairfax Press, 1977.

Schley, Winfield S. *Forty-five Years under the Flag.* New York: D. Appleton, 1904.

Seager, Robert, II. *Alfred Thayer Mahan: The Man and His Letters.* Annapolis, Md.: Naval Institute Press, 1977.

Semmes, Raphael. *The Confederate Raider* Alabama. 1869. Reprint, New York: Fawcett Publications, 1962.

Shingleton, Royce. *High Seas Confederate: The Life and Times of John Newland Maffitt.* Columbia: University of South Carolina Press, 1994.

Smith, Mason P. *Confederates Downeast: Confederate Operations in and around Maine.* Portland, Maine: Provincial Press, 1985.

Snead, Thomas L. "The Conquest of Arkansas." *Battles and Leaders.* Vol. 3. New York: Thomas Yoseloff, 1887–1888. Reprint, New York: Thomas Yoseloff, 1956.

Snow, Edward R. *An Island Citadel.* Braintree, Mass.: Glenrose Press, n.d.

————. *Historic Fort Warren.* Braintree, Mass.: Glenrose Press, n.d.

Southern Historical Collection. *Transactions of the Southern Historical Society.* Baltimore: Turnbull Brothers, 1874.

Soley, James R. *The Blockade and Cruisers.* New York: Charles Scribner's Sons, 1883.

————. *Historic Sketch of the United States Naval Academy.* Washington, D.C.: Government Printing Office, 1872.

Still, William N., Jr. *Iron Afloat: The Story of the Confederate Armorclads.* Columbia: University of South Carolina Press, 1985.

Sweetman, Jack. *The U.S. Naval Academy.* Annapolis, Md.: Naval Institute Press, 1979.

Taylor, John M. *Confederate Raider: Raphael Semmes of the* Alabama. Washington, D.C.: Brassey's, 1994.

von Clausewitz, Carl. *On War.* Edited by Anatol Rapoport. New York: Pelican Books, 1968.

Weems, Bob. *Charles Read: Confederate Buccaneer.* Jackson, Miss.: Heritage Books, 1982.

Welles, Gideon. *Diary of Gideon Welles.* Boston and New York: Houghton Mifflin, 1911.

Williams, Mrs. H. Dwight. *A Year in China and A Narrative of Capture and Imprisonment When Homeward Bound, On Board the Rebel Pirate* Florida. New York: Hurd and Houghton, 1864.

Winters, John D. *The Civil War in Louisiana.* Baton Rouge: Louisiana State University Press, 1963.

Wise, Stephen R. *Lifeline of the Confederacy: Blockade Running during the Civil War.* Columbia: University of South Carolina Press, 1988.

INDEX

(Page references in *italics* refer to information contained in photographs/captions. Photographs in inset identified by "*ph.*")

A

Aldebaran, 100–101
Alexander, Lt. Joseph W., 128–33, 135–37, 158
Alfred H. Partridge, 110
Andrews, Maj. George, 126, 127
Appomattox Court House, 159
CSS *Archer*
  in Portland (Me.), 4, 5, 10
  Savez commandeers, 121
CSS *Arkansas*
  construction of, 63–67
  crew of, 78, 79
  destroyed, 81–83, *ph.18*
  runs Farragut's fleet, 73–76, *ph.17*
  at Vicksburg, 77–80
  vs. USS *Carondelet*, 71–73
  on Yazoo River, 68–73
CSS *Atlanta*, 127, 144

B

Baton Rouge, 61, 81, 83
Battery Semmes, 143, *ph.28*

Battery Wood, 143
battle, sea, nature of, 173
Bibber, Albert, 5, 7, 11, 122
Billups, John, 105, 126, 143, 157
Blake, Capt. George S., 19
blockades, 31–37, 86–90
Breckenridge, Gen. John, 81, 83
Bridgetown (Barb.), 99–100
USS *Brooklyn*, 31, 89
Brown, Charles, 125
Brown, Eugene H., 5, 81, 86
Brown, Lt. Isaac Newton, 63–64, 69, 81, 83, *ph.16*. See also CSS *Arkansas*
Buchanan, Adm. Franklin, 86–87
Butler, Maj. Gen. Benjamin, 139, 141, 143
"Buttons," 126
Byzantium, 117

C

Cairo (Ill.), 40
Caleb Cushing, 2, 4, 5–14, *ph.26*
Calhoun, 35

Cardenas (Cuba), 94
USS *Carondelet*, 71–73
USS *Cayuga*, 53–54
Chesapeake, 5, 10–15
City of Dallas, 171
City Point, *140*, 152
Civil War, outbreak of, 26
CSS *Clarence*
   captured by *Florida*, 104–6,
     ph.22
   captures *Alfred H. Partridge*, 110
   captures *M. A. Shindler*, 112
   captures *Mary Alvina*, 110
   captures *Tacony*, 112, *ph.23*
   captures *Whistling Wind*, 110
   commandeered, 104–6
   meets *Forrester*, 108
Colombia, 170
Columbus (Ky.), 39–40
commerce raiders, 30, 173
Commonwealth, 103
Confederate Navy
   at start of Civil War, 29, 30
Corris Ann, 93
Cuba, 92–94
Cuyler, 89–90

D

Davenport, Lt. Dudley, 2, 6–7, 8
Davis, Capt. Charles Henry, 61
DeSoto Point, 66
Drayton, A. L., 107, 109, 174
Dutch Gap Canal, 143

E

Emmons, Cmdr. George F., 89–90
escape attempts, 128–33, 135–37
Essex, 79, 80

Estelle, 91
exchanges, prisoner, 133, 137,
   139–42

F

Fairbanks, Charles B., 52–53
Farragut, David Glasgow
   at New Orleans, 46, 47, 48, 52,
     58, 59, *ph.12*
   at Vicksburg, 68, 69, 78–79
Fernando de Noronha, 104
fire rafts, 48, 56–57
CSS *Florida*, 14, 84, 85
   in Barbados, 99–100
   captures *Aldebaran*, 100–101
   captures *Clarence*, 104–5, *ph.22*
   captures *Commonwealth*, 103
   captures *Corris Ann*, 93
   captures *Estelle*, 91
   captures *Henrietta*, 103
   captures *Jacob Bell*, 97–99
   captures *Lapwing*, 102
   captures *M. J. Colcord*, 102
   captures *Oneida*, 103
   captures *Star of Peace*, 100, 101
   captures *Windward*, 93
   in Cuban waters, 92–94
   Oreto II, 102
   runs blockade at Mobile, 86–90
Foote, Andrew Hull, 1, 44, 45, 61
Forest City, 2, 8, 9
Fort Brady, 148
Fort Donelson, 40
Fort Henry, 40
Fort Jackson, 48, 50–51
Fort Morgan, 86
Fort Pillow, 46, 61–62
Fort Preble, Savez imprisoned in,
   127

Fort Randolf, 61
Fort St. Philip, 48, 50–51
Fort Sumter, 27
Fort Warren
   escape attempts, 128–33, 135–37
   imprisoned in, 127–36, 167,
     ph.27

G

CSS General Polk, 39
Gift, Lt. George, 66, 71, 72, 74,
   83
Goldsborough, Comdr. Louis M.,
   17–18, 19
Goodspeed, 118
Greeley, Horace, 118
Grimball, Lt. John, 66, 71, 72

H

Hall, Rosa, 27, 171
USS *Hartford*, *ph.15*
Havana (Cuba), 92
Henrietta, 103
Huger, Lt. Thomas B., 29, 45, 46,
   ph.5. See also CSS *McRae*
Hunt, Robert, 126

I

imprisonment, 125–36
insurance, shipping, 123
USS *Iroquois*, 54
Isaac Webb, 116–17
Island No. 10, 40–*41*, 44–45, *ph.10*
Ivy, 35

J

CSS *Jackson*, 35, 39
Jackson (Miss.), 15–16

Jacob Bell, 97–99, *ph.20*
James River, *140*, 143
   raids upon, 144–46
   squadron, 142, 147–52, *ph.29*
Jewett, Jedidiah, 9, 14

K

Kate Stewart, 113, 116
Kennon, Lt. Beverly, 50

L

USS *Lafayette*, 162, 163
USS *Lancaster*, 74
Lapwing, 102
Lewis, Lt. John, 152
Liverpool Landing, 64–65
Livingston, 39
Lockwood, Henry H., 19
CSS *Louisiana*, 47, 51
Louisiana, State of
   navy of, 50, 53
Lyceum, 20
Lynch, Comdr. William F., 65, 69

M

M. A. Shindler, 112
Maffitt, Capt. John N., 84, 85, 86,
   105–6, *ph.19. See also*
   CSS *Florida*
Mallory, Stephen, 27, 30, 86, 135,
   147
Manassas, 35–36
USS *Manhattan*, 162
Mary Alvina, 110
USS *Massachusetts*, 32
Matherson, J. W., 105, 143
May, Nebraska, 171
McLellan, Jacob, 10, 14

CSS *McRae*, *ph.6*
  conversion to raider, 30–31
  history of, 30
  at New Madrid, 38–45
  in New Orleans, 31–37, 47–57
  Savez assigned to, 27, 29–30
  sunk, 58–59, 141
Meade, Lt. Comdr. Richard W.,
  Jr., 126
Memphis (Tenn.), 61–62
merchant shipping, 123
Merryman, Lt. James H., 2, 8, 13–
  14
Micawaber, 117
mines, 148
CSS *Mississippi*, 47, *ph.14*
Mississippi, secession of, 26
Mississippi River
  control of, 38, 61, 80
  map of, 49
  CSS *Webb* on, 161–67
Mitchell, Comdr. John K., 50, 142,
  147–52
M. J. Colcord, 102
Mobile Bay (Ala.), 86–90
Morgan, Jimmy, 33, 142, 148, 169,
  ph.7
Morse, Ruggles Sylvester, 2

N

Nassau, 95
Naval Academy. *See* United States
  Naval Academy
New Madrid, 41–44
New Orleans
  blockade of, 31–37
  command problems at, 50
  defenses of, 34–35, 47–50

in early 1862, 47
loss of, to Union, 47–57, 141,
  ph.13
merchant shipping of, 29
newspaper business, 16

O

Oneida, 103
USS *Onondaga*, 145
Oreto II, 102
Ould, Col. Robert, 141

P

CSS *Patrick Henry*, 142
Pinkney, Comdr. Robert F., 46, 61,
  65
USS *Pinola*, 74
USS *Plymouth*, summer cruise on,
  21–25, *ph.3*
Pope, Brig. Gen. John, 42–44
Porter, David D., 127
Portland (Me.), 1–5
  attack on, by Savez, 5–10
  harbor map, 3
  merchant shipping, 4
USS *Powhatan*, assigned to, 25–26,
  ph.4
Prime, Capt. Nathaniel, 10, 13–14
prison, 125–36
prisoner exchanges, 133, 137,
  139–42
Pryde, Nicholas B., 105, 130

Q

USS *Queen of the West*, 71, 73, 80

R

Read, Charles William "Savez." *See* Savez (Charles William Read)
Read, Edmund Gaines, 170
Read, Elizabeth (sister), 27–28
Read, John (brother), 27
Read, John (grandfather), 28
Read, Maria Louise (mother), 15, 16
Read, Nebraska (wife), 171
Read, Rose (wife), 27, 171
Read, William (brother), 27
Read, William (father), 15
Resolute, 58
USS *Richmond*, 36, 74–75, 166–67, *ph.8*, *ph.11*
River Defense Fleet, 53

S

sail plan, of USS *Constitution*, 177
Saunders, Maj. Reid, 129, 137
Savez (Charles William Read), *ph.1*, *ph.31–33*. *See also under* specific ships
  academic skills, 18, 25
  acquires nickname, 19
  after War, 169–72
  CSS *Archer*, commands, 121–23
  birth and early years, 15–16
  captured, 13
  children, 171
  CSS *Clarence*, commands, 107–12
  death, 172
  escape attempts, 128–33, 135–37
  CSS *Florida*, assigned to, 84–106
  James River raids, 142–46, 152–55
  with James River Squadron, 147–52
  CSS *McRae*, assigned to, 27–84
  USS *Powhatan*, assigned to, 25–26
  as prisoner of war, 125–37
  resigns from U.S. Navy, 26
  ships captured by, 175–76
  starts a newspaper, 16
  surrenders to Schley, 167–68
  CSS *Tacony*, commands, 113–21
  at U.S. Naval Academy, 17–25, *ph.1*
  CSS *William H. Webb*, commands, 157–67
Schley, Winfield Scott, 20, 167
Sherman, Thomas, 130
Ship Island, 31, 46
ships, captured by Savez, 175–76
slaves, former, captured, 133, 141
Southwest Passage, Battle at the, *ph.8*
Star of Peace, 100, 101
steam engines, 33, 47
Stevens, Lt. Henry, 71, 81–83
Stevenson, Capt. John, 50
surrender, of Army of Northern Virginia, 159–60

T

CSS *Tacony*, 112
  bounty offered for, 119
  burned and abandoned, 121, *ph.25*
  captures *Archer*, 121
  captures *Byzantium*, 117
  captures fishing schooners, 120, *ph.24*

captures *Goodspeed*, 118
captures *Isaac Webb*, 116–17
captures *Kate Steward*, 113, *ph.23*
captures *Micawaber*, 117
captures *Umpire*, 116
Savez commandeers, 112–13
ships sent after, 115–19
telegraph lines, 163–64
20th Maine, 2
Thurston, James, 129–33
Tiptonville, 45, 46
Titcomb, Elbridge, 5, 7, 122
torpedoes, 144, 145, 148
Tuscarora, 35, 39
USS *Tyler*, 71, 73

U

Umpire, 116
United Fruit Company, 171
United States Naval Academy, 16–
    25, *ph.2. See also* United
    States Navy
  daily life at, 17–19
  summer cruise on *Plymouth*,
    21–25
United States Navy. *See also* United
    States Naval Academy

at New Orleans, 47–57
at outbreak of Civil War, 26–27,
    29
at Vicksburg, 68

V

USS *Vanderbilt*, 97
Van Dorn, Maj. Gen. Earl, 67–68
Vicksburg, 66–69, 76, 78–79

W

USS *Wachusett*, 92–93
Ward, Artemus, 125
Warley, Lt. Alexander, 32
Welles, Gideon, 1, 114, 119
Whistling Wind, 110
White, Isaac, 100
Wilkes, Rear Adm. Charles,
    92–93, 100
CSS *William H. Webb*, 157–67,
    ph.30
Windward, 93

Y

Yazoo City, 63
Yazoo River, 66